The

Cotton

Kingdom

American

History

Landmarks

Edited by

David Freeman Hawke

Frederick Law Olmsted

The

Cotton

Kingdom

A Selection

The Bobbs-Merrill Company, Inc.
Indianapolis & New York

Frederick Law Olmsted: 1822–1903

Contents

Editor's Introduction

1

Frederick Law Olmsted had the luck to be born well-to-do and the greater luck to have a tolerant father willing to give him time to find himself. Olmsted had reached his mid-thirties and experimented with several careers before settling down to one. Even then he did not so much choose a profession as create one—that of landscape architect. Central Park in New York City, Fairmount Park in Philadelphia, and Golden Gate Park in San Francisco number among his achievements as an architect, but they fail to eclipse the equally impressive achievements of his earlier career as a newspaper correspondent. Out of that experience came three books on the antebellum South which, on the eve of the Civil War, were combined into *The Cotton Kingdom*. "Few books on economic and social observation ever written in any land possess the enduring interest of Olmsted's," the historian Allan Nevins has said, a judgment no fair-minded critic, regardless of his views on slavery or the South, has found reason to dispute.

The dispassionate and realistic account of slavery that appears in *The Cotton Kingdom* came, strangely, from a man reared in a region of abolitionists. Olmsted was born in Hartford, Connecticut, in 1822, the son of a prosperous merchant who liked to spend the summers roaming with his family on foot and by horse and carriage through the New England countryside, a sedate form of the vagabond life that gave Olmsted a love for travel he never lost. The family planned to send him to Yale, but at the age of fourteen a severe case of sumac poisoning left him with eyes too weak for hard study. The permissive parents let the boy "run wild," and, as he later recalled, his days were spent "roaming afield and day-dreaming under a tree." An attempt to combine an outdoor life with a career led to an informal apprenticeship to a topographical engineer.

Olmsted soon abandoned that experiment and, when eighteen years old, went to work for an import house in New York City. That job, too, bored him, and after a year and a half he left it to attend Yale as a special student. He tried college for a year, then in 1843 shipped out as an ordinary seaman on a vessel bound for China. (Richard H. Dana's *Two Years Before the Mast* had been published three years earlier, and that romantic account of life at sea may have influenced Olmsted's decision.) He returned from China still at loose ends. Once again, although now twenty-four, he signed up for classes at Yale.

The second year at Yale came during the Mexican War, which in the North had provoked loud and heated discussions about the spread of slavery beyond the South's traditional boundaries. Olmsted's closest friend at Yale was Charles Loring Brace, a "red hot abolitionist." Olmsted deplored slavery, but he also rejected every tenet of abolition; gradual emancipation, with colonization in Africa, was his favored solution to the race problem. He also believed that the Constitution gave Southerners the right "to continue their peculiar institution as it is and where it is." Brace could not budge him from this moderate stand.

Sometime during this second exposure to academic life Olmsted settled on a new career. This time he determined to become a farmer. His father, with an apparently bottomless reservoir of patience, in 1847 bought his son a plot of land along the Connecticut seashore where he could test the strength of his latest enthusiasm. Olmsted displayed enough aptitude and interest in agriculture to persuade his father the next year to buy him a 130-acre farm on Staten Island, off the tip of Manhattan, which was close enough to let the unsettled son enjoy the best of town and country. Olmsted worked hard at the business of farming. He experimented with fruit-tree grafts and fertilizers and invested in the latest machinery, and, as an enlightened gentleman, he published the results of his progressive methods in agricultural journals. At the age of twenty-six he seemed set on the life of a "well-to-do working farmer," as he put it.

Farming became more than a hobby but never an obsession. In slack seasons he found time to slip across the bay and into

Manhattan to buy prints and such books as John Ruskin's *Modern Painters.* In 1850 he left for a tour of Europe with his younger brother John and his college friend Charles Brace. To make the trip seem more than a frivolous vacation, the three planned to study the "varying developments of human nature under different biases and institutions." They spent the first months hiking through the countryside of England and Wales, moved on to Scotland, then at a more leisurely pace toured through Belgium, France, and Germany.

After returning home Olmsted spent the winter on the farm writing up the first part of the trip. The book that resulted, *Walks and Talks of an American Farmer in England,* was published in 1852, reprinted in 1854, and again in a revised edition in 1859 (reissued in 1967). Olmsted aimed, so he said, to pass along to fellow American farmers all the "practical agricultural information" he had picked up during the previous summer. Actually, he sought mainly to capture the flavor of the land and people of rural England, and in this sense *Walks and Talks* served as a testing ground for a literary style developed more fully in the later volumes on the South. With anecdotes, through conversations that skillfully reproduced local accents, and in leisurely yet vivid descriptions of the landscape he reported what he saw and heard and then let readers form "their own views from the facts that I give them." When he let his opinions intrude, he assumed readers had enough information to take them "for only just what they shall seem to be worth."

With the arrival of spring and the completion of *Walks and Talks* the farm reclaimed Olmsted's attention, but not for long. Agitation over the Compromise of 1850, with its (to the North) obnoxious Fugitive Slave Law, had revived the debates between Olmsted and Brace over slavery. The publication of *Uncle Tom's Cabin* in 1852 added fuel to the discussions. As the debate wound through the year, it occurred to both men that Olmsted's ambivalence about the South and slavery might be resolved by a trip through the slave states, where he could see firsthand the effects of bondage on those who endured and those who imposed it. Because Olmsted's puritanical New England mentality balked at the thought of a trip designed only to indulge his curiosity and love of travel, Brace arranged to give the expedition a broader purpose by suggesting to Henry J. Raymond, editor of the *New-York Daily Times,* as it was then called, that he hire Olmsted as a special correspondent. Raymond took five minutes to size up Olmsted as a person — he may have prejudged him as a writer through *Walks and Talks* — and accepted the proposition. The assignment carried no strings. Raymond asked only that the reports from the South be confined "to personal observations" and told Olmsted not to worry about being "constrained by regard to consistency with the general position of the paper or anything else."

2

No abler, friendlier, or less self-righteous observer than Olmsted ever traveled the South prior to the Civil War. "Few men could have been so little inclined to establish previously formed opinion as I was," he remarked after his return. Though born and bred in the North, he went with no axe to grind, but only "to see for myself," he said in his first dispatch, "the ordinary condition of the laborers in the South." If anything, he was too open-minded, according to abolitionist friends, for the moral issue involved in slavery counted little with him. His experience as a farmer gave him an advantage over other visitors, for in a land that ran mainly to farms he could talk sensibly to people from all classes about their work and problems. An eye for the ludicrous, an affection for people, and a boundless curiosity enlivened his reports to the *Times.* No sense of mission seeped into a line he wrote. The South could not have asked for anything more. If books could avert wars, those Olmsted eventually turned out about the South should have helped forestall the bloodiest conflict America ever knew.

The first trip lasted three months — from December 1852 to February 1853. Olmsted started out from Washington, moved through eastern Virginia at a leisurely pace, down into the Carolinas and Georgia, then westward into Alabama. He took a steamboat from Mobile to New Orleans and after a pause in that city pushed northward to Memphis. He then crossed the Appalachian mountains, skirting their eastern base as he moved through a land of "poor whites," and ended the trek in northwestern Virginia. The *Times* published the first account of his adventures on February 16, 1853, shortly after Olmsted had returned to New York. The series ran under the title of "The South" and the by-line "Yeoman." It extended to fifty letters and appeared for a solid year. Extremists condemned the series — abolitionists believed it soft-pedaled the evils of slavery, and professional Southerners called the letters insulting — but moderates in both the North and South complimented the author. "This is exactly what we wish all well-disposed and well-behaved Northern people, who desire to know something of the South would do," commented one Southern paper.

The *Times* asked Olmsted to make a second trip as soon as possible. This time he headed for Texas, carrying along his brother John, who was suffering from tuberculosis. Medical opinion in those days held that a long trip in the open air offered the best chance to cure the disease, and to this end the brothers mapped out an expedition by horseback across Texas. They left New York in mid-November, 1853, while the reports on the first trip were still appearing. The trek through Texas extended two thousand miles and lasted five months. The adventure ended at New Orleans, where John left for home while Frederick stayed behind to finish his dispatches, the first of which had appeared in March, 1854. The second series comprised only fifteen articles, partly because far-off Texas aroused less interest in the North, but mainly because the Kansas-Nebraska Bill, then agitating Congress as well as the whole country, preempted the bulk of available news-paper space.

After finishing the pieces on Texas, Olmsted set out once more on horseback, this time traveling through the highlands or backcountry from Alabama up to Virginia. This journey, the final one, lasted four months. Altogether Olmsted had spent fourteen months in the South. In that time he had visited thirteen Southern states and talked to scores of Negroes and, by his own count, some five hundred white people who "told me something of their own lives and fortunes, across their own tables, and with the means of measuring the weight of their words before my eyes."

Shortly after arriving back in New York, Olmsted set about turning the newspaper articles into books. The volume covering the first trip — *A Journey in the Seaboard Slave States, with Remarks on Their Economy* — was published early in 1856. The newspaper articles had been expanded with new material on the Southern economy, but the chief difference appeared in Olmsted's sharper tone toward the South and its peculiar institution. He apologized in the Preface for being "too fault-finding," and warned the reader he would be traveling "in company with an honest growler."

Less than a year later came *A Journey Through Texas; or a Saddle-Trip on the Southwestern Frontier,* in which the original fifteen dispatches had been lengthened — with John Olmsted's help — into five hundred pages. The third volume came more slowly, delayed partly by the death of his brother and the collapse of a publishing firm Olmsted had invested in, but principally by the load of work that had come with his appointment in the autumn of 1857 as superintendent of Central Park. *A Journey in the Back Country* finally appeared in the summer of 1860. In style and content it reflected the tension between North and South that had increased steadily during the months Olmsted was writing. Though he still sought to be fair and friendly to the South, he was less than ever content just to describe what he had seen and let the reader make his own evaluation. Now he must intrude his own views. "Facts of general observation and conclusions of judgment form a larger part of this volume than of the others," he admitted in the Preface.

Back Country ended, so far as Olmsted knew at the time, what he had to say about the slave states. In November Lincoln was elected president, and soon after the Southern states began to secede. Olmsted had warned near the end of his final volume that the North would regard secession as a cause for war. Privately, he admitted even before Lincoln took office that "my mind is made up for a fight."

But before the fight came, Olmsted turned out one more book about the South. In January of 1861 an English publishing house asked him to condense his three volumes into two slim ones for British readers. The invitation attracted him, for he knew the potential importance of Great Britain, the South's major customer for cotton, in any war between the North and South. His writings might contribute to the shaping of anti-Southern feeling in the British government and among the people. Olmsted accepted the offer; then, with the hope of getting off a manuscript before the war broke and British opinion congealed, he took on a Washington journalist named Daniel R. Goodloe to help speed the job of pruning and reducing the three volumes. The two men worked swiftly and well together, once Olmsted had made it clear he wanted no interpolations from his collaborator. The deadly business of condensation fell largely to Goodloe, who performed his assignment with considerable skill. He cut 1,732 pages to 768 pages, all this in spite of several lengthy additions by Olmsted — among them, mainly for English readers, an introductory chapter on "The Present Crisis" and a long letter by an Illinois farmer on the South. Work on *The Cotton Kingdom*, Olmsted's title for the new volume, was completed in three months, during which time Olmsted had continued to carry on his work with the Central Park project. English printers began to set it in type in June, 1861, and in October, Olmsted had a copy in hand of the two trim volumes. Within a few weeks an American edition made from the British plates was on the market.

3

The English edition was entitled, *Journeys and Explorations in the Cotton Kingdom*. The American publisher reversed emphasis and called it *The Cotton Kingdom: A Traveller's Observations on Cotton and Slavery in the American Slave States*. Whoever discarded *Our Slave States*, the original title of Olmsted's trilogy, for the jazzier *Cotton Kingdom*, succeeded, purposely or not, in perpetrating a myth about the South the author takes care to contradict from his earliest pages to the end of the book. Olmsted has barely cleared Virginia and edged into the Carolinas before it becomes obvious that the

South produces not one staple crop but several. Gradually, as he moves from a lumbering region to a rice-growing area, from a tobacco section to one where sugar cane predominates, it becomes apparent that as the crops vary so does the South. Not cotton but the Negro blends and compresses a region that stretches from the plains of Texas through a mountainous country of small farms to the rolling countryside of Maryland into a unified region called the South.

Other travelers had previously remarked on the unifying effect of Negro slavery on a diverse South. Others, too, had commented perceptively on the effects of the Negro and slavery on white Southerners and their way of life. But no one before had investigated the variety of Southern life at such length, in such depth, and with less bias. In the words of Allan Nevins, Olmsted "did more than any other man of the time to make the discussion of slavery realistic by examining in detail its practical workings, and describing all its concomitants in the life of the people." The stereotypes of *Uncle Tom's Cabin* vanished in his books. A humane master talks about the necessity of whipping his slaves to keep them in line. A free Negro does not hesitate, given the chance, to accumulate slaves of his own. A harried overseer becomes one of the driven himself—on one side by the master, on the other by the Negroes. Southern hospitality becomes a mythical virtue.

Olmsted took nothing on faith. He checked into every assumption about the Negro and slavery made by abolitionists and Southerners and came up with answers that satisfied neither group. Was cruelty an integral part of the slave system? (To a degree, yes.) Did the Negro of the South eat better than the poor of New York City? (Yes, probably.) What sort of man was the slaveowner? (He varied as men everywhere varied.) Was slavery economically profitable? (For the large, well-run plantation, yes; for the South as a whole, no.) Did slavery corrupt the whites as well as the Negroes? (Yes.) But Olmsted's judgments for the modern reader matter less than the facts and observations they are founded upon. This abbreviated version of *The Cotton Kingdom* has been edited to let the modern reader see the South as Olmsted saw it more than a century ago. As much as possible, Olmsted's conclusions have been eliminated so that the reader can draw his own generalizations about the South and slavery. In other words, the purpose of this volume adheres to that Olmsted set for himself—to let the reader "see things for himself, as far as possible, and to see them carefully and fairly, but cheerfully and kindly," and "also to search for the causes and extenuating circumstances, past and present, of those phenomena which are commonly reported to the prejudice of the slaveholding community; and especially of those features which are manifestly most to be regretted in the actual condition of the older Slave States."

Note on the Text

The chapters of this edition follow the order of the original edition, with the exception of that on "The Exceptional Large Planters," which has been transposed to keep the narrative thread intact. Spellings have been Americanized, as they would have been if the book had originally been printed in the United States, and usages have been made consistent. The word "Negro" has been capitalized to conform to modern custom. No other changes have been made in the text.

This version of *The Cotton Kingdom* has been drawn from the original two-volume English edition published in 1861. The material in Chapter 1 comes from Volume I, pages 38–41, 46–54, 55–56, 57, 59–64, 69–78, 81–83, 86–90, 92–106; Chapter 2, pages 141–143, 144–148, 154–157, 168–176, 188–191, 197–202, 206–290, 213–222; Chapter 3, pages 227, 235–240, 242–255, 258, 259–271; Chapter 4, pages 272–278, 281–282; Chapter 5, pages 285, 287–289, 296–300, 317–341; Chapter 6, pages 342–343, 344–345, 346–352, 353–358, 365–376; Chapter 7 comes from Volume II, pages 9–10, 12–14, 16–21, 23–25, 29, 30–32, 42–50, 52–54; Chapter 8, pages 171–183, Chapter 9, pages 95–114, 119–123, 125–129, 134–142.

The

Cotton

Kingdom

1.

Virginia

Richmond, Dec. 16th—From Washington to Richmond, Virginia, by the regular great southern route—steamboat on the Potomac to Acquia Creek, and thence direct by rail. The boat makes 55 miles in 3½ hours, including two stoppages (12½ miles an hour); fare $2 (3.6 cents a mile). Flat rail; distance, 75 miles; time 5½ hours (13 miles an hour); fare, $3.50 (4⅔ cents a mile).

Not more than a third of the country, visible on this route, I should say, is cleared; the rest mainly a pine forest. Of the cleared land, not more than one quarter seems to have been lately in cultivation; the rest is grown over with briars and bushes, and a long, coarse grass of no value. But two crops seem to be grown upon the cultivated land—maize and wheat. The last is frequently sown in narrow beds and carefully surface drained, and is looking remarkably well.

A good many old plantation mansions are to be seen; generally standing in a grove of white oaks, upon some hilltop. Most of them are constructed of wood, of two stories, painted white, and have, perhaps, a dozen rude looking little log cabins scattered around them, for the slaves. Now and then, there is one of more pretension, with a large porch or gallery in front, like that of Mount Vernon. These are generally in a heavy, compact style; less often, perhaps, than similar establishments at the North, in markedly bad, or vulgar taste, but seem in sad need of repairs.

The more common sort of habitations of the white people are either of logs or loosely boarded frames, a brick chimney running up outside, at one end: everything very slovenly and dirty about them. Swine, hounds, and black and white children, are commonly lying very promiscuously together on the ground about the doors.

I am struck with the close cohabitation and association of black and white—Negro women are carrying black and white

3

babies together in their arms; black and white children are playing together (not going to school together); black and white faces are constantly thrust together out of the doors, to see the train go by.

A fine looking, well-dressed, and well-behaved colored young man sat, together with a white man, on a seat in the cars. I suppose the man was his master; but he was much the less like a gentleman of the two. The railroad company advertises to take colored people only in second-class trains; but servants seem to go with their masters everywhere. Once, today, seeing a lady entering the car at a way-station, with a family behind her, and that she was looking about to find a place where they could be seated together, I rose, and offered her my seat, which had several vacancies round it. She accepted it, without thanking me, and immediately installed in it a stout Negro woman; took the adjoining seat herself, and seated the rest of her party before her. It consisted of a white girl, probably her daughter, and a bright and very pretty mulatto girl. They all talked and laughed together; and the girls munched confectionary out of the same paper, with a familiarity and closeness of intimacy that would have been noticed with astonishment, if not with manifest displeasure, in almost any chance company at the North. When the Negro is definitely a slave, it would seem that the alleged natural antipathy of the white race to associate with him is lost.

I am surprised at the number of fine looking mulattoes, or nearly white-colored persons, that I see. The majority of those with whom I have come personally in contact are such. I fancy I see a peculiar expression among these—a contraction of the eyebrows and tightening of the lips—a spying, secretive, and counsel-keeping expression.

But the great mass, as they are seen at work, under overseers, in the fields, appear very dull, idiotic, and brute like; and it requires an effort to appreciate that they are, very much more than the beasts they drive, our brethren—a part of ourselves. They are very ragged, and the women especially, who work in the field with the men, with no apparent distinction in their labor, disgustingly dirty. They seem to move very awkwardly, slowly, and undecidedly, and almost invariably stop their work while the train is passing.

One tannery and two or three saw-mills afforded the only indications I saw, in seventy-five miles of this old country — settled before any part of Massachusetts — of any industrial occupation other than corn and wheat culture, and firewood chopping. At Fredericksburg we passed through the streets of a rather busy, poorly built town; but altogether, the country seen from the railroad, bore less signs of an active and prospering people than any I ever travelled through before, for an equal distance.

Richmond, at a glance from adjacent high ground, through a dull cloud of bituminous smoke, upon a lowering winter's day, has a very picturesque appearance, and I was reminded of the sensation produced by a similar *coup d' oeil* of Edinburgh. It is somewhat similarly situated upon and among some considerable hills; but the moment it is examined at all in detail, there is but one spot, in the whole picture, upon which the eye is at all attracted to rest. This is the Capitol, a Grecian edifice, standing alone, and finely placed on open and elevated ground, in the center of the town. It was built soon after the Revolution, and the model was obtained by Mr. Jefferson, then Minister to France, from the Maison Carrée.

A considerable part of the town, which contains a population of 28,000, is compactly and somewhat substantially built, but is without any pretensions to architectural merit, except in a few modern private mansions. The streets are not paved, and but few of them are provided with sidewalks other than of earth or gravel. The town is lighted with gas, and furnished with excellent water by an aqueduct.

In what I suppose to be the fashionable streets, there were many more well-dressed and highly dressed colored people than white; and among this dark gentry the finest French cloths, embroidered waistcoats, patent leather shoes, resplendent brooches, silk hats, kid gloves, and *eau de mille fleurs,* were quite common. Nor was the fairer, or rather the softer sex, at all left in the shade of this splendor. Many of the colored ladies were dressed not only expensively, but with good taste and effect, after the latest Parisian mode. Some of them were very attractive in appearance, and would have produced a decided sensation in any European drawing room. Their walk and carriage were more often stylish and graceful. Nearly a fourth part seemed to me to have lost all African peculiarity of feature, and to have acquired, in place of it, a good deal of that voluptuousness of expression which characterizes many of the women of the South of Europe.

There was no indication of their belonging to a subject race, except that they invariably gave the way to the white people they met. Once, when two of them, engaged in conversation and looking at each other, had not noticed his approach, I saw a Virginian gentleman lift his walking stick and push a woman aside with it. In the evening I saw three rowdies, arm-in-arm, taking the whole of the sidewalk, hustle a black man off it, giving him a blow, as they passed, that sent him staggering into the middle of the street. As he recovered himself he began to call out to, and threaten them. Perhaps he saw me stop, and thought I should support him, as I was certainly inclined to: "Can't you find anything else to do than to be knockin' quiet people round! You jus' come back here, will you? Here, you! *don't care if you is white.* You jus' come back here, and I'll teach you how to behave — knockin' people round! — don't care if I does hab to go to der watchhouse." They passed on without noticing him further, only laughing jeeringly — and he continued: "You come back here, and I'll make you laugh; you is jus' three white nigger cowards, dat's what *you* be."

I observe, in the newspapers, complaints of growing insolence and insubordination among the Negroes, arising, it is thought, from too many privileges being permitted them by their masters, and from too merciful administration of the police laws with regard to them. Except in this instance, however, I have seen not the slightest evidence of any independent manliness on the part of the Negroes towards the whites. As far as I have yet observed, they are treated very kindly and even generously as servants, but their manner to white people is invariably either sullen, jocose, or fawning.

The pronunciation and dialect of the Negroes, here, is generally much more idiomatic and peculiar than with us. As I write, I hear a man shouting, slowly and deliberately, meaning to say *there:* "*Dah! dah!* DAH!"

Among the people you see in the streets, full half, I should think, are more or less of Negro blood, and a very decent, civil people these seem, in general, to be; more so than the laboring class of whites, among which there are many very ruffianly looking fellows. There is a considerable population of foreign origin, generally of the least valuable class; very dirty German Jews, especially, abound, and their characteristic shops (with their characteristic smells, quite as bad as in Cologne) are thickly set in the narrowest and meanest streets, which seem to be otherwise inhabited mainly by Negroes.

Immense wagons, drawn by six mules each, the teamster always riding on the back of the near wheeler, are a characteristic feature of the streets. On the canal, a long, narrow, canoe-like boat, perhaps fifty feet long and six wide, and drawing but a foot or two of water, is nearly as common as the ordinary large boats, such as are used on our canals. They come out of some of the small, narrow, crooked streams, connected with the canals, in which a difficult navigation is effected by poling. They are loaded with tobacco, flour, and a great variety of raw country produce. The canal boatmen seem rude, insolent, and riotous, and every facility is evidently afforded them, at Richmond, for indulging their peculiar appetites and tastes. A great many low eating, and, I should think, drinking, shops are frequented chiefly by the Negroes. Dancing and other amusements are carried on in these at night.

From reading the comments of Southern statesmen and newspapers on the crime and misery which sometimes result from the accumulation of poor and ignorant people, with no intelligent masters to take care of them, in our Northern towns, one might get the impression that Southern towns — especially those not demoralized by foreign commerce — were comparatively free from a low and licentious population. From what I have seen, however, I am led to think that there is at least as much vice, and of what we call rowdyism, in Richmond, as in any Northern town of its size.

Richmond. — Yesterday morning, during a cold, sleety storm, against which I was struggling, with my umbrella, to the post office, I met a comfortably dressed Negro leading three others by a rope; the first was a middle-aged man; the second a girl of, perhaps, twenty; and the last a boy, considerably younger.

The arms of all three were secured before them with handcuffs, and the rope by which they were led passed from one to another; being made fast at each pair of handcuffs. They were thinly clad, the girl especially so, having only an old ragged handkerchief around her neck, over a common calico dress, and another handkerchief twisted around her head. They were dripping wet, and icicles were forming, at the time, on the awning bars.

The boy looked most dolefully, and the girl was turning around with a very angry face, and shouting, "O pshaw! Shut up!"

"What are they?" said I, to a white man, who had also stopped, for a moment, to look at them. "What's he going to do with them?"

"Come in a canal boat, I reckon: sent down here to be sold. — That ar's a likely gal."

Our ways lay together, and I asked further explanation. He informed me that the Negro-dealers had confidential servants always in attendance, on the arrival of the railroad trains and canal packets, to take any Negroes that might have come consigned to them, and bring them to their marts.

Nearly opposite the post office was another singular group of Negroes. They consisted of men and boys, and each carried a coarse, white blanket, drawn together at the corners so as to hold some articles; probably, extra clothes. They stood in a row, in lounging attitudes, and some of them, again, were quarrelling, or reproving one another. A villainous looking white man stood in front of them. Presently, a stout, respectable man, dressed in black according to the custom, and without any overcoat or umbrella, but with a large, golden headed walking stick, came out of the door of an office, and, without saying a word, walked briskly up the street; the Negroes immediately followed, in file; the other white man bringing up the rear. They were slaves that had been sent into the town to be hired out as servants or factory hands. The gentleman in black was, probably, the broker in the business.

Near the post office, opposite a large livery and sale stable, I turned into a short, broad street, in which were a number of establishments, the signs on which indicated that they were occupied by "Slave Dealers," and that "Slaves, for Sale or to Hire," were to be found within them. They were much like Intelligence Offices, being large rooms partly occupied by ranges of forms, on which sat a few comfortably and neatly clad Negroes, who appeared perfectly cheerful, each grinning obsequiously, but with a manifest interest or anxiety, when I fixed my eye on them for a moment.

The hotel at which I am staying, "The American," Milberger Smith, from New York, proprietor, is an excellent one. I have never, this side the Atlantic, had my comforts provided for better, in my private room, with so little annoyance from the servants. The chamber servants are Negroes, and are accomplished in their business; (the dining room servants are Irish). A man and a woman attend together upon a few assigned rooms, in the hall adjoining which they are constantly in waiting; your bell is answered immediately, your orders are quickly and quietly followed, and your particular personal wants anticipated as much as possible, and provided for, as well as the usual offices performed, when you are out. The man becomes your servant while you are in your room; he asks, at night, when he comes to request your boots, at what time he shall come in the morning, and then, without being very exactly punctual, he comes quietly in, makes your fire, sets the boots before it, brushes and arranges your clothes, lays out your linen, arranges your dressing gear, asks if you want anything else of him before breakfast, opens the shutters, and goes off to the next room. I took occasion to speak well of him to my neighbor one day, that I might judge whether I was particularly favored.

"Oh, yes," he said, "Henry was a very good boy, very — valuable servant — quite so — would be worth two thousand dollars, if he was a little younger — easy."

At dinner, a venerable looking man asked another —

"Niggers are going high now, aint they?"

"Yes, sir."

"What would you consider a fair price for a woman thirty years old, with a young one two years old?"

"Depends altogether on her physical condition, you know. — Has she any other children?"

"*Yes; four.*"

" — Well — I reckon about seven to eight hundred."

"I bought one yesterday — gave six hundred and fifty."

"Well, sir, if she's tolerable likely, you did well."

This morning I visited a farm, situated on the bank of James River, near Richmond.

The labor upon it was entirely performed by slaves. I did not inquire their number, but I judged there were from twenty to forty. Their "quarters" lined the approach road to the mansion, and were well made and comfortable log cabins, about thirty feet long by twenty wide, and eight feet tall, with a high loft and shingle roof. Each divided in the middle, and having a brick chimney outside the wall at either end, was intended to be occupied by two families. There were square windows, closed by wooden ports, having a single pane of glass in the center. The house servants were neatly dressed, but the field hands wore very coarse and ragged garments.

During the three hours, or more, in which I was in company with the proprietor, I do not think ten consecutive minutes passed uninterrupted by some of the slaves requiring his personal direction or assistance. He was even obliged, three times, to leave the dinner table.

"You see," said he, smiling, as he came in the last time," a farmer's life, in this country, is no sinecure." Then turning the conversation to slavery, he observed, in answer to a remark of mine, "I only wish your philanthropists would contrive some satisfactory plan to relieve us of it; the trouble and the responsibility of properly taking care of our Negroes, you may judge, from what you see yourself here, is anything but enviable. But what can we do that is better? Our free Negroes — and I believe it is the same at the North as it is here — are a miserable set of vagabonds, drunken, vicious, worse off, it is my honest opinion, than those who are retained in slavery. I am satisfied, too, that our slaves are better off, as they are, than the majority of your free laboring classes at the North."

I expressed my doubts.

"Well, they certainly are better off than the English agricultural laborers, or, I believe, those of any other Christian

country. Free labor might be more profitable to us: I am inclined
to think it would be. The slaves are excessively careless and
wasteful, and, in various ways — which, without you lived
among them, you could hardly be made to understand — subject
us to very annoying losses.

"To make anything by farming, here, a man has got to live a
hard life. You see how constantly I am called upon — and, often,
it is about as bad at night as by day. Last night I did not sleep
a wink till near morning; I am quite worn out with it, and my
wife's health is failing. But I cannot rid myself of it."

I asked why he did not employ an overseer.

"Because I do not think it right to trust to such men as we
have to use, if we use any, for overseers."

"Is the general character of overseers bad?"

"They are the curse of this country, sir; the worst men in the
community. . . . But lately, I had another sort of fellow offer — a
fellow like a dancing master, with kid gloves, and wristbands
turned up over his coat sleeves, and all so nice, that I was almost
ashamed to talk to him in my old coat and slouched hat. Half
a bushel of recommendations he had with him, too. Well, he
was not the man for me — not half the gentleman, with all his
airs, that Ned here is" — (a black servant, who was bursting with
suppressed laughter, behind his chair).

"Oh, they are interesting creatures, sir," he continued, "and,
with all their faults, have many beautiful traits. I can't help
being attached to them, and I am sure they love us." In his own
case, at least, I did not doubt it; his manner towards them was
paternal — familiar and kind; and they came to him like children
who have been given some task, and constantly are wanting to
be encouraged and guided, simply and confidently. At dinner,
he frequently addressed the servant familiarly, and drew him
into our conversation as if he were a family friend, better informed, on some local and domestic points, than himself.

Petersburg. — The train was advertised to leave at 3:30 P.M. At
that hour the cars were crowded with passengers, and the engineer, punctually at the minute, gave notice that he was at his
post, by a long, loud whistle of the locomotive. Five minutes
afterwards he gave us an impatient jerk; ten minutes afterwards

we advanced three rods; twelve minutes afterwards, returned to first position: continued, "backing and filling," upon the bridge over the rapids of the James River, for half an hour. At precisely four o'clock, crossed the bridge and fairly started for Petersburg.

Ran twenty miles in exactly an hour and thirty minutes (thirteen miles an hour; mail train, especially recommended by advertisement as "fast"). Brakes on three times, for cattle on the track; twenty minutes spent at way-stations. Flat rail. Locomotive built at Philadelphia. I am informed that most of those used on the road—perhaps all those of the *slow* trains—are made at Petersburg.

There were, in the train, two first-class passenger cars, and two freight cars. The latter were occupied by about forty Negroes, most of them belonging to traders, who were sending them to the cotton States to be sold. Such kind of evidence of activity in the slave trade of Virginia is to be seen every day; but particulars and statistics of it are not to be obtained by a stranger here. Most gentlemen of character seem to have a special disinclination to converse on the subject; and it is denied, with feeling, that slaves are often reared, as is supposed by the Abolitionists, with the intention of selling them to the traders. It appears to me evident, however, from the manner in which I hear the traffic spoken of incidentally, that the cash value of a slave for sale, above the cost of raising it from infancy to the age at which it commands the highest price, is generally considered among the surest elements of a planter's wealth. Such a nigger is worth such a price, and such another is too old to learn to pick cotton, and such another will bring so much, when it has grown a little more, I have frequently heard people say, in the street, or the public houses. That a slave woman is commonly esteemed least for her working qualities, most for those qualities which give value to a brood mare is, also, constantly made apparent.

A gentleman with whom I was conversing on the subject of the cost of slave labor, in answer to an inquiry—What proportion of all the stock of slaves of an old plantation might be reckoned upon to do full work?—answered, that he owned ninety-six Negroes; of these, only thirty-five were field hands, the rest being either too young or too old for hard work. He reckoned his whole force as only equal to twenty-one strong men, or "*prime* field hands." But this proportion was somewhat smaller than usual, he added, "because his women were uncommonly good breeders; he did not suppose there was a lot of women anywhere that bred faster than his; he never heard of babies coming so fast as they did on his plantation; it was perfectly surprising; and every one of them, in his estimation, was worth two hundred dollars, as Negroes were selling now, the moment it drew breath."

I asked what he thought might be the usual proportion of workers to slaves, supported on plantations, throughout the South. On the large cotton and sugar plantations of the more Southern States, it was very high, he replied; because their hands were nearly all bought and *picked for work;* he supposed, on these, it would be about one-half; but, on any old plantation, where the stock of slaves had been an inheritance, and none had been bought or sold, he thought the working force would rarely be more than one-third, at most, of the whole number.

This gentleman was out of health, and told me, with frankness, that such was the trouble and annoyance his Negroes occasioned him—although he had an overseer—and so wearisome did he find the lonely life he led on his plantation, that he could not remain upon it; and as he knew everything would go to the dogs if he did not, he was seriously contemplating to sell out, retaining only his foster mother and a body servant. He thought of taking them to Louisiana and Texas, for sale; but, if he should learn that there was much probability that Lower California would be made a Slave State, he supposed it would pay him to wait, as probably, if that should occur, he could take them there and sell them for twice as much as they would now bring in New Orleans. He knew very well, he said, that, as they were, raising corn and tobacco, they were paying nothing at all like a fair interest on their value.

Some of his best hands he now rented out, to work at a furnace, and for the best of these he had been offered, for next year, two hundred dollars. He did not know whether he ought to let them go, though. They were worked hard, and had too much liberty, and were acquiring bad habits. They earned money by overwork, and spent it for whisky, and got a habit of roaming about and *taking care of themselves;* because when they were not at work in the furnace, nobody looked out for them.

I begin to suspect that the great trouble and anxiety of Southern gentlemen is:—How, without quite destroying the capabilities of the Negro for any work at all, to prevent him from learning to take care of himself.

Petersburg, Dec. 28th.—It was early on a fine, mild, bright morning, like the pleasantest we ever have in March, that I alighted from a train of cars, at a country station. Besides the shanty that stood for a station house, there was a small, comfortable farmhouse on the right, and a country store on the left, and around them, perhaps, fifty acres of clear land, now much flooded with muddy water—all framed in by thick pine wood.

A few Negro children, staring as fixedly and posed as lifelessly as if they were really figures "carved in ebony," stood, lay, and lounged on the sunny side of the ranks of locomotive firewood; a white man, smoking a cigar, looked out of the door of the store, and another, chewing tobacco, leaned against a gatepost in front of the farmhouse; I advanced to the latter, and asked him if I could hire a horse in the neighborhood.

"How d'ye do, sir?" he replied, spitting and bowing with ceremony; "I have some horses—none on 'em very good ones, though—rather hard riders; reckon, perhaps, they wouldn't suit you."

"Thank you; do you think I could find anything better about here?"

"Colonel Gillin, over here to the store, 's got a right nice saddle horse, if he'll let you take her. I'll go over there with you, and see if he will. . . . Mornin', Colonel;—here's a gentleman that wants to go to Thomas W.'s: couldn't you let him have your saddle horse?"

"How do you do, sir; I suppose you'd come back tonight?"

"That's my intention; but I might be detained till tomorrow, unless it would be inconvenient to you to spare your horse."

"Well, yes, sir, I reckon you can have her;—Tom!—Tom!— *Tom!* Now, has that devilish nigger gone again? Tom! *Oh,* Tom! saddle the filly for this gentleman.—Have you ever been to Mr. W.'s, sir?"

"No, I have not."

"It isn't a very easy place for strangers to go to from here; but I reckon I can direct you, so you'll have no difficulty."

He accordingly began to direct me; but the way appeared so difficult to find, I asked him to let me make a written memorandum, and, from this memorandum, I now repeat the directions he gave me.

"You take this road here — you'll see where it's most travelled, and it's easy enough to keep on it for about a mile; then there's a fork, and you take the right; pretty soon, you'll cross a creek and turn to the right — the creek's been up a good deal lately, and there's some big trees fallen along there, and if they ha'n't got them out of the way, you may have some difficulty in finding where the road is; but you keep bearing off to the right, where it's the most open [i.e., the wood], and you'll see it again pretty soon. Then you go on, keeping along in the road — you'll see where folks have travelled before — for may be a quarter of a mile, and you'll find a cross road; you must take that to the left; pretty soon you'll pass two cabins; one of 'em's old and all fallen in, the other one's new, and there's a white man lives into it: you can't mistake it. About a hundred yards beyond it, there's a fork, and you take the left — it turns square off, and it's fenced for a good bit; keep along by the fence, and you can't miss it. It's right straight beyond that till you come to a school-house, there's a gate opposite to it, and off there there's a big house — but I don't reckon you'll see it neither, for the woods. But somewhere, about three hundred yards beyond the school-house, you'll find a little road running off to the left through an old field; you take that, and in less than half a mile you'll find a path going square off to the right; you take that, and keep on it till you pass a little cabin in the woods; ain't nobody lives there now: then it turns to the left, and when you come to a fence and a gate, you'll see a house there, that's Mr. George Rivers' plantation — it breaks in two, and you take the right, and when you come to the end of the fence, turn the corner — don't keep on, but turn there. Then it's straight, till you come to the creek again — there's a bridge there; don't go over the bridge, but turn to the left and keep along nigh the creek, and pretty soon you'll see a meeting house in the woods; you go to that, and

you'll see a path bearing off to the right—it looks as if it was
going right away from the creek, but you take it, and pretty
soon it'll bring you to a sawmill on the creek, up higher a piece;
you just cross the creek there, and you'll find some people at
the mill, and they'll put you right straight on the road to
Mr. W.'s."

"How far is it all, sir?"

"I reckon it's about two hours' ride, when the roads are good,
to the sawmill. Mr. W.'s gate is only a mile or so beyond that,
and then you've got another mile, or better, after you get to the
gate, but you'll see some nigger quarters—the niggers belong
to Mr. W., and I reckon ther'll be some of 'em round, and they'll
show you just where to go."

After reading over my memorandum, and finding it correct,
and agreeing with him that I should pay two dollars a day for
the mare, we walked out, and found her saddled and waiting
for me.

I remarked that she was very good looking.

"Yes, sir; she ain't a bad filly; out of a mare that came of Lady
Rackett by old Lord-knows-who, the best horse we ever had in
this part of the country: I expect you have heard of him. Oh!
Jane's maybe a little playful, but you'll find her a pleasant
riding horse."

The filly was just so pleasantly playful, and full of well-bred
life, as to create a joyful, healthy, sympathetic, frolicsome heed-
lessness in her rider, and, in two hours, we had lost our way,
and I was trying to work up a dead reckoning.

Within less than a quarter of a mile there was a fork in the
road to the left, which seemed a good deal more travelled than
the straight one; nevertheless I kept the latter, and was soon
well satisfied that I had done so. It presently led me up a slope
out of the oak woods into a dark evergreen forest; and though it
was a mere bridlepath, it must have existed, I thought, before
the trees began to grow, for it was free of stumps, and smooth
and clean as a garden walk, and the pines grew thickly up,
about four feet apart, on each side of it, their branches meeting,
just clear of my head, and making a dense shade. There was an
agreeable, slightly balsamic odor in the air; the path was
covered with a deep, elastic mat of pine leaves, so that our foot-

steps could hardly be heard; and for a time we greatly enjoyed going along at a lazy, pacing walk of Jane's. It was noonday, and had been rather warmer than was quite agreeable on the open road, and I took my hat off, and let the living pine leaves brush my hair. But, after a while, I felt slightly chilly; and when Jane, at the same time, gave a little sympathizing caper, I bent my head down, that the limbs might not hit me, until it nearly rested on her neck, dropped my hands and pressed my knees tightly against her. Away we bounded!

A glorious gallop Jane had inherited from her noble grandfather!

Out of the cool dark green alley, at last, and soon, with a more cautious step, down a steep, stony declivity, set with deciduous trees — beech, ash, oak, gum — "gum," beloved of the "minstrels." A brawling shallow brook at the bottom, into which our path descended, though on the opposite shore was a steep, high bank, faced by an impenetrable brake of bush and brier.

Have we been following a path only leading to a watering place, then? I see no continuance of it. Jane does not hesitate at all; but, as if it was the commonest thing here to take advantage of nature's engineering in this way, walking into the water, turns her head up stream.

For more than a mile we continued following up the brook, which was all the time walled in by insurmountable banks, overhung by large trees. Sometimes it swept strongly through a deep channel, contracted by boulders; sometimes purled and tinkled over a pebbly slope; and sometimes stood in broad, silent pools, around the edges of which remained a skirt of ice, held there by bushes and long broken water grasses.

At length came pine woods again. Jane was now for leaving the brook. I let her have her own way, and she soon found a beaten track in the woods. It certainly was not the "straight road" we had been directed to follow; but its course was less crooked than that of the brook, and after some time it led us out into a more open country, with young pines and enclosed fields. Eventually we came to a gate and lane, which we followed till we came to another cross lane leading straight to a farmhouse.

As soon as we turned into the cross lane, half a dozen little Negro boys and girls were seen running toward the house, to give alarm. We passed a stable, with a cattle-pen by its side, opposite which was a vegetable garden, enclosed with split palings; then across a running stream of water; then by a small cabin on the right; and a corncrib and large pen, with a number of fatting hogs in it, on the left; then into a large, irregular yard, in the midst of which was the farmhouse, before which were now collected three white children, six black ones, two Negro women, and an old lady wearing spectacles.

"How dy do, sir?" said the old lady, as we reined up, lifted our hat, and put our black foot foremost.

"Thank you, madam, quite well; but I have lost my way to Mr. Thomas W.'s, and will trouble you to tell me how to go from here to get to his house."

By this time a black man came cautiously walking in from the field back of the house, bringing an axe; a woman, who had been washing clothes in the brook, left her work and came up on the other side, and two more girls climbed upon a great heap of logs that had been thrown upon the ground, near the porch, for fuel. The swine were making a great noise in their pen, as if feeding time had come; and a flock of turkeys were gobbling so incessantly and loudly that I was not heard. The old lady ordered the turkeys to be driven away, but nobody stirred to do it, and I rode nearer and repeated my request. No better success. "Can't you shew away them turkeys?" she asked again; but nobody "shewed." A third time I endeavored to make myself understood. "Will you please direct me how to go to Mr. W.'s?"

"No, sir—not here."

"Excuse me—I asked if you would direct me to Mr. W.'s."

"If some of you niggers don't shew them turkeys, I'll have you all whipped as soon as your mass John comes home," exclaimed the old lady, now quite excited. The man with the axe, without moving towards them at all, picked up a billet of wood, and threw it at the biggest cock turkey, who immediately collapsed; and the whole flock scattered, chased by the two girls who had been on the log heap.

"An't dat Colonel Gillin's mare, master?" asked the black man, coming up on my left.

"You want to go to Thomas W.'s?" asked the old lady.

"Yes, madam."

"It's a good many years since I have been to Thomas W.'s, and I reckon I can't tell you how to go there now."

"If master'll go over to Missy Abler's, I reckon dey ken tell 'em dah, sar."

"And how shall I go to Mrs. Abler's?"

"You want to go to Missy Abler's; you take dat path right over 'yond dem bars, dar, by de hog pen, dat runs along by dat fence into de woods, and dat'll take you right straight dar."

"Is you come from Colonel Gillin's, massa?" asked the wash woman.

"Yes."

"Did you see a black man dar, dey calls Tom, sar?"

"Yes."

"Tom's my husband, massa; if you's gwine back dah, wish you'd tell um, ef you please, sar, dat I wants to see him partiklar; will ou, massa?"

"Yes."

"Tank you, massa."

I bowed to the old lady, and, in turning to ride off, saw two other Negro boys who had come out of the woods, and were now leaning over the fence, and staring at us, as if I were a giant and Jane was a dragoness.

We trotted away, found the path, and in course of a mile had our choice of at least twenty forks to go "straight to Mrs. Abler's." At length, cleared land again, fences, stubble fields and a lane, that took us to a little cabin, which fronted, much to my surprise, upon a broad and well-travelled road. Over the door of the cabin was a sign, done in black, upon a hogshead stave, showing that it was a "*Grosery*," which, in Virginia, means the same thing as in Ireland—a dram shop.

I hung the bridle over a rack before the door, and walked in. At one end of the interior was a range of shelves, on which were two decanters, some dirty tumblers, a box of crackers, a canister, and several packages in paper; under the shelves a table and a barrel. At the other end of the room was a fireplace; near this, a chest, and another range of shelves, on which stood plates and cooking utensils: between these and the grocery end were a bed and a spinning-wheel. Near the spinning-wheel sat a tall, bony, sickly, sullen young woman, nursing a languishing infant. The faculty would not have discouraged either of them from trying hydropathic practice. In a corner of the fireplace sat a man, smoking a pipe. He rose, as I entered, walked across to the grocery shelves, turned a chair round at the table, and asked me to take a seat. I excused myself, and requested him to direct me to Mr. W.'s. He had heard of such a man living somewhere about there, but he did not know where. He repeated this, with an oath, when I declined to "take" anything, and added, that he had not lived here long, and he was sorry he had ever come here. It was the worst job, for himself, ever he did, when he came here, though all he wanted was to just get a living.

I rode on till I came to another house, a very pleasant little house, with a steep, gabled roof, curving at the bottom, and extending over a little gallery, which was entered, by steps, from the road; back of it were stables and Negro cabins, and by its side was a small garden, and beyond that a peach orchard. As I approached it, a well-dressed young man, with an intelligent and pleasant face, came out into the gallery. I asked him if he could direct me to Mr. W.'s. "Thomas W.'s?" he inquired.

"Yes, sir."

"You are not going in the right direction to go to Mr. W.'s. The shortest way you can take to go there is, to go right back to the Court House."

I told him I had just come out of the lane by the grocery on to the road. "Ah! well, I'll tell you; you had better turn round, and keep right straight upon this road till you get to the Court House, and anybody can tell you, there, how to go."

"How far is it, sir?"

"To the Court House?—not above a mile."

"And to Mr. W.'s?"

"To Mr. W.'s, I should think it was as much as ten miles, and long ones, too."

I rode to the Court House, which was a plain brick building in the center of a small square, around which there were twenty or thirty houses, two of them being occupied as stores, one as a saddler's shop, one had the sign of "Law Office" upon it; one was a jail; two were occupied by physicians, one other looked as if it might be a meeting house or schoolhouse, or the shop of any mechanic needing much light for his work, and two were "Hotels." At one of these we stopped to dine; Jane had "corn and fodder" (they had no oats or hay in the stable), and I had ham and eggs (they had no fresh meat in the house). I had several other things, however, that were very good, besides the company of the landlady, who sat alone with me, at the table, in a long dining hall, and was very pretty, amiable, and talkative.

In a course of apologies, which came in the place of soup, she gave me the clue to the assemblage of Negroes I had seen at the mill. It was Christmas week; all the servants thought they must go, for at least one day, to have a frolic, and today (as luck would have it, when I was coming,) her cook was off with some others; she did not suppose they'd be back till tomorrow, and then, likely as not, they'd be drunk. She did not think this custom, of letting servants go so, at Christmas, was a good one; niggers were not fit to be let to take care of themselves, anyhow. It was very bad for them, and she didn't think it was *right*. Providence had put the servants into our hands to be looked out for, and she didn't believe it was intended they should be let to do all sorts of wickedness, even if Christmas did come but once a year. She wished, for her part, it did not come but once in ten years.

(The Negroes, who were husking maize near the cabin where the white man lived, were, no doubt, slaves, who had hired themselves out by the day, during the holiday week, to earn a little money on their own account.)

In regard to the size of the dining hall, and the extent of sheds in the stable yard, the landlady told me that though at other times they very often did not have a single guest in a day, at "Court time" they always had more than they could comfortably accommodate. I judged, also, from her manners and the general appearance of the house, as well as from the charges, that, at such times, the company might be of a rather respectable character. The appearance of the other public house indicated that it expected a less select patronage.

When I left, my direction was to keep on the main road until I came to a fork, about four miles distant, then take the left, and

keep *the best-travelled road,* until I came to a certain house,
which was so described that I should know it, where I was
advised to ask further directions.

 The sky was now clouding over; it was growing cold; and we
went on, as fast as we conveniently could, until we reached the
fork in the road. The direction to keep the best-travelled road,
was unpleasantly prominent in my mind; it was near sunset,
I reflected, and however jolly it might be at twelve o'clock at
noon, it would be quite another thing to be knocking about
among those fierce hogs in the pine forest, if I should be lost,
at twelve o'clock at night. Besides, as the landlady said about
her Negroes, I did not think it was right to expose Jane to this
danger, unnecessarily. A little beyond the fork, there was a
large, gray, old house, with a grove of tall poplars before it; a
respectable, country-gentleman-of-the-old-school look it had. —
These old Virginians are proverbially hospitable. — It's rather
impudent; but I hate to go back to the Court House, and I am — I
will ride on, and look it in the face, at any rate.

 Zigzag fences up to a large, square yard, growing full of
Lombardy poplar sprouts, from the roots of eight or ten old
trees, which were planted some fifty years ago, I suppose, in a
double row, on two sides of the house. At the further end of
this yard, beyond the house, a gate opened on the road, and
out of this was just then coming a black man.

 I inquired of him if there was a house, near by, at which I
could get accommodation for the night. Reckoned his master'd
take me in, if I'd ask him. Where was his master? In the house:
I could go right in here (at a place where a panel of the paling
had fallen over) and see him if I wanted to. I asked him to hold
my horse, and went in.

 It was a simple two-story house, very much like those built
by the wealthier class of people in New England villages, from
fifty to a hundred years ago, except that the chimneys were
carried up outside the walls. There was a porch at the front
door, and a small wing at one end, in the rear: from this wing
to the other end extended a broad gallery.

 A dog had been barking at me after I had dismounted; and
just as I reached the steps of the gallery, a vigorous, middle-
aged man, with a rather sullen and suspicious expression of

face, came out without any coat on, to see what had excited him.

Doubting if he were the master of the house, I told him that I had come in to inquire if it would be convenient to allow me to spend the night with them. He asked where I came from, whither I was going, and various other questions, until I had given him an epitome of my day's wanderings and adventures; at the conclusion of which he walked to the end of the gallery to look at my horse; then without giving me any answer, but muttering indistinctly something about servants, walked into the house, shutting the door behind him!

Well, thought I, this is not overwhelmingly hospitable. What can it mean?

While I was considering whether he expected me to go without any further talk—his curiosity being, I judged, satisfied— he came out again, and said, "Reckon you can stay, sir, if you'll take what we'll give you." (The good man had been in to consult his wife.) I replied that I would do so thankfully, and hoped they would not give themselves any unnecessary trouble, or alter their usual family arrangements. I was then invited to come in, but I preferred to see my horse taken care of first. My host called for "Sam," two or three times, and then said he reckoned all his "people" had gone off, and he would attend to my horse himself. I offered to assist him, and we walked out to the gate, where the Negro, not being inclined to wait for my return, had left Jane fastened to a post. Our host conducted us to an old square log cabin which had formerly been used for curing tobacco, there being no room for Jane, he said, in the stables proper.

The floor of the tobacco house was covered with lumber, old plows, scythes and cradles, a part of which had to be removed to make room for the filly to stand. She was then induced, with some difficulty, to enter it through a low, square doorway; saddle and bridle were removed, and she was fastened in a corner by a piece of old plowline. We then went to a fodder stack, and pulled out from it several small bundles of maize leaves. Additional feed and water were promised when "some of the niggers" came in; and, after righting up an old door that had fallen from one hinge, and setting a rail against it to keep it in its place, we returned to the house.

My host (whom I will call Mr. Newman) observed that his buildings and fences were a good deal out of order. He had owned the place but a few years, and had not had time to make much improvement about the house yet.

I learned that there were no white laboring men here who hired themselves out by the month. The poor white people that had to labor for their living, never would work steadily at any employment. "They generally followed boating"—hiring as hands on the bateaus that navigate the small streams and canals, but never for a longer term at once than a single trip of a boat, whether that might be long or short. At the end of the trip they were paid by the day. Their wages were from fifty cents to a dollar, varying with the demand and individual capacities. They hardly ever worked on farms except in harvest, when they usually received a dollar a day, sometimes more. In harvest time, most of the rural mechanics closed their shops and hired out to the farmers at a dollar a day, which would indicate that their ordinary earnings are considerably less than this. At other than harvest time, the poor white people, who had no trade, would sometimes work for the farmers by the job; not often any regular agricultural labor, but at getting rails or shingles, or clearing land.

He did not know that they were particular about working with Negroes, but no white man would ever do certain kinds of work (such as taking care of cattle, or getting water or wood to be used in the house); and if you should ask a white man you had hired, to do such things, he would get mad and tell you he wasn't a nigger. Poor white girls never hired out to do servants' work, but they would come and help another white woman about her sewing and quilting, and take wages for it. But these girls were not very respectable generally, and it was not agreeable to have them in your house, though there were some very respectable ladies that would go out to sew. Farmers depended almost entirely upon their Negroes; it was only when they were hard pushed by their crops, that they ever got white hands to help them.

Negroes had commanded such high wages lately, to work on railroads and in tobacco factories, that farmers were tempted to hire out too many of their people, and to undertake to do too much work with those they retained; and thus they were often driven to employ white men, and to give them very high wages by the day, when they found themselves getting much behind-hand with their crops. He had been driven very hard in this way this last season; he had been so unfortunate as to lose one of his best women, who died in childbed just before harvest. The loss of the woman and her child, for the child had died also, just at that time, came very hard upon him. He would not have taken a thousand dollars of any man's money for them. He had had to hire white men to help him, but they were poor sticks, and would be half the time drunk, and you never know what to depend upon with them. One fellow that he had hired, who had agreed to work for him all through harvest, got him to pay him some wages in advance (he said it was to buy him some clothes with, so that he could go to meeting on Sunday, at the Court House), and went off the next day, right in the middle of harvest, and he had never seen him since. He had heard of him — he was on a boat — but he didn't reckon he should ever get his money again.

Of course, he did not see how white laborers were ever going to come into competition with Negroes here, at all. You never could depend on white men, and you couldn't *drive* them any; they wouldn't stand it. Slaves were the reliable laborers — you could command them and make them do what was right.

From the manner in which he talked of the white laboring people, it was evident that, although he placed them in some sort of an equality with himself, and that in his intercourse with them he wouldn't think of asserting for himself any superior dignity, or even feel himself to be patronizing them in not doing so, yet he, all the time, recognized them as a distinct and a rather despicable class, and wanted to have as little to do with them as he conveniently could.

I have been once or twice told that the poor white people, meaning those, I suppose, who bring nothing to market to ex-change for money but their labor, although they may own a cabin and a little furniture, and cultivate land enough to supply themselves with (maize) bread, are worse off in almost all respects than the slaves. They are said to be extremely ignorant and immoral, as well as indolent and unambitious. That their condition is not so unfortunate by any means as that of Negroes, however, is most obvious, since from among them, men sometimes elevate themselves to positions and habits of usefulness, and respectability. They are said to "corrupt" the Negroes, and to encourage them to steal, or to work for them at night and on Sundays, and to pay them with liquor, and also to constantly associate licentiously with them. They seem, nevertheless, more than any other portion of the community, to hate and despise the Negroes.

The country passed through, in the early part of my second day's ride, was very similar in general characteristics to that I have already described; only that a rather larger portion of it was cleared, and plantations were more frequent. About eleven o'clock I crossed a bridge and came to the meeting house I had been expecting to reach by that hour the previous day. It was in the midst of the woods, and the small clearing around it was still dotted with the stumps of the trees out of whose trunks it had been built; for it was a log structure.

Half an hour after this I arrived at the Negro quarters — a little hamlet of ten or twelve small and dilapidated cabins. Just beyond them was a plain farm gate, at which several Negroes were standing: one of them, a well-made man, with an intelligent countenance and prompt manner, directed me how to find my way to his owner's house. It was still nearly a mile distant; and yet, until I arrived in its immediate vicinity, I saw no cultivated field, and but one clearing. In the edge of this clearing, a number of Negroes, male and female, lay stretched out upon the ground near a small smoking charcoal pit. Their master afterwards informed me that they were burning charcoal for the plantation blacksmith, using the time allowed them for holidays — from Christmas to New Year's Day — to earn a little money for themselves in this way. He paid them by the bushel for it. When I said that I supposed he allowed them to take what wood they chose for this purpose, he replied that he had five hundred acres covered with wood, which he would be very glad to have any one burn, or clear off in any way.

Mr. W.'s house was an old family mansion, which he had himself remodeled "in the Grecian style," and furnished with a large wooden portico. An oak forest had originally occupied the ground where it stood; but this having been cleared and the soil worn out in cultivation by the previous proprietors, pine woods now surrounded it in every direction, a square of a few acres only being kept clear immediately about it. A number of the old oaks still stood in the rear of the house, and, until Mr. W. commenced "his improvements," there had been some in its front. But as he deemed these to have an aspect of negligence and rudeness, not quite proper to be associated with a fine house, he had cut them away, and substituted formal rows of miserable little ailanthus trees. I could not believe my ears till this explanation had been twice repeated to me.

On three sides of the outer part of the cleared square, which was called "the lawn," but which was no more like a lawn than it was like a sea beach, there was a row of Negro cabins, stables, tobacco houses, and other offices, all built of rough logs.

Mr. W. was one of the few large planters of his vicinity who still made the culture of tobacco their principal business. He said there was a general prejudice against tobacco, in all the tidewater region of the state, because it was through the culture of tobacco that the once fertile soils had been impoverished; but he did not believe that, at the present value of Negroes, their labor could be applied to the culture of grain, with any profit, except under peculiarly favorable circumstances. Possibly, the use of guano might make wheat a paying crop, but he still doubted. He had not used it, himself. Tobacco required fresh land, and was rapidly exhausting, but it returned more money, for the labor used upon it, than anything else; enough more, in his opinion, to pay for the wearing out of the land. If he was well paid for it, he did not know why he should not wear out his land.

His tobacco fields were nearly all in a distant and lower part of his plantation; land which had been neglected before his time, in a great measure, because it had been sometimes flooded, and was, much of the year, too wet for cultivation. He was draining and clearing it, and it now brought good crops.

He had had an Irish gang draining for him, by contract. He thought a Negro could do twice as much work, in a day, as an Irishman. He had not stood over them and seen them at work, but judged entirely from the amount they accomplished: he thought a good gang of Negroes would have got on twice as fast. He was sure they must have "trifled" a great deal, or they would have accomplished more than they had. He complained much, also, of their sprees and quarrels. I asked why he should employ Irishmen, in preference to doing the work with his own hands. "It's dangerous work and a Negro's life is too valuable to be risked at it. If a Negro dies, it's a considerable loss, you know."

He afterwards said that his Negroes never worked so hard as to tire themselves — always were lively, and ready to go off on a frolic at night. He did not think they ever did half a fair day's work. They could not be made to work hard: they never would lay out their strength freely, and it was impossible to make them do it.

This is just what I have thought when I have seen slaves at work — they seem to go through the motions of labor without putting strength into them. They keep their powers in reserve for their own use at night, perhaps.

Mr. W. also said that he cultivated only the coarser and lower priced sorts of tobacco, because the finer sorts required more painstaking and discretion than it was possible to make a large gang of Negroes use. "You can make a nigger work," he said, "but you cannot make him think."

Although Mr. W. was so wealthy (or, at least, would be considered anywhere at the North), and had been at college, his style of living was very farmerlike, and thoroughly Southern. On their plantations, generally, the Virginia gentlemen seem to drop their full dress and constrained town habits, and to live a free, rustic, shooting-jacket life. We dined in a room that extended out, rearwardly, from the house, and which, in a Northern establishment, would have been the kitchen. The cooking was done in a detached log cabin, and the dishes brought some distance, through the open air, by the servants. The outer door was left constantly open, though there was a fire in an enormous old fireplace, large enough, if it could have been distributed sufficiently, to have lasted a New York seamstress the best part of the winter. By the door there was indiscriminate admittance to Negro children and foxhounds, and, on an average, there were four of these, grinning or licking their chops, on either side of my chair, all the time I was at the table. A stout woman acted as head waitress, employing two handsome little mulatto boys as her aids in communicating with the kitchen, from which relays of hot cornbread, of an excellence quite new to me, were brought at frequent intervals. There was no other bread, and but one vegetable served — sweet potato, roasted in ashes, and this, I thought, was the best sweet potato, also, that I ever had eaten; but there were four preparations of swine's flesh, besides fried fowls, fried eggs, cold roast turkey, and opossum, cooked, I know not how, but it somewhat resembled baked sucking pig. The only beverages on the table were milk and whisky.

———. ———. I have been visiting a farm, cultivated entirely by free labor. The proprietor told me that he was first led to disuse slave labor, not from any economical considerations, but because he had become convinced that there was an essential wrong in holding men in forced servitude with any other purpose than to benefit them alone, and because he was not willing to allow his own children to be educated as slave masters. His father had been a large slaveholder, and he felt very strongly the bad influence it had had on his own character. He wished me to be satisfied that Jefferson uttered a great truth when he asserted that slavery was more pernicious to the white race than the black. Although, therefore, a chief part of his inheritance had been in slaves, he had liberated them all.

Most of them had, by his advice, gone to Africa. These he had frequently heard from. Except a child that had been drowned, they were, at his last account, all alive, in general good health, and satisfactorily prospering. He had lately received a letter from one of them, who told him that he was "*trying* to preach the Gospel," and who had evidently greatly improved, both intellectually and morally, since he left here. With regard to those going North, and the common opinion that they encountered much misery, and would be much better off here, he said that it entirely depended on the general character and habits of the individual: it was true of those who were badly brought up, and who had acquired indolent and vicious habits, especially if they were drunkards, but, if of some intelligence and well trained, they generally represented themselves to be successful and contented.

He mentioned two remarkable cases, that had come under his own observation, of this kind. One was that of a man who had been free, but, by some fraud and informality of his papers, was re-enslaved. He ran away, and afterwards negotiated, by correspondence, with his master, and purchased his freedom. This man he had accidentally met, fifteen years afterwards, in a Northern city; he was engaged in profitable and increasing business, and showed him, by his books, that he was possessed of property to the amount of ten thousand dollars. He was living a great deal more comfortably and wisely than ever his old master had done. The other case was that of a colored woman, who had obtained her freedom, and who became apprehensive that she also was about to be fraudulently made a slave again. She fled to Philadelphia, where she was nearly starved, at first. A little girl, who heard her begging in the streets to be allowed to work for bread, told her that her mother was wanting some washing done, and she followed her home. The mother, not knowing her, was afraid to trust her with the articles to be washed. She prayed so earnestly for the job, however—suggesting that she might be locked into a room until she had completed it—that it was given her.

So she commenced life in Philadelphia. Ten years afterwards he had accidentally met her there; she recognized him immediately, recalled herself to his recollection, manifested the greatest joy at seeing him, and asked him to come to her house, which he found a handsome three-story building, furnished really with elegance; and she pointed out to him, from the window, three houses in the vicinity that she owned and rented. She showed great anxiety to have her children well educated, and was employing the best instructors for them which she could procure in Philadelphia.

He considered the condition of slaves to have much improved since the Revolution, and very perceptibly during the last twenty years. The original stock of slaves, the imported Africans, he observed, probably required to be governed with much greater severity, and very little humanity was exercised or thought of with regard to them. The slaves of the present day are of a higher character; in fact, he did not think more than half of them were full-blooded Africans. Public sentiment condemned the man who treated his slaves with cruelty. The owners were mainly men of some cultivation, and felt a family attachment to their slaves, many of whom had been the play-mates of their boyhood. Nevertheless, they were frequently punished severely, under the impulse of temporary passion, often without deliberation, and on unfounded suspicion. This was especially the case where they were left to overseers, who, though sometimes men of intelligence and piety, were more often coarse, brutal, and licentious; drinking men, wholly unfitted for the responsibility imposed on them.

With regard to the value of slave labor, this gentleman is confident that, at present, he has the advantage in employing free men instead of it. It has not been so until of late, the price of slaves having much advanced within ten years, while immigration has made free white laborers more easy to be procured.

He has heretofore had some difficulty in obtaining hands when he needed them, and has suffered a good deal from the demoralizing influence of adjacent slave labor, the men, after a few months residence, inclining to follow the customs of the slaves with regard to the amount of work they should do in a day, or their careless mode of operation. He has had white and black Virginians, sometimes Germans, and latterly Irish. Of all these, he has found the Irish on the whole the best. The poorest have been the native white Virginians; next, the free blacks: and though there have been exceptions, he has not generally paid these as high as one hundred dollars a year, and has thought them less worth their wages than any he has had. At present, he has two white natives and two free colored men, but both the latter were brought up in his family, and are worth twenty dollars a year more than the average. The free black, he thinks, is generally worse than the slave, and so is the poor white man. He also employs, at present, four Irish hands, and is expecting two more to arrive, who have been recommended to him, and sent for by those he has. He pays the Irishmen $120 a year, and boards them. He has had them for $100; but these are all excellent men, and well worth their price. They are less given to drinking than any men he has ever had; and one of them first suggested improvements to him in his farm, that he is now carrying out with prospects of considerable advantage. Housemaids, Irish girls, he pays $3 and $6 a month.

He does not apprehend that in future he shall have any difficulty in obtaining steady men, who will accomplish much more work than any slaves. There are some operations, such as carting and spreading dung, and all work with the fork, spade, or shovel, at which his Irishmen will do, he thinks, over fifty per cent more in a day than any Negroes he has ever known. On the whole, he is satisfied that at present free labor is more profitable than slave labor, though his success is not so evident that he would be willing to have attention particularly called to it. His farm, moreover, is now in a transition state from one system of husbandry to another, and appearances are temporarily more unfavorable on that account.

The wages paid for slaves, when they are hired for agricultural labor, do not differ at present, he says, from those which he pays for his free laborers. In both cases the hiring party boards the laborer, but, in addition to money and board, the slave employer has to furnish clothing, and is subject, without redress, to any losses which may result from the carelessness or malevolence of the slave. He also has to lose his time if he is unwell, or when from any cause he is absent or unable to work.

The slave, if he is indisposed to work, and especially if he is not treated well, or does not like the master who has hired him, will sham sickness—even make himself sick or lame—that he need not work. But a more serious loss frequently arises, when the slave, thinking he is worked too hard, or being angered by punishment or unkind treatment, "getting the sulks," takes to "the swamp," and comes back when he has a mind to. Often this will not be till the year is up for which he is engaged, when he will return to his owner, who glad to find his property safe, and that it has not died in the swamp, or gone to Canada, forgets to punish him, and immediately sends him for another year to a new master.

"But, meanwhile, how does the Negro support life in the swamp?" I asked.

"Oh, he gets sheep and pigs and calves, and fowls and turkeys; sometimes they will kill a small cow. We have often seen the fires, where they were cooking them, through the woods, in the swamp yonder. If it is cold, he will crawl under a fodder stack, or go into the cabins with some of the other Negroes, and in the same way, you see, he can get all the corn, or almost anything else he wants."

"He steals them from his master?"

"From any one; frequently from me. I have had many a sheep taken by them."

"It is a common thing, then?"

"Certainly, it is, very common, and the loss is sometimes exceedingly provoking. One of my neighbors here was going to build, and hired two mechanics for a year. Just as he was ready to put his house up, the two men, taking offense at something, both ran away, and did not come back at all till their year was out, and then their owner immediately hired them out again to another man."

These Negroes "in the swamp," he said, were often hunted after, but it was very difficult to find them, and, if caught, they would run again, and the other Negroes would hide and assist them. Dogs to track them he had never known to be used in Virginia.

Saturday, Dec. 25th. — From Christmas to New Year's Day, most of the slaves, except house servants, enjoy a freedom from labor; and Christmas is especially holiday, or Saturnalia, with them. The young ones began last night firing crackers, and I do not observe that they are engaged in any other amusement today; the older ones are generally getting drunk, and making business for the police. I have seen large gangs coming in from the country, and these contrast much in their general appearance with the town Negroes. The latter are dressed expensively, and frequently more elegantly than the whites. They seem to be spending money freely, and I observe that they, and even the slaves that wait upon me at the hotel, often have watches, and other articles of value.

The slaves have a good many ways of obtaining "spending money," which though in law belonging to their owner, as the property of a son under age does to his father, they are never dispossessed of, and use for their own gratification, with even less restraint than a wholesome regard for their health and moral condition may be thought to require. A Richmond paper, complaining of the liberty allowed to slaves in this respect, as calculated to foster an insubordinate spirit, speaks of their "champagne suppers." The police broke into a gambling cellar a few nights since, and found about twenty Negroes at "high play," with all the usual accessories of a first-class "Hell." It is mentioned that, among the number taken to the watchhouse, and treated with lashes the next morning, there were some who had previously enjoyed a high reputation for piety, and others of a very elegant or foppish appearance.

Passing two Negroes in the street, I heard the following:

"—Workin' in a tobacco factory all de year roun', an' come Christmas only twenty dollars! Workin' mighty hard, too—up to twelve o'clock o' night very often—an' then to hab a nigger oberseah!"

"A nigger!"

"Yes—dat's it, yer see. Wouldn't care if 'twarn't for dat. Nothin' but a dirty nigger! orderin' 'round, jes' as if he was a wite man!"

It is the custom of tobacco manufacturers to hire slaves and free Negroes at a certain rate of wages per year. A task of 45 lbs. per day is given them to work up, and all that they choose to do more than this they are paid for—payment being made once a fortnight; and invariably this over-wages is used by the slave for himself, and is usually spent in drinking, licentiousness, and gambling. The man was grumbling that he had saved but $20 to spend at the holidays.

Sitting with a company of smokers last night, one of them, to show me the manner in which a slave of any ingenuity or cunning would manage to avoid working for his master's profit, narrated the following anecdote. He was executor of an estate in which, among other Negroes, there was one very smart man, who, he knew perfectly well, ought to be earning for the estate $150 a year, and who could do it if he chose, yet whose wages for a year, being let out by the day or job, had amounted to but $18, while he had paid for medical attendance upon him $45. Having failed in every other way to make him earn anything, he proposed to him that he should purchase his freedom and go to Philadelphia, where he had a brother. He told him that if he would earn a certain sum ($400 I believe), and pay it over to the estate for himself, he would give him his free papers. The man agreed to the arrangement, and by his overwork in a tobacco factory, and some assistance from his free brother, soon paid the sum agreed upon, and was sent to Philadelphia. A few weeks afterwards he met him in the street, and asked him why he had returned. "Oh, I don't like dat Philadelphy, massa; an't no chance for colored folks dere; spec' if I'd been a runaway, de wite folks dere take care o' me; but I couldn't git anythin' to do, so I jis borrow ten dollar of my broder, and cum back to old Virginny."

"But you know the law forbids your return. I wonder that you are not afraid to be seen here; I should think Mr. —— (an officer of police) would take you up."

"Oh! I look out for dat, massa; I juss hire myself out to Mr. —— himself, ha! ha! He tink I your boy."

And so it proved; the officer, thinking that he was permitted to hire himself out, and tempted by the low wages at which he offered himself, had neglected to ask for his written permission, and had engaged him for a year. He still lived with the officer, and was an active, healthy, good servant to him.

A well-informed capitalist and slaveholder remarked, that Negroes could not be employed in cotton factories. I said that I understood they were so in Charleston, and some other places at the South.

"It may be so, yet," he answered, "but they will have to give it up."

The reason was, he said, that the Negro could never be trained to exercise judgment; he cannot be made to use his mind; he always depends on machinery doing its own work, and cannot be made to watch it. He neglects it until something is broken or there is great waste. "We have tried rewards and punishments, but it makes no difference. It's his nature and you cannot change it. All men are indolent and have a disinclination to labor, but this is a great deal stronger in the African race than in any other. In working niggers, we must always calculate that they will not labor at all except to avoid punishment, and they will never do more than just enough to save themselves from being punished, and no amount of punishment will prevent their working carelessly and indifferently. It always seems on the plantation as if they took pains to break all the tools and spoil all the cattle that they possibly can, even when they know they'll be directly punished for it."

As to rewards, he said, "They only want to support life: they will not work for anything more; and in this country it would be hard to prevent their getting that." I thought this opinion of the power of rewards was not exactly confirmed by the narrative we had just heard, but I said nothing. "If you could move," he continued, "all the white people from the whole seaboard district of Virginia and give it up to the Negroes that are on it now, just leave them to themselves, in ten years' time there would not be an acre of land cultivated, and nothing would be produced, except what grew spontaneously."

I said I supposed that they were much better off, more improved intellectually, and more kindly treated in Virginia than further South. He said I was mistaken in both respects—that in Louisiana, especially, they were more intelligent, because the amalgamation of the races was much greater, and they were treated with more familiarity by the whites; besides which, the laws of Louisiana were much more favorable to them. For instance, they required the planter to give slaves 200 pounds of pork a year: and he gave a very apt anecdote, showing the effect of this law, but which, at the same time, made it evident that a Virginian may be accustomed to neglect providing sufficient food for his force, and that they sometimes suffer greatly for want of it. I was assured, however, that this was very rare—that, generally, the slaves were well provided for—always allowed a sufficient quantity of meal, and, generally, of pork—were permitted to raise pigs and poultry, and in summer could always grow as many vegetables as they wanted. It was observed, however, that they frequently neglect to provide for themselves in this way, and live mainly on meal and bacon. If a man does not provide well for his slaves, it soon becomes known; he gets the name of a "nigger killer," and loses the respect of the community.

The general allowance of food was thought to be a peck and a half of meal, and three pounds of bacon a week. This, it was observed, is as much meal as they can eat, but they would be glad to have more bacon; sometimes they receive four pounds, but it is oftener that they get less than three. It is distributed to them on Saturday nights; or, on the better managed plantations, sometimes on Wednesday, to prevent their using it extravagantly, or selling it for whisky on Sunday. This distribution is called the "drawing," and is made by the overseer to all the heads of families or single Negroes. Except on the smallest plantations, where the cooking is done in the house of the proprietor, there is a cook house, furnished with a large copper for boiling, and an oven. Every night the Negroes take their "mess," for the next day's breakfast and dinner, to the cook, to be prepared for the next day. Custom varies as to the time it is served out to them; sometimes at morning and noon, at other times at noon and night. Each Negro marks his meat by cuts, so that he shall know it from the rest, and they observe each other's rights with regard to this, punctiliously.

After breakfast has been eaten early in the cabins, at sunrise, or a little before in winter, and perhaps a little later in summer, they go to the field. At noon dinner is brought to them, and, unless the work presses, they are allowed two hours' rest. Very punctually at sunset they stop work and are at liberty, except that a squad is detached once a week for shelling corn, to go to the mill for the next week's drawing of meal. Thus they work in the field about eleven hours a day, on an average. Returning to the cabins, wood "ought to have been" carted for them; but if it has not been, they then go to the woods and "tote" it home for themselves. They then make a fire — a big, blazing fire at this season, for the supply of fuel is unlimited — and cook their own supper, which will be a bit of bacon fried, often with eggs, cornbread baked in the spider after the bacon, to absorb the fat, and perhaps some sweet potatoes roasted in the ashes. Immediately after supper they go to sleep, often lying on the floor or a bench in preference to a bed. About two o'clock they very generally rouse up and cook and eat, or eat cold, what

they call their "mornin' bit"; then sleep again till breakfast.
They generally save from their ration of meal: commonly as
much as five bushels of meal was sent to town by my infor-
mant's hands every week, to be sold for them. Upon inquiry, he
almost always found that it belonged to only two or three
individuals, who had traded for it with the rest; he added, that
too often the exchange was for whisky, which, against his rules,
they obtained of some rascally white people in the neighborhood, and kept concealed. They were very fond of whisky, and
sometimes much injured themselves with it.

To show me how well they were supplied with eggs, he said
that once a vessel came to anchor, becalmed, off his place, and
the captain came to him and asked leave to purchase some eggs
of his people. He gave him permission, and called the cook to
collect them for him. The cook asked how many she should
bring. "Oh, all you can get," he answered — and she returned
after a time, with several boys assisting her, bringing nearly
two bushels, all the property of the slaves, and which they
were willing to sell at four cents a dozen.

One of the smokers explained to me that it is bad economy,
not to allow an abundant supply of food to "a man's force." If
not well provided for, the Negroes will find a way to provide for
themselves. It is, also, but simple policy to have them well
lodged and clothed. If they do not have comfortable cabins and
sufficient clothing, they will take cold, and be laid up. He lost a
valuable Negro, once, from having neglected to provide him
with shoes.

The houses of the slaves are usually log cabins, of various
degrees of comfort and commodiousness. At one end there is a
great open fireplace, which is exterior to the wall of the house,
being made of clay in an enclosure, about eight feet square and
high, of logs. The chimney is sometimes of brick, but more
commonly of lath or split sticks, laid up like log work and
plastered with mud. They enjoy great roaring fires, and, as the
common fuel is pine, the cabin, at night when the door is open,
seen from a distance, appears like a fierce furnace. The chimneys
often catch fire, and the cabin is destroyed. Very little precaution can be taken against this danger. Several cabins are placed
near together, and they are called "the quarters." On a planta-

tion of moderate size there will be but one "quarters." The situation chosen for it has reference to convenience of obtaining water from springs and fuel from the woods.

As to the clothing of the slaves on the plantations, they are said to be usually furnished by their owners or masters, every year, each with a coat and trousers, of a coarse woollen or woollen and cotton stuff (mostly made, especially for this purpose, in Providence, R. I.) for winter, trousers of cotton osnaburghs for summer, sometimes with a jacket also of the same; two pairs of strong shoes, or one pair of strong boots and one of lighter shoes for harvest; three shirts, one blanket, and one felt hat.

The women have two dresses of striped cotton, three shifts, two pairs of shoes, etc. The women lying in are kept at knitting short sacks, from cotton, which, in Southern Virginia, is usually raised for this purpose on the farm, and these are also given to the Negroes. They also purchase clothing for themselves, and, I notice especially, are well supplied with handkerchiefs, which the men frequently, and the women nearly always, wear on their heads. On Sundays and holidays they usually look very smart, but when at work, very ragged and slovenly.

At the conclusion of our barroom session, some time after midnight, as we were retiring to our rooms, our progress upstairs and along the corridors was several times impeded, by Negroes lying fast asleep, in their usual clothes only, upon the floor. I asked why they were not abed, and was answered by a gentleman, that Negroes never wanted to go to bed; they always preferred to sleep on the floor.

That "slaves are liars," or, as they say here, "niggers will lie," always has been proverbial. "They will lie in their very prayers to God," said one, and I find illustrations of the trouble that the vice occasions on every hand here. I just heard this, from a lady. A housemaid, who had the reputation of being especially devout, was suspected by her mistress of having stolen from her bureau several trinkets. She was charged with the theft, and vociferously denied it. She was watched, and the articles discovered openly displayed on her person as she went to church. She still, on her return, denied having them — was searched, and they were found in her pockets. When reproached by her mistress, and lectured on the wickedness of lying and stealing, she replied with the confident air of knowing the ground she stood upon, "Law, mam, don't say I's wicked; ole Aunt Ann says it allers right for us poor colored people to 'popiate whatever of de wite folk's blessins de Lord puts in our way"; old Aunt Ann being a sort of mother in the colored Israel of the town.

It is told me as a singular fact, that everywhere on the plantations, the agrarian notion has become a fixed point of the Negro system of ethics: that the result of labor belongs of right to the laborer, and on this ground, even the religious feel justified in using "massa's" property for their own temporal benefit. This they term "taking," and it is never admitted to be a reproach to a man among them that he is charged with it, though "stealing," or taking from another than their master, and particularly from one another, is so. They almost universally pilfer from the household stores when they have a safe opportunity.

2.

The Carolinas

Norfolk. — In order to be in time for the train of cars in which I was to leave Petersburg for Norfolk, I was called up at an unusual hour in the morning and provided with an apology for breakfast, on the ground that there had not been time to prepare anything better (though I was charged full time on the bill), advised by the landlord to hurry when I seated myself at the table, and two minutes afterwards informed that, if I remained longer, I should be too late.

Thanks to these kind precautions, I reached the station twenty minutes before the train left, and was afterwards carried, with about fifty other people, at the rate of ten miles an hour, to City-point, where all were discharged under a dirty shed, from which a wharf projected into James River.

The train was advertised to connect here with a steamboat for Norfolk. Finding no steamboat at the wharf, I feared, at first, that the delay in leaving Petersburg and the slow speed upon the road had detained us so long that the boat had departed without us. But observing no disappointment or concern expressed by the other passengers, I concluded the boat was to call for us, and had yet to arrive. An hour passed, during which I tried to keep warm by walking up and down the wharf; rain then commenced falling, and I returned to the crowded shed and asked a young man, who was engaged in cutting the letters G. W. B., with a dirk knife, upon the head of a tobacco cask, what was supposed to have detained the steamboat.

"Detained her? there aint no detention to her, as I know on; 'taint hardly time for her to be along yet."

Another half-hour, in fact, passed, before the steamboat arrived, nor was any impatience manifested by the passengers. All seemed to take this hurrying and waiting process as the regular thing. The women sat sullenly upon trunks and packing cases, and watched their baggage and restrained their children; the men chewed tobacco and read newspapers;

41

lounged first on one side and then on the other; some smoked, some walked away to a distant tavern; some reclined on the heaps of freight and went to sleep, and a few conversed quietly and intermittently with one another.

The shores of the James River are low and level — the scenery uninteresting; but frequent planters' mansions, often of considerable size and of some elegance, stand upon the bank, and sometimes these have very pretty and well-kept grounds about them, and the plantations surrounding them are culti-vated with neatness and skill. Many men distinguished in law and politics here have their homes.

I was pleased to see the appearance of enthusiasm with which some passengers, who were landed from our boat at one of these places, were received by two or three well-dressed Negro servants, who had come from the house to the wharf to meet them. Black and white met with kisses; and the effort of a long-haired sophomore to maintain his dignity, was quite ineffectual to kill the kindness of a fat mulatto woman, who joyfully and pathetically shouted, as she caught him off the gangplank, "Oh Massa George, is you come back!" Field Negroes, standing by, looked on with their usual besotted expression, and neither offered nor received greetings.

Jan. 10th. — Norfolk is a dirty, low, ill-arranged town, nearly divided by a morass. It has a single creditable public building, a number of fine private residences, and the polite society is reputed to be agreeable, refined, and cultivated, receiving a character from the families of the resident naval officers. It has all the immoral and disagreeable characteristics of a large seaport, with very few of the advantages that we should expect to find as relief to them. No lyceum or public libraries, no public gardens, no galleries of art, and though there are two "Bethels," no "home" for its seamen; no public resorts of healthful amusement; no place better than a filthy, tobacco-impregnated barroom or a licentious dance cellar, so far as I have been able to learn, for the stranger of high or low degree to pass the hours unoccupied by business.

Jan. 18th. — The "Great Dismal Swamp," together with the

smaller "Dismals" (for so the term is used here), of the same character, along the North Carolina coast, have hitherto been of considerable commercial importance as furnishing a large amount of lumber, and especially of shingles for our Northern use, as well as for exportation. The district from which this commerce proceeds is all a vast quagmire, the soil being entirely composed of decayed vegetable fiber, saturated and surcharged with water; yielding or *quaking* on the surface to the tread of a man, and a large part of it, during most of the year, half inundated with standing pools. It is divided by creeks and water veins, and in the center is a pond six miles long and three broad, the shores of which, strange to say, are at a higher elevation above the sea, than any other part of the swamp, and yet are of the same miry consistency. The Great Dismal is about thirty miles long and ten miles wide, on an average; its area about 200,000 acres. And the little Dismal, Aligator, Catfish, Green, and other smaller swamps, on the shores of Albemarle and Pamlico, contain over 2,000,000 acres.

The swamp belongs to a great many proprietors. Most of them own only a few acres, but some possess large tracts and use a heavy capital in the business. One, whose acquaintance I made, employed more than a hundred hands in getting out shingles alone. The value of the swamp land varies with the wood upon it, and the facility with which it can be got off, from 12½ cents to $10 an acre. It is made passable in any desired direction in which trees grow, by laying logs, cut in lengths of eight or ten feet, parallel and against each other on the surface of the soil, or "sponge," as it is called. Mules and oxen are used to some extent upon these roads, but transportation is mainly by hand to the creeks, or to ditches communicating with them or the canal.

Except by those log roads, the swamp is scarcely passable in many parts, owing not only to the softness of the sponge, but to the obstruction caused by innumerable shrubs, vines, creepers, and briars, which often take entire possession of the surface, forming a dense brake or jungle. This, however, is sometimes removed by fires, which of late years have been frequent and very destructive to the standing timber. The most common shrubs are various smooth-leaved evergreens, and their dense, bright, glossy foliage was exceedingly beautiful in the wintry season of my visit. There is a good deal of game in the swamp — bears and wildcats are sometimes shot, raccoons and opossums are plentiful, and deer are found in the drier parts and on the outskirts. The fishing, in the interior waters, is also said to be excellent.

Nearly all the valuable trees have now been cut off from the swamp. The whole ground has been frequently gone over, the best timber selected and removed at each time, leaving the remainder standing thinly, so that the wind has more effect upon it; and much of it, from the yielding of the soft soil, is uprooted or broken off. The fires have also greatly injured it. The principal stock, now worked into shingles, is obtained *from beneath the surface* — old trunks that have been preserved by the wetness of the soil, and that are found by "sounding" with poles, and raised with hooks or pikes by the Negroes.

The quarry is giving out, however; and except that lumber, and especially shingles, have been in great demand at high prices of late, the business would be almost at an end. As it is, the principal men engaged in it are turning their attention to other and more distant supplies. A very large purchase had been made by one company in the Florida everglades, and a schooner, with a gang of hands trained in the "Dismals," was about to sail from Deep Creek, for this new field of operations.

The labor in the swamp is almost entirely done by slaves; and the way in which they are managed is interesting and instructive. They are mostly hired by their employers at a rent, perhaps of one hundred dollars a year for each, paid to their owners. They spend one or two months of the winter — when it is too wet to work in the swamp — at the residence of their master. At this period little or no work is required of them; their time is their own, and if they can get any employment, they will generally keep for themselves what they are paid for it. When it is sufficiently dry — usually early in February — they go into the swamp in gangs, each gang under a white overseer. Before leaving, they are all examined and registered at the Court House; and "passes," good for a year, are given them, in which their features and the marks upon their persons are minutely described. Each man is furnished with a quantity of provisions and clothing, of which, as well as of all that he afterwards draws from the stock in the hands of the overseer, an exact account is kept.

Arrived at their destination, a rude camp is made; huts of logs, poles, shingles, and boughs being built, usually, upon some places where shingles have been worked before, and in which the shavings have accumulated in small hillocks upon the soft surface of the ground.

The slave lumberman then lives measurably as a free man; hunts, fishes, eats, drinks, smokes and sleeps, plays and works, each when and as much as he pleases. It is only required of him that he shall have made, after half a year has passed, such a quantity of shingles as shall be worth to his master so much money as is paid to his owner for his services, and shall refund the value of the clothing and provisions he has required.

No "driving" at his work is attempted or needed. No force is used to overcome the indolence peculiar to the Negro. The overseer merely takes a daily account of the number of shingles each man adds to the general stock, and employs another set of hands, with mules, to draw them to a point from which they can be shipped, and where they are, from time to time, called for by a schooner.

At the end of five months the gang returns to dry land, and a statement of account from the overseer's book is drawn up, something like the following: —

Sam Bo to John Doe, Dr.

Feb. 1. To clothing (outfit)	$	5.00
Mar. 10. To clothing, as per overseer's account		2.25
Feb. 1. To bacon and meal (outfit)		19.00
July 1. To stores drawn in swamp, as per overseer's account		4.75
July 1. To half-yearly hire, paid his owner . .		50.00
		$ 81.00

Per Contra, Cr.

July 1. By 10,000 shingles, as per overseer's account, 10c.	100.00	
Balance due Sambo	————	$19.00

which is immediately paid him, and of which, together with the proceeds of sale of peltry which he has got while in the swamp, he is always allowed to make use as his own. No liquor is sold or served to the Negroes in the swamp, and, as their first want when they come out of it is an excitement, most of their money goes to the grog shops.

After a short vacation, the whole gang is taken in the schooner to spend another five months in the swamp as before. If they are good hands and work steadily, they will commonly be hired again, and so continuing, will spend most of their lives at it. They almost invariably have excellent health, as have also the white men engaged in the business. They all consider the water of the "Dismals" to have a medicinal virtue, and quite probably it is a mild tonic. It is greenish in color, and I thought I detected a slightly resinous taste upon first drinking it. Upon entering the swamp also, an agreeable resinous odor, resembling that of a hemlock forest, was perceptible.

The Negroes working in the swamp were more sprightly and straightforward in their manner and conversation than any field-hand plantation Negroes that I saw at the South; two or three of their employers with whom I conversed spoke well of them, as compared with other slaves, and made no complaints of "rascality" or laziness.

Norfolk, Jan. 20th. — While driving a chaise from Portsmouth to Deep River, I picked up on the road a jaded-looking Negro, who proved to be a very intelligent and good-natured fellow. His account of the lumber business, and of the life of the lumbermen in the swamps, in answer to my questions, was clear and precise, and was afterwards verified by information obtained from his master.

He told me that his name was Joseph, that he belonged (as property) to a church in one of the inland counties, and that he was hired from the trustees of the church by his present master. He expressed contentment with his lot, but great unwillingness to be sold to go on to a plantation. He liked to "mind himself," as he did in the swamps. Whether he would still more prefer to be entirely his own master, I did not ask.

The Dismal Swamps are noted places of refuge for runaway

Negroes. They were formerly peopled in this way much more than at present; a systematic hunting of them with dogs and guns having been made by individuals who took it up as a business about ten years ago. Children were born, bred, lived, and died here. Joseph Church told me he had seen skeletons, and had helped to bury bodies recently dead. There were people in the swamps still, he thought, that were the children of runaways, and who had been runaways themselves "all their lives." What a life it must be! born outlaws; educated self-stealers; trained from infancy to be constantly in dread of the approach of a white man as a thing more fearful than wildcats or serpents, or even starvation.

There can be but few, however, if any, of these "natives" left. They cannot obtain the means of supporting life without coming often either to the outskirts to steal from the plantations, or to the neighborhood of the camps of the lumbermen. They depend much upon the charity or the wages given them by the latter. The poorer white men, owning small tracts of the swamps, will sometimes employ them, and the Negroes frequently. In the hands of either they are liable to be betrayed to the Negro-hunters. Joseph said that they had huts in "back places" hidden by bushes, and difficult of access; he had, apparently, been himself quite intimate with them. When the shingle Negroes employed them, he told me, they made them get up logs for them, and would give them enough to eat, and some clothes, and perhaps two dollars a month in money. But some, when they owed them money, would betray them, instead of paying them.

I asked if they were ever shot. "Oh, yes," he said; when the hunters saw a runaway, if he tried to get from them, they would call out to him, that if he did not stop they would shoot, and if he did not, they would shoot, and sometimes kill him.

"But some on 'em would rather be shot than be took, sir," he added, simply.

A farmer living near the swamp confirmed this account, and said he knew of three or four being shot in one day.

No particular breed of dogs is needed for hunting Negroes: bloodhounds, foxhounds, bulldogs, and curs were used, and one white man told me how they were trained for it, as if it were a common or notorious practice. They are shut up when puppies, and never allowed to see a Negro except while training to catch him. A Negro is made to run from them, and they are encouraged to follow him until he gets into a tree, when meat is given them. Afterwards they learn to follow any particular Negro by scent, and then a shoe or a piece of clothing is taken off a Negro, and they learn to find by scent who it belongs to, and to tree him, etc. All this the farmer told me. I don't think dogs are employed in the ordinary "driving" in the swamp, but only to overtake some particular slave, as soon as possible, after it is discovered that he has fled from a plantation. Joseph said that it was easy for the drivers to tell a fugitive from a regularly employed slave in the swamps.

"How do they know them?"

"Oh, dey looks *strange*."

"How do you mean?"

"*Skeared* like, you know, sir, and kind o' strange, cause dey hasn't much to eat, and ain't decent (not decently clothed), like we is."

When the hunters take a Negro who has not a pass, or "free papers," and they don't know whose slave he is, they confine him in jail, and advertise him. If no one claims him within a year he is sold to the highest bidder, at a public sale, and this sale gives title in law against any subsequent claimant.

The country from Portsmouth to Gaston, eighty miles, partly in Virginia, and partly in North Carolina, is almost all pine forest, or cypress swamp; and on the little land that is cultivated, I saw no indication of any other crop than maize. The soil is light and poor. Between Weldon and Gaston there are heavier soils, and we passed several cotton fields, and planters' mansions. On the low, flat lands bordering the banks of the Roanoke, the soil is of the character of that of James River, fine, fertile, mellow loam; and the maize crop seemed to have been heavy.

Gaston is a village of some twenty houses, shops, and cabins, besides the railroad storehouses, the hotel, and a nondescript building, which may be either a fancy barn, or a little church, getting high. From the manner in which passengers are forced, by the management of the trains arriving here, to patronize it, the hotel, I presume, belongs to the railroad companies. It is ill-kept, but affords some entertainment from its travesty of certain metropolitan vulgarities. I was chummed with a Southern gentleman, in a very small room. Finding the sheets on both our beds had been soiled by previous occupants, he made a row about it with the servants, and, after a long delay, had them changed; then observing that it was probably the mistress's fault, and not the servants', he paid the Negro, whom he had been berating, for his trouble.

Among our inside passengers, in the stagecoach, was a free colored woman; she was treated in no way differently from the white ladies. My roommate said this was entirely customary at the South, and no Southerner would ever think of objecting to it. Notwithstanding which, I have known young Southerners to get very angry because Negroes were not excluded from the public conveyances in which they had taken passage themselves, at the North; and I have always supposed that when they were so excluded, it was from fear of offending Southern travellers, more than anything else.

Sitting near some men lounging on the river bank, I took notes of the following interesting information, delivered in a high-keyed, blatant drawl: —

"The best medicine there is, is this here Idee of Potasun. It's made out of two minerals; one on 'em they gets in the mountains of Scotland — that's the Idee; the other's steel filings, and they mixes them eschemically until they works altogether into a solid stuff like saltpetre. Now, I tell you that's the stuff for medicine. It's the best thing a man can ever put into his self. It searches out every narve in his body."

The train by which we were finally able to leave Gaston arrived the next day an hour and a half after its advertised time. The road was excellent and the speed good, a heavy U rail having lately been substituted for a flat one. A new equipment of the road, throughout, is nearly complete. The cars of this train were very old, dirty, and with dilapidated and moth-eaten furniture. They furnished me with a comfort, however, which I have never been able to try before — a full-length lounge, on which, with my overcoat for a pillow, the car being warmed, and unintentionally well ventilated, I slept soundly after dark. Why night trains are not furnished with sleeping apartments, has long been a wonder to me. We have now smoking rooms and water closets on our trains; why not sleeping, dressing, and refreshment rooms? With these additions, and good ventilation, we could go from New York to New Orleans, by rail, without stopping: as it is, a man of ordinary constitution cannot go a quarter that distance without suffering serious indisposition. Surely such improvements could not fail to be remunerative, particularly on lines competing with water communication.

The country passed through, so far as I observed, was almost entirely covered with wood; and such of it as was cultivated, very unproductive.

The city of Raleigh (old Sir Walter), the capital of North Carolina, is a pleasing town—the streets wide, and lined with trees, and many white wooden mansions, all having little courtyards of flowers and shrubbery around them. The Statehouse is, in every way, a noble building, constructed of brownish-gray granite, in Grecian style. It stands on an elevated position, near the center of the city, in a square field, which is shaded by some tall old oaks, and could easily be made into an appropriate and beautiful little park; but which, with singular negligence, or more singular economy (while $500,000 has been spent upon the simple edifice), remains in a rude state of undressed nature, and is used as a hog pasture. A trifle of the expense, employed with doubtful advantage, to give a smooth exterior face to the blocks of stone, if laid out in grading, smoothing, and dressing its ground base, would have added indescribably to the beauty of the edifice. An architect should always begin his work upon the ground.

It is hard to admire what is common; and it is, perhaps, asking too much of the citizens of Raleigh, that they should plant for ornament, or even cause to be retained about such institutions as their Lunatic Asylum, the beautiful evergreens that crowd about the town; but can any man walk from the Capitol oaks to the pine grove, a little beyond the Deaf and Dumb Institution, and say that he would not far rather have the latter than the former to curtain in his habitation? If he can in summer, let him try it again, as I did, in a soft winter's day, when the evergreens fill the air with a balsamic odor, and the green light comes quivering through them, and the foot falls silently upon the elastic carpet they have spread, deluding one with all the feelings of spring.

The country, for miles about Raleigh, is nearly all pine forest, unfertile, and so little cultivated, that it is a mystery how a town of 2,500 inhabitants can obtain sufficient supplies from it to exist.

The public house at which I stayed was, however, not only well supplied, but was excellently well kept, for a house of its class, in all other respects. The landlord superintended his business personally, and was always attentive and obliging to his guests; and the servants were sufficiently numerous, intelligent, and well instructed. Though I had no acquaintances in Raleigh, I remained, finding myself in such good quarters, several days. I think the house was called "The Burlinghame."

After this stay, rendered also partly necessary for the repair of damages to my clothing and baggage on the Weldon stage, I engaged a seat one day on the coach, advertised to leave at nine o'clock for Fayetteville. At half-past nine, tired of waiting for its departure, I told the agent, as it was not ready to start, I would walk on a bit, and let them pick me up. I found a rough road — for several miles a clayey surface and much water — and was obliged to pick my way a good deal through the woods on either side. Stopping frequently, when I came to cultivated land, to examine the soil and the appearance of the stubble of the maize — the only crop — in three different fields I made five measurements at random, of fifty feet each, and found the stalks had stood, on an average, five feet by two feet one inch apart, and that, generally, they were not over an inch in diameter at the butt. In one old field, in process of clearing for new cultivation, I examined a most absurd little plow, with a share not more than six inches in depth, and eight in length on the sole, fastened by a socket to a stake, to which was fitted a short beam and stilts. It was drawn by one mule, and its work among the stumps could only be called scratching. A farmer told me that he considered twenty-five bushels of corn a large crop, and that he generally got only as much as fifteen. He said that no money was to be got by raising corn, and very few farmers here "made" any more than they needed for their own force. It cost too much to get it to market, and yet sometimes they had to buy corn at a dollar a bushel, and wagon it home from Raleigh, or further, enough not having been raised in the country for home consumption. Cotton was the only crop they got any money for. I, nevertheless, did not see a single cotton-field during the day. He said that the largest crop of corn that he knew of, reckoned to be fifty bushels to the acre, had been raised on some reclaimed swamp, while it was still so wet that horses would mire on it all the summer, and most of it had been tended entirely with hoes.

After walking a few miles, the country became more flat, and was covered with old forests of yellow pine, and, at nine miles south of Raleigh, there were occasionally young long-leaved pines: exceedingly beautiful they are while young, the color being more agreeable than that of any other pine, and the leaves, or "straw," as its foliage is called here, long, graceful, and lustrous. As the tree gets older, it becomes of a stiffer character and darker color.

I do not think I passed, in ten miles, more than half a dozen homesteads, and of these but one was at all above the character of a hut or cabin. The same remarkable appearance of listless-ness, which I had noticed so often in Virginia, characterized the men who stood leaning against the logs of the hovels. They blinked at me as I passed, as if unable to withdraw their hands from their pockets to shade their eyes. Every dwelling sent its pack of curs to meet me, and as often as they opened cry, a woman, with a pipe in her mouth, would come to the door and call them off; the men and boys blinking on in rest and silence.

A little after one o'clock I reached "Banks's," a plantation where the stage horses are changed, eleven miles from Raleigh. Here I waited nearly an hour, till the coach arrived, when, fresh horses having been put on, I took an outside seat.

"There ain't a man in North Car'lina could drive them horses up the hills without a whip," said the driver. "You ought to get yesef a whip, massa," said one of the Negroes. "Durnation! think I'm going to buy whips! the best whip in North Car'lina wouldn't last a week on this road." "Dat's a fac—dat ar is a fac;

but look yeah, massa, ye let me hab yer stick, and I'll make a whip for ye; ye nebber can make Bawley go widout it, no how." The stick was a sapling rod, of which two or three lay on the coach top; the Negro fastened a long leather thong to it. "Dah! ye can fetch old Bawley wi' dat." "Bawley" had been tackled in as the leader of the "spike team"; but, upon attempting to start, it was found that he couldn't be driven in that way at all, and the driver took him out and put him to the pole, within reach of the butt of his stick, and another horse was put on the lead.

One Negro now took the leader by the head, and applied a stick lustily to his flanks; another, at the near wheeler, did the same; and the driver belabored Bawley from the box. But as soon as they began to move forward, and the Negro let go the leader's head, he would face about. After this had been repeated many times, a new plan of operations was arranged that proved successful. Leaving the two wheelers to the care of the Negroes, the driver was enabled to give all his attention to the leader. When the wheelers started, of course he was struck by the pole, upon which he would turn tail and start for the stable. The Negroes kept the wheelers from following him, and the driver with his stick, and another Negro with the bough of a tree, thrashed his face; he would then turn again, and, being hit by the pole, start ahead. So, after ten minutes of fearful outcry we got off.

"How far is it to Mrs. Barclay's?" a passenger had asked. "Thirteen miles," answered a Negro; "but I tell 'ou, massa, dais a heap to be said and talk 'bout 'fore 'ou see Missy Barclay's wid dem hosses." There was, indeed.

"Bawley—*you!* Bawley—Bawley! wha' 'bout?—ah!"

"*Rock!* wha' you doin'?—(durned sick horse—an't fit to be in a stage, nohow)."

"Bawley! you! g'up!"

"Oh! you dod-rotted Bob—*Bob!*—(he don't draw a pound, and he an't a gwine to)—*you*, Bob!—(well, he can't stop, can he, as long as the wheelers keep movin'?) Bob! I'll break yer legs, you don't git out the way."

"Oh, Bawley!—(no business to put such a lame hoss into the stage.) Blamnation, Bawley! Now, if you stop, I'll kill you."

"Wha' 'bout, Rock? Dod burn that Rock! You stop if you dare! (I'll be durned to Hux if that 'ere hoss arn't all used up.)"

"You, *Bob!* get out de way, or I'll be ——."

"Oh! d'rot yer soul, Bawley—y're gwine to stop! G'up! G'up! *Rock!* You all-fired ole villain! Wha' 'bout? (If they jus' git to stoppin', all hell couldn't git the mails through tonight.)"

After about three miles of this, they did stop. The driver threw the reins down in despair. After looking at the wheels, and seeing that we were on a good piece of road, nothing unusual to hinder progress, he put his hands in his pockets, and sat quietly a minute, and then began, in a businesslike manner, to swear, no longer confining himself to the peculiar idiomatic profanity of the country, but using real, outright, old-fashioned, uncompromising English oaths, as loud as he could yell. Then he stopped, and after another pause, began to talk quietly to the horses:

"You, Bob, you won't draw? Didn't you git enough last night? (I jabbed my knife into his face twice when we got into that fix last night"; and the wounds on the horse's head showed that he spoke the truth.) "I swar, Bob, if I have to come down thar, I'll cut your throat."

He stopped again, and then sat down on the footboard, and began to beat the wheelers as hard and as rapidly as possible with the butt of his stick. They started, and, striking Bob with the pole, he jumped and turned round; but a happy stroke on "the raw" in his face brought him to his place; and the stick being applied just in time to the wheelers, he caught the pole and jumped ahead. We were off again.

"Turned over in that 'ere mire hole last night," said the driver. "Couldn't do anythin' with 'em—passengers camped out—thar's were they had their fire, under that tree; didn't get to Raleigh till nine o'clock this mornin'. That's the reason I weren't along after you any sooner—hadn't got my breakfast; that's the reason the hosses don't draw no better today, too, I s'pose. *You,* Rock!—*Bawley!*—BOB!"

After two miles more, the horses stopped once more. The driver now quietly took the leader off (he had never drawn at all), and tied him behind the coach. He then began beating the near wheeler, a passenger did the same to Bawley—both standing on the ground — while I threw off my overcoat and walked on. For a time I could occasionally hear the cry, "Bawl — Rock!" and knew that the coach was moving again; gradually I outwalked the sound.

Fayetteville. — The Negroes employed in the turpentine business, to which during the last week I have been giving some examination, seem to me to be unusually intelligent and cheerful, decidedly more so than most of the white people inhabiting the turpentine forest. Among the latter there is a large number, I should think a majority, of entirely uneducated, poverty stricken vagabonds. I mean by vagabonds, simply, people without habitual, definite occupation or reliable means of livelihood. They are poor, having almost no property but their own bodies; and the use of these, that is, their labor, they are not accustomed to hire out statedly and regularly, so as to obtain capital by wages, but only occasionally by the day or job, when driven to it by necessity. A family of these people will commonly hire, or "squat" and build, a little log cabin, so made that it is only a shelter from rain, the sides not being chinked, and having no more furniture or pretension to comfort than is commonly provided a criminal in the cell of a prison. They will cultivate a little corn, and possibly a few roods of potatoes, cowpeas, and coleworts. They will own a few swine, that find their living in the forest; and pretty certainly, also, a rifle and dogs; and the men, ostensibly, occupy most of their time in hunting. I am, mainly, repeating the statements of one of the turpentine distillers, but it was confirmed by others, and by my own observation, so far as it went.

A gentleman of Fayetteville told me that he had, several times, appraised, under oath, the whole household property of families of this class at less than $20. If they have need of money to purchase clothing, etc., they obtain it by selling their game or meal. If they have none of this to spare, or an insufficiency, they will work for a neighboring farmer for a few days, and they usually get for their labor fifty cents a day, *finding themselves* [i.e., providing their own room and board]. The farmers and distillers say, that they do not like to employ them, because they cannot be relied upon to finish what they undertake, or to work according to directions; and because, being white men, they cannot "drive" them. That is to say, their labor is even more inefficient and unmanageable than that of slaves.

That I have not formed an exaggerated estimate of the proportion of such a class, will appear to the reader more probable from the testimony of a pious colporteur, given before a public meeting in Charleston, in February, 1855. I quote from a Charleston paper's report. The colporteur had been stationed at ——— county, N.C.: — "*The larger portion* of the inhabitants seemed to be totally given up to a species of mental hallucination, which carried them captive at its will. They nearly all believed implicitly in witchcraft, and attributed everything that happened, good or bad, to the agency of persons whom they supposed possessed of evil spirits."

The majority of what I have termed turpentine farmers — meaning the small proprietors of the long-leafed pine forest land — are people but a grade superior, in character or condition, to these vagabonds. They have habitations more like houses — log cabins, commonly, sometimes chinked, oftener not — without windows of glass, but with a few pieces of substantial old-fashioned heirloom furniture; a vegetable garden, in which, however, you will find no vegetable but what they call "collards" (colewort) for "greens"; fewer dogs, more swine, and larger clearings for maize, but no better crops than the poorer class. Their property is, nevertheless, often of considerable money value, consisting mainly of Negroes, who, associating intimately with their masters, are of superior intelligence to the slaves of the wealthier classes.

Some of the larger proprietors, who are also often cotton planters, cultivating the richer low lands, are said to be gentlemen of good estate — intelligent, cultivated, and hospitable.

North Carolina has a proverbial reputation for the ignorance and torpidity of her people; being, in this respect, at the head of the Slave States. I do not find the reason of this in any innate quality of the popular mind; but, rather, in the circumstances under which it finds its development. Owing to the general poverty of the soil in the eastern part of the State, and to the almost exclusive employment of slave labor on the soils productive of cotton; owing, also, to the difficulty and expense of reaching market with bulky produce from the interior and

western districts, population and wealth are more divided than
in the other Atlantic States; industry is almost entirely rural,
and there is but little communication or concert of action among
the small and scattered proprietors of capital. For the same
reason, the advantages of education are more difficult to be
enjoyed, the distance at which families reside apart preventing
children from coming together in such numbers as to give
remunerative employment to a teacher. The teachers are,
generally, totally unfitted for their business; young men, as a
clergyman informed me, themselves not only unadvanced
beyond the lowest knowledge of the elements of primary school
learning, but often coarse, vulgar, and profane in their language
and behavior, who take up teaching as a temporary business,
to supply the demand of a neighborhood of people as ignorant
and uncultivated as themselves.

The native white population of North Carolina is 550,267
The whole white population under 20 years is 301,106
Leaving white adults over 20 249,161
Of these there are natives who cannot read and write 73,226

Being more than one-fourth of the native white adults.

But the aspect of North Carolina with regard to slavery, is,
in some respects, less lamentable than that of Virginia. There
is not only less bigotry upon the subject, and more freedom of
conversation, but I saw here, in the institution, more of patriarchal character than in any other State. The slave more
frequently appears as a family servant—a member of his
master's family, interested with him in his fortune, good or
bad. This is a result of the less concentration of wealth in
families or individuals, occasioned by the circumstances I
have described. Slavery thus loses much of its inhumanity.
It is still questionable, however, if, as the subject race approaches civilization, the dominant race is not proportionately
detained in its onward progress. One is forced often to question, too, in viewing slavery in this aspect, whether humanity
and the accumulation of wealth, the prosperity of the master,
and the happiness and improvement of the subject, are not in
some degree incompatible.

These later observations are made after having twice again

passed through the State, once in a leisurely way on horse-back. In some of the western and northern central parts of the State, there is much more enterprise, thrift, and comfort than in the eastern part, where I had my first impressions.

I left Fayetteville in a steamboat (advertised for 8 o'clock, left at 8:45) bound down Cape Fear River to Wilmington.

We reached Wilmington, the port at the mouth of the river, at half-past nine. Taking a carriage, I was driven first to one hotel and afterwards to another. They were both so crowded with guests, and excessive business duties so prevented the clerks from being tolerably civil to me, that I feared if I remained in either of them I should have another Norfolk experience. While I was endeavoring to ascertain if there was a third public house, in which I might, perhaps, obtain a private room, my eye fell upon an advertisement of a new railroad line of passage to Charleston. A boat, to take passengers to the railroad, was to start every night, from Wilmington, at ten o'clock. It was already something past ten; but being pretty sure that she would not get off punctually, and having a strong resisting impulse to being packed away in a close room, with any chance stranger the clerk of the house might choose to couple me with, I shouldered my baggage and ran for the wharves. At half-past ten I was looking at Wilmington over the stern of another little wheelbarrow steamboat, pushing back up the river. When or how I was to be taken to Charleston, I had not yet been able to ascertain. The captain assured me it was all right, and demanded twenty dollars. Being in his power I gave it to him, and received in return a pocketful of tickets, guaranteeing the bearer passage from place to place; of not one of which places had I ever heard before, except Charleston.

The cabin was small, dirty, crowded, close, and smoky. Finding a warm spot in the deck, over the furnace, and to lee-ward of the chimney, I pillowed myself on my luggage and went to sleep.

The ringing of the boat's bell awoke me, after no great lapse of time, and I found we were in a small creek, heading south-ward. Presently we reached a wharf, near which stood a locomotive and train. A long, narrow plank having been run out, half a dozen white men, including myself, went on shore. Then followed as many Negroes, who appeared to be a recent purchase of their owner. Owing, probably, to an unusually low tide, there was a steep ascent from the boat to the wharf, and I was amused to see the anxiety of this gentleman for the safe landing of his property, and especially to hear him curse them for their carelessness, as if their lives were of much greater value to him than to themselves. One was a woman. All carried over their shoulders some little baggage, probably all their personal effects, slung in a blanket; and one had a dog, whose safe landing caused him nearly as much anxiety as his own did *his* owner.

"Gib me da dog, now," said the dog's owner, standing half way up the plank.

"Damn the dog," said the Negro's owner; "give me your hand up here. Let go of the dog; d'ye hear! Let him take care of himself."

But the Negro hugged the dog, and brought him safely on shore.

After a short delay the train started: the single passenger car was a fine one (made at Wilmington, Delaware), and just sufficiently warmed. I should have slept again if it had not been that two of the six inmates were drunk—one of them uproariously.

Passing through long stretches of cypress swamps, with occasional intervals of either pine barrens, or clear water ponds, in about two hours we came, in the midst of the woods, to the end of the rails. In the vicinity could be seen a small tent, a shanty of loose boards, and a large, subdued fire, around which, upon the ground, a considerable number of men were stretched out asleep. This was the camp of the hands engaged in laying the rails, and who were thus daily extending the distance which the locomotive could run.

The conductor told me that there was here a break of about eighty miles in the rail, over which I should be transferred by a stagecoach, which would come as soon as possible after the driver knew that the train had arrived. To inform him of this, the locomotive trumpeted loud and long.

The Negro property, which had been brought up in a freight

car, was immediately let out on the stoppage of the train. As it stepped on to the platform, the owner asked, "Are you all here?"

"Yes, massa, we is all heah," answered one. "Do dysef no harm, for we's all heah," added another, in an undertone.

The Negroes immediately gathered some wood, and taking a brand from the railroad hands, made a fire for themselves; then, all but the woman, opening their bundles, wrapped themselves in their blankets and went to sleep. The woman, bareheaded, and very inadequately clothed as she was, stood for a long time alone, erect and statuelike, her head bowed, gazing in the fire. She had taken no part in the light chat of the others, and had given them no assistance in making the fire. Her dress, too, was not the usual plantation apparel. It was all sadly suggestive.

The principal other freight of the train was one hundred and twenty bales of Northern hay. It belonged, as the conductor told me, to a planter who lived some twenty miles beyond here, and who had bought it in Wilmington at a dollar and a half a hundred weight, to feed his mules. Including the steamboat and railroad freight, and all the labor of getting it to his stables, its entire cost to him would not be much less than two dollars a hundred, or at least four times as much as it would have cost to raise and make it in the interior of New York or New England. There are not only several forage crops which can be raised in South Carolina, that cannot be grown on account of the severity of the winter in the Free States, but, on a farm near Fayetteville, a few days before, I had seen a crop of natural grass growing in half-cultivated land, dead upon the ground; which, I think, would have made, if it had been cut and well treated in the summer, three tons of hay to the acre. The owner of the land said that there was no better hay than it would have made, but he hadn't had time to attend to it. He had as much as his hands could do of other work at the period of the year when it should have been made.

Probably the case was similar with the planter who had bought this Northern hay at a price four times that which it would have cost a Northern farmer to make it. He had preferred to employ his slaves at other business.

The inference must be, either that there was most improbably foolish, bad management, or that the slaves were more profitably employed in cultivating cotton, than they could have been in cultivating maize, or other forage crops.

I put the case, some days afterwards, to an English merchant, who had had good opportunities, and made it a part of his business to study such matters.

"I have no doubt," said he, "that if hay cannot be obtained here, other valuable forage can, with less labor than anywhere at the North; and all the Southern agricultural journals sustain this opinion, and declare it to be purely bad management that neglects these crops, and devotes labor to cotton, so exclusively. Probably, it is so—at the present cost of forage. Nevertheless, the fact is also true, as the planters assert, that they cannot afford to apply their labor to anything else but cotton. And yet, they complain that the price of cotton is so low that there is no profit in growing it, which is evidently false. You see that they prefer buying hay to raising it at, to say the least, three times what it costs your Northern farmers to raise it. Of course, if cotton could be grown in New York and Ohio, it could be afforded at one-third the cost it is here—say at three cents per pound. And that is my solution of the slavery question. Bring cotton down to three cents a pound, and there would be more abolitionists in South Carolina than in Massachusetts. If that can be brought about, in any way—and it is not impossible that we may live to see it, as our railways are extended in India, and the French enlarge their free-labor plantations in Algiers— there will be an end of slavery."

It was just one o'clock when the stagecoach came for us. There was but one passenger beside myself—a Philadelphia gentleman, going to Columbia. We proceeded very slowly for about three miles, across a swamp, upon a "corduroy road"; then more rapidly, over rough ground, being tossed about in the coach most severely, for six or eight miles further.

The country was very thinly peopled; lone houses often being several miles apart. The large majority of the dwellings were of logs, and even those of the white people were often without glass windows. In the better class of cabins, the roof is usually built with a curve, so as to project eight or ten feet beyond the log wall; and a part of this space, exterior to the logs, is enclosed with boards, making an additional small room — the remainder forms an open porch. The whole cabin is often elevated on four corner posts, two or three feet from the ground, so that the air may circulate under it. The fireplace is built at the end of the house, of sticks and clay, and the chimney is carried up outside, and often detached from the log walls; but the roof is extended at the gable, until in a line with its outer side. The porch has a railing in front, and a wide shelf at the end, on which a bucket of water, a gourd, and hand basin, are usually placed. There are chairs, or benches, in the porch, and you often see women sitting at work in it, as in Germany.

The logs are usually hewn but little; and, of course, as they are laid up, there will be wide interstices between them — which are increased by subsequent shrinking. These, very commonly, are not "chinked," or filled up in any way; nor is the wall lined on the inside. Through the chinks, as you pass along the road, you may often see all that is going on in the house; and, at night, the light of the fire shines brightly out on all sides.

Cabins, of this class, would almost always be flanked by two or three Negro huts. The cabins of the poor whites, much the largest in number, were of a meaner sort — being mere square pens of logs, roofed over, provided with a chimney, and usually with a shed of boards, supported by rough posts, before the door.

Occasionally, where, near the banks of a water course, the silvery sand was darkened by a considerable intermixture of mould, there would be a large plantation, with Negro quarters, and a cotton press and gin house. We passed half a dozen of these, perhaps, during the day. Where the owners resided in them, they would have comfortable-looking residences, not unlike the better class of New England farmhouses. On the largest, however, there was no residence for the owner, at all, only a small cottage, or whitewashed cabin, for the overseer. The Negro cabins, here, were the smallest I had seen — I thought not more than twelve feet square, inside. They stood in two rows, with a wide street between them. They were built of logs, with no windows — no opening at all, except the doorway, with a chimney of sticks and mud; with no trees about them, no porches, or shades, of any kind. Except for the chimney—the purpose of which I should not readily have guessed if I had seen one of them in New England—I should have conjectured that it had been built for a powder house, or perhaps an ice house—never for an animal to sleep in.

We stopped, for some time, on this plantation, near where some thirty men and women were at work, repairing the road. The women were in majority, and were engaged at exactly the same labor as the men; driving the carts, loading them with dirt, and dumping them upon the road; cutting down trees, and drawing wood by hand, to lay across the miry places; hoeing, and shovelling. They were dressed in coarse gray gowns, generally very much burned, and very dirty; which, for greater convenience of working in the mud, were reefed up with a cord drawn tightly around the body, a little above the hips—the spare amount of skirt bagging out between this and the waist proper. On their legs were loose leggings, or pieces of blanket or bagging wrapped about, and lashed with thongs; and they wore very heavy shoes. Most of them had hand-kerchiefs, only, tied around their heads; some wore men's caps, or old slouched hats, and several were bareheaded.

The overseer rode about among them, on a horse, carrying in his hand a rawhide whip, constantly directing and encouraging them; but, as my companion and I, both, several times noticed, as often as he visited one end of the line of operations, the hands at the other end would discontinue their labor, until he turned to ride towards them again. Clumsy, awkward, gross, elephantine in all their movements; pouting, grinning, and leering at us; sly, sensual, and shameless, in all their expressions and demeanor; I never before had witnessed, I thought, anything more revolting than the whole scene.

At length, the overseer dismounted from his horse, and, giving him to a boy to take to the stables, got upon the coach, and rode with us several miles. From the conversation I had with him, as well as from what I saw of his conduct in the field, I judged that he was an uncommonly fit man for his duties; at least ordinarily amiable in disposition, and not passionate; but deliberate, watchful, and efficient. I thought he would be not only a good economist, but a firm and considerate officer or master.

If these women, and their children after them, were always naturally and necessarily to remain of the character and capacity stamped on their faces—as is probably the opinion of their owner, in common with most wealthy South Carolina planters—I don't know that they could be much less miserably situated, or guided more for their own good and that of the world, than they were. They were fat enough, and didn't look as if they were at all overworked, or harassed by cares, or oppressed by a consciousness of their degradation. If that is all—as some think.

We took supper at a neat log cabin, standing a short distance off the road, with a beautiful evergreen oak, the first I had observed, in front of it. There was no glass in the windows, but drapery of white muslin restrained the currents of air, and during the day would let in sufficient light, while a blazing wood fire both warmed and lighted the room by night. A rifle and powder horn hung near the fireplace, and the master of the house, a fine, hearty, companionable fellow, said that he had lately shot three deer, and that there were plenty of cats, and foxes, as well as turkeys, hares, squirrels, and other small game in the vicinity. It was a perfectly charming little back-woods farmhouse—good wife, supper, and all; but one disagreeable blot darkened the otherwise most agreeable picture of rustic civilization—we were waited upon at table by two excessively dirty, slovenly dressed, Negro girls. In the rear of the cabin were two hovels, each lighted by large fires, and apparently crowded with other slaves belonging to the family.

Between nine and ten at night, we reached the end of the completed railroad, coming up in search for that we had left the previous night. There was another camp and fire of the workmen, and in a little white frame house we found a company of engineers. There were two trains and locomotives on the track, and a gang of Negroes was loading cotton into one of them.

I strolled off until I reached an opening in the woods, in which was a cotton field and some Negro cabins, and beyond it large girdled trees, among which were two Negroes with dogs, barking, yelping, hacking, shouting, and whistling, after 'coons and 'possums. Returning to the railroad, I found a comfortable, warm passenger car, and, wrapped in my blanket, went to sleep. At midnight I was awakened by loud laughter, and, looking out, saw that the gang of Negroes had made a fire, and were enjoying a right merry repast. Suddenly, one raised such a sound as I never heard before; a long, loud, musical shout, rising and falling, and breaking into falsetto, his voice ringing through the woods in the clear, frosty night air, like a bugle call. As he finished, the melody was caught up by another, and then another, and then by several in chorus. When there was silence again, one of them cried out, as if bursting with amusement: "Did yer see de dog? — when I began eeohing, he turn roun' an' look me straight into der face; ha! ha! ha!" and the whole party broke into the loudest peals of laughter, as if it was the very best joke they had ever heard.

After a few minutes I could hear one urging the rest to come to work again, and soon he stepped towards the cotton bales, saying, "Come, brederen, come; let's go at it; come now, eoho! roll away! eeoho-eeoho-weeioho-i!" — and the rest taking it up as before, in a few moments they all had their shoulders to a bale of cotton, and were rolling it up the embankment.

About half-past three, I was awakened again by the whistle of the locomotive, answering, I suppose, the horn of a stage-coach, which in a few minutes drove up, bringing a mail. A Negro man and woman who had been sleeping near me, replenished the fire; two other passengers came in, and we started.

In the woods, I saw a Negro by a fire, while it was still night, shaving shingles very industriously. He did not even stop to look at the train. No doubt he was a slave, working by task, and of his own accord at night, that he might have the more daylight for his own purposes.

The Negroes enjoy fine blazing fires in the open air, and make them at every opportunity. The train on this road was provided with a man and maid-servant to attend to the fire and wait on the passengers — a very good arrangement, by the way, yet to be adopted on our own long passenger trains. When we arrived at a junction where we were to change cars, as soon as all the passengers had left the train, they also left; but instead of going into the station house with us, they immediately collected some pine branches and chips, and getting a brand from the locomotive, made a fire upon the ground, and seated themselves by it. Other Negroes soon began to join them, and as they approached were called to: "Doan' yer cum widout som' wood! Doan' yer cum widout som' wood!" and every one had to make his contribution. At another place, near a cotton plantation, I found a woman collecting pine leaves into heaps, to be carted to the cattle pens. She, too, had a fire near her. "What are you doing with a fire, aunty?" "Oh, jus' to warm my hans wen dey gits cold, massa." The weather was then almost uncomfortably warm.

We were running during the forenoon, for a hundred miles, or more, in a southerly direction, on nearly a straight course, through about the middle of the State of South Carolina. The greater part of this distance, the flat, sandy pine barrens continued, scarcely a foot of grading, for many miles at a time, having been required in the construction of the railroad. As the swamps, which were still frequent, were crossed on piles and tresselwork, the roads must have been built very cheaply — the land damages being nothing. We passed from the track of one company to that of another, several times during the day — the speed was from fifteen to twenty miles an hour, with long stoppages at the stations. A conductor said they could easily run forty miles, and had done it, including stoppages; but they were forbidden now to make fast time, from the injury it did the road — the superstructure being much more shaken and liable to displacement in these light sands than on our Northern roads. The locomotives that I saw were all made in Philadelphia; the cars were all from the Hartford, Conn., and Worcester, Mass., manufactories, and invariably, elegant and comfortable. The roads seemed to be doing a heavy freighting business with cotton. We passed at the turnouts half a dozen trains, with nearly a thousand bales on each, but the number of passengers was always small. A slave country can never, it is evident, furnish a passenger traffic of much value. A majority of the passenger trains, which I saw used in the South, were not paying for the fuel and wages expended in running them.

For an hour or two we got above the sandy zone, and into the second, middle, or "wave" region of the State. The surface here was extremely undulating, gracefully swelling and dipping in bluffs and dells — the soil a mellow brown loam, with some indications of fertility, especially in the valleys. Yet most of the ground was occupied by pine woods (probably old-field pines, on exhausted cotton fields). For a few miles, on a gently sloping surface of the same sort of soil, there were some enormously large cotton fields.

I saw women working again, in large gangs with men. In one case they were distributing manure — ditch scrapings it appeared to be — and the mode of operation was this: the manure had been already carted into heaps upon the ground; a number of the women were carrying it in from the heap in baskets, on their heads, and one in her apron, and spreading it with their hands between the ridges on which the cotton grew last year; the rest followed with great, long-handled, heavy, clumsy hoes, and pulled down the ridges over the manure, and so made new ridges for the next planting. I asked a young planter who continued with me a good part of the day, why they did not use plows. He said this was rather rough land, and a plow wouldn't work in it very well. It was light soil, and smooth enough for a parade ground. The fact is, in certain parts of South Carolina, a plow is yet an almost unknown instrument of tillage.

About noon we turned east, on a track running direct to Charleston. Pine barrens continued alternating with swamp, with some cotton and corn fields on the edges of the latter. A few of the pines were "boxed" for turpentine; and I understood that one or two companies from North Carolina had been operating here for several years. Plantations were not very often seen along the road through the sand; but stations, at which cotton was stored and loading, were comparatively frequent.

At one of the stations an empty car had been attached to the train; I had gone into it, and was standing at one end of it, when an elderly countryman with a young woman and three little children entered and took seats at the other. The old man took out a roll of deerskin, in which were bankbills, and some small change.

"How much did he say 'twould be?" he inquired.

"Seventy cents."

"For both on us?"

"For each on us."

"Both on us, I reckon."

"Reckon it's each."

"I've got jess seventy-five cents in hard money."

"Give it to him, and tell him it's all yer got; reckon he'll let us go."

At this I moved, to attract their attention; the old man started, and looked towards me for a moment, and said no more. I soon afterwards walked out on the platform, passing him, and the conductor came in, and collected their fare; I then returned, and stood near them, looking out of the window of the door. The old man had a good-humored, thin, withered, very brown face, and there was a speaking twinkle in his eye. He was dressed in clothes much of the Quaker cut — a broad-brimmed, low hat; white cotton shirt, open in front, and without cravat, showing his hairy breast; a long-skirted, snuff-colored coat, of very coarse homespun; short trousers, of brown drilling; red woollen stockings, and heavy cowhide shoes. He presently asked the time of day; I gave it to him, and we continued in conversation, as follows: —

"Right cold weather."

"Yes."

"G'wine to Branchville?"

"I am going beyond there — to Charleston."

"Ah — come from Hamburg this mornin'?"

"No — from beyond there."

"Did ye? — where'd you come from?"

"From Wilmington."

"How long yer ben comin'?"

"I left Wilmington night before last, about ten o'clock. I have been ever since on the road."

"Reckon yer a nightbird."

"What?"

"Reckon you are a nightbird — what we calls a nighthawk; keeps a goin' at night, you know."

"Yes — I've been going most of two nights."

"Reckon so; kinder red your eyes is. Live in Charleston, do ye?"

"No, I live in New York."

"New York—that's a good ways, yet, ain't it?"

"Yes."

"Reckon yer arter a chicken, up here."

"No."

"Ah, ha—reckon ye are."

The young woman laughed, lifted her shoulder, and looked out of the window.

"Reckon ye'll get somebody's chicken."

"I'm afraid not."

The young woman laughed again, and tossed her head.

"Oh, reckon ye will—ah, ha! But yer mustn't mind my fun."

"Not at all, not at all. Where did *you* come from?"

"Up here to ——; g'wine hum; g'wine to stop down here, next deeper. How do you go, w'en you get to Charleston?"

"I am going on to New Orleans."

"Is New York beyond New Orleans?"

"Beyond New Orleans? Oh, no."

"In New Orleans, is't?"

"What?"

"New York is somewhere in New Orleans, ain't it?"

"No; it's the other way—beyond Wilmington."

"Oh! Been pretty cold thar?"

"Yes; there was a foot and a half of snow there, last week, I hear."

"Lord o'massy! why! have to feed all the cattle!—whew!—ha!—whew! don't wonner ye com' away."

"You are a farmer."

"Yes."

"Well, I am a farmer, too."

"Be ye—to New York?"

"Yes; how much land have you got?"

"A hundred and twenty-five acres; how much have you?"

"Just about the same. What's your land worth, here?"

"Some on't —what we call swampland—kinder low and wet like, you know—that's worth five dollars an acre; and mainly it's worth a dollar and a half or two dollars — that's takin' a common trac' of upland. What's yours worth?"

"A hundred and fifty to two hundred dollars."

"What!"

"A hundred and fifty to two hundred."

"Dollars?"

"Yes."

"Not an acre?"

"Yes."

"Good Lord! yer might as well buy niggers to onst. Do you work any niggers?"

"No."

"May be they don't have niggers — that is, slaves — to New York."

"No, we do not. It's against the law."

"Yes, I heerd 'twas, some place. How do yer get yer work done?"

"I hire white men — Irishmen generally."

"Do they work good?"

"Yes, better than Negroes, I think, and don't cost nearly as much."

"What do yer have to give 'em?"

"Eight or nine dollars a month, and board, for common hands, by the year."

"Hi, Lordy! and they work up right smart, do they? Why, yer can't get any kind of a good nigger less'n twelve dollars a month."

"And board?"

"And board 'em? yes; and clothe, and blank, and shoe 'em, too."

He owned no Negroes himself and did not hire any. "They," his family, "made their own crap." They raised maize, and sweet potatoes, and cowpeas. He reckoned, in general, they made about three barrels of maize to the acre; sometimes, as much as five. He described to me, as a novelty, a plow, with "a sort of a wing, like, on one side," that pushed off, and turned over a slice of the ground; from which it appeared that he had, until recently, never seen a mould board; the common plows of this country being constructed on the same principles as those of the Chinese, and only rooting the ground, like a hog or a mole — not cleaving and turning. He had never heard of working a plow with more than one horse. He was frank and good natured; embarrassed his daughter by coarse jokes about herself and her babies, and asked me if I would not go home with him, and, when I declined, pressed me to come and see them when I returned. That I might do so, he gave me directions how to get to his farm; observing that I must start pretty early in the day — because it would not be safe for a stranger to try to cross the swamp after dark. The moment the train began to check its speed, before stopping at the place at which he was to leave, he said to his daughter, "Come, gal! quick now; gather up yer young ones!" and stepped out, pulling her after him, on to the platform. As they walked off, I noticed that he strode ahead, like an Indian or a gypsy man, and she carried in her arms two of the children and a bundle, while the third child held to her skirts.

A party of fashionably dressed people took the train for Charleston — two families, apparently, returning from a visit to their plantations. They came to the station in handsome coaches. Some minutes before the rest, there entered the car, in which I was then again alone, and reclining on a bench in the corner, an old nurse, with a baby, and two young Negro women, having care of half a dozen children, mostly girls, from three to fifteen years of age. As they closed the door, the Negro girls seemed to resume a conversation, or quarrel. Their language was loud and obscene, such as I never heard before from any but the most depraved and beastly women of the streets. Upon observing me, they dropped their voices, but not with any appearance of shame, and continued their altercation, until their mistresses entered. The white children, in the mean time, had listened, without any appearance of wonder or annoyance. The moment the ladies opened the door, they became silent.

3.

The Rice District

Plantation, February. — I left [Savannah] yesterday morning, on horseback, with a letter in my pocket to Mr. X., under whose roof I am now writing.

Mr. X. has two plantations on the river, besides a large tract of poor pine forest land, extending some miles back upon the upland, and reaching above the malarious region. In the upper part of this pine land is a house, occupied by his overseer during the malarious season, when it is dangerous for any but Negroes to remain during the night in the vicinity of the swamps or rice fields. Even those few who have been born in the region, and have grown up subject to the malaria, are said to be generally weakly and short-lived. The Negroes do not enjoy as good health on rice plantations as elsewhere; and the greater difficulty with which their lives are preserved, through infancy especially, shows that the subtle poison of the miasma is not innocuous to them; but Mr. X. boasts a steady increase of his Negro stock, of five per cent per annum, which is better than is averaged on the plantations of the interior.

The plantation which contains Mr. X.'s winter residence has but a small extent of rice land, the greater part of it being reclaimed upland swamp soil, suitable for the culture of Sea Island cotton. The other plantation contains over five hundred acres of rice land, fitted for irrigation; the remainder is unusually fertile reclaimed upland swamp, and some hundred acres of it are cultivated for maize and Sea Island cotton.

There is a "Negro settlement" on each; but both plantations, although a mile or two apart, are worked together as one, under one overseer — the hands being drafted from one to another as their labor is required. Somewhat over seven hundred acres are at the present time under the plow in the two plantations: the whole number of Negroes is two hundred, and they are reckoned to be equal to about one hundred prime hands — an unusual strength for that number of all classes. The overseer lives, in winter, near the settlement of the larger plantation, Mr. X. near that of the smaller.

It is an old family estate, inherited by Mr. X.'s wife, who, with her children, was born and brought up upon it in close intimacy with the Negroes, a large proportion of whom were also included in her inheritance, or have been since born upon the estate. Mr. X. himself is a New England farmer's son, and has been a successful merchant and manufacturer.

The patriarchal institution should be seen here under its most favorable aspects; not only from the ties of long family association, common traditions, common memories, and, if ever, common interests, between the slaves and their rulers, but, also, from the practical talent for organization and administration, gained among the rugged fields, the complicated looms, and the exact and comprehensive counting houses of New England, which directs the labor.

The house servants are more intelligent, understand and perform their duties better, and are more appropriately dressed, than any I have seen before. The labor required of them is light, and they are treated with much more consideration for their health and comfort than is usually given to that of free domestics. They live in brick cabins, adjoining the house and stables, and one of these, into which I have looked, is neatly and comfortably furnished. Several of the house servants, as is usual, are mulattoes, and good looking. The mulattoes are generally preferred for indoor occupations. Slaves brought up to housework dread to be employed at field labor; and those accustomed to the comparatively unconstrained life of the Negro settlement, detest the close control and careful movements required of the house servants. It is a punishment for a lazy field hand, to employ him in menial duties at the house, as it is to set a sneaking sailor to do the work of a cabin servant; and it is equally a punishment to a neglectful house servant, to banish him to the field gangs. All the household economy is, of course, carried on in a style appropriate to a wealthy gentleman's residence — not more so, nor less so, that I observe, than in an establishment of similar grade at the North.

It is a custom with Mr. X., when on the estate, to look each day at all the work going on, inspect the buildings, boats, embankments, and sluiceways, and examine the sick. Yesterday I accompanied him in one of these daily rounds.

After a ride of several miles through the woods, in the rear of the plantations we came to his largest Negro settlement. There was a street, or common, two hundred feet wide, on which the cabins of the Negroes fronted. Each cabin was a framed building, the walls boarded and whitewashed on the outside, lathed and plastered within, the roof shingled; forty-two feet long, twenty-one feet wide, divided into two family tenements, each twenty-one by twenty-one; each tenement divided into three rooms—one, the common household apartment, twenty-one by ten; each of the others (bedrooms), ten by ten. There was a brick fireplace in the middle of the long side of each living room, the chimneys rising in one, in the middle of the roof. Besides these rooms, each tenement had a cock loft, entered by steps from the household room. Each tenement is occupied, on an average, by five persons. There were in them closets, with locks and keys, and a varying quantity of rude furniture. Each cabin stood two hundred feet from the next, and the street in front of them being two hundred feet wide, they were just that distance apart each way. The people were nearly all absent at work, and had locked their outer doors, taking the keys with them. Each cabin has a front and back door, and each room a window, closed by a wooden shutter, swinging outward, on hinges. Between each tenement and the next house, is a small piece of ground, enclosed with palings, in which are coops of fowl with chickens, hovels for nests, and for sows with pig. There were a great many fowls in the street. The Negroes' swine are allowed to run in the woods, each owner having his own distinguished by a peculiar mark. In the rear of the yards were gardens—a half-acre to each family. Internally the cabins appeared dirty and disordered, which was rather a pleasant indication that their homelife was not much interfered with, though I found certain police regulations were enforced.

The cabin nearest the overseer's house was used as a nursery. Having driven up to this, Mr. X. inquired first of an old nurse how the children were; whether there had been any births since his last visit; spoke to two convalescent young mothers, who were lounging on the floor of the portico, with the children, and then asked if there were any sick people.

"Nobody, oney dat boy, Sam, sar."

"What Sam is that?"

"Dat little Sam, sar; Tom's Sue's Sam, sar."

"What's the matter with him?"

"Don' 'spec dere's noting much de matter wid him now, sar. He came in Sa'dy, complainin' he had de stomach ache, an' I gin him some ile, sar; 'spec he mus' be well, dis time, but he din go out dis mornin.' "

"Well, I'll see to him."

Mr. X. went to Tom's Sue's cabin, looked at the boy, and, concluding that he was well, though he lay abed, and pretended to cry with pain, ordered him to go out to work. Then, meeting the overseer, who was just riding away, on some business of the plantation, he remained some time in conversation with him, while I occupied myself in making a sketch of the nursery and street of the settlement in my notebook. On the verandah and the steps of the nursery, there were twenty-seven children, most of them infants, that had been left there by their mothers, while they were working their tasks in the fields. They probably make a visit to them once or twice during the day, to nurse them, and receive them to take to their cabins, or where they like, when they have finished their tasks — generally in the middle of the afternoon. The older children were fed with porridge, by the general nurse. A number of girls, eight or ten years old, were occupied in holding and tending the youngest infants. Those a little older — the crawlers — were in the pen, and those big enough to toddle were playing on the steps, or before the house. Some of these, with two or three bigger ones, were singing and dancing about a fire that they had made on the ground. They were not at all disturbed or interrupted in their amusement by the presence of their owner and myself. At twelve years of age, the children are first put to regular field work; until then no labor is required of them, except, perhaps, occasionally they are charged with some light kind of duty, such as frightening birds from corn. When first sent to the field, one quarter of an able-bodied hand's day's work is ordinarily allotted to them, as their task.

From the settlement, we drove to the "mill" — not a flouring mill, though I believe there is a run of stones in it — but a monster barn, with more extensive and better machinery for threshing and storing rice, driven by a steam engine, than I have ever seen used for grain before. Adjoining the millhouse were shops and sheds, in which blacksmiths, carpenters, and other mechanics — all slaves, belonging to Mr. X. — were at work. He called my attention to the excellence of their workmanship, and said that they exercised as much ingenuity and skill as the ordinary mechanics that he was used to employ in New England. He pointed out to me some carpenter's work, a part of which had been executed by a New England mechanic, and a part by one of his own hands, which indicated that the latter was much the better workman.

I was gratified by this, for I had been so often told, in Virginia, by gentlemen anxious to convince me that the Negro was incapable of being educated or improved to a condition in which it would be safe to trust him with himself — that no Negro mechanic could ever be taught, or induced to work carefully or nicely — that I had begun to believe it might be so.

We were attended through the millhouse by a respectable looking, orderly, and quiet-mannered mulatto, who was called, by his master, "the watchman." His duties, however, as they were described to me, were those of a steward, or intendant. He carried, by a strap at his waist, a very large number of keys, and had charge of all the stores of provisions, tools, and materials of the plantations, as well as of all their produce, before it was shipped to market. He weighed and measured out all the rations of the slaves and the cattle; superintended the mechanics, and made and repaired, as was necessary, all the machinery, including the steam engine.

In all these departments, his authority was superior to that of the overseer. The overseer received his private allowance of family provisions from him, as did also the head servant at the mansion, who was his brother. His responsibility was much greater than that of the overseer; and Mr. X. said he would trust him with much more than he would any overseer he had ever known.

The watchman was a fine-looking fellow: as we were returning from church, on Sunday, he had passed us, well dressed and well mounted, and as he raised his hat, to salute us, there was nothing in his manner or appearance, except his color, to distinguish him from a gentleman of good breeding and fortune.

When we were leaving the house, to go to church, on Sunday, after all the white family had entered their carriages, or mounted their horses, the head house servant also mounted a horse — as he did so, slipping a coin into the hands of the boy who had been holding him. Afterwards, we passed a family of Negroes, in a light wagon, the oldest among them driving the horse. On my inquiring if the slaves were allowed to take horses to drive to church, I was informed that in each of these three cases, the horses belonged to the Negroes who were driving or riding them. The old man was infirm, and Mr. X. had given him a horse, to enable him to move about. He was probably employed to look after the cattle at pasture, or at something in which it was necessary, for his usefulness, that he should have a horse: I say this, because I afterwards found, in similar cases on other plantations, that it was so. But the watchman and the house servant had bought their horses with money. The watchman was believed to own three horses; and, to account for his wealth, Mr. X.'s son told me that his father considered him a very valuable servant, and frequently encouraged his good behavior with handsome gratuities. He receives, probably, considerably higher wages, in fact (in the form of presents), than the white overseer. He knew his father gave him two hundred dollars at once, a short time ago. The watchman has a private house, and, no doubt, lives in considerable luxury.

Will it be said, "therefore, slavery is neither necessarily degrading nor inhumane"? On the other hand, so far as it is not, there is no apology for it. It is possible, though not probable, that this fine fellow, if he had been born a free man, would be no better employed than he is here; but, in that case, where is the advantage? Certainly not in the economy of the arrangement. And if he were self-dependent, if, especially, he had to provide for the present and future of those he loved, and was able to do so, would he not necessarily live a happier, stronger, better, and more respectable man?

After passing through toolrooms, corn rooms, mule stables, storerooms, and a large garden, in which vegetables to be distributed among the Negroes, as well as for the family, are grown, we walked to the rice land. It is divided by embankments into fields of about twenty acres each, but varying somewhat in size, according to the course of the river. The arrangements are such that each field may be flooded independently of the rest, and they are subdivided by open ditches into rectangular plots of a quarter acre each. We first proceeded to where twenty or thirty women and girls were engaged in raking together, in heaps and winrows, the stubble and rubbish left on the field after the last crop, and burning it. The main object of this operation is to kill all the seeds of weeds, or of rice, on the ground. Ordinarily it is done by tasks—a certain number of the small divisions of the field being given to each hand to burn in a day; but owing to a more than usual amount of rain having fallen lately, and some other causes, making the work harder in some places than others, the women were now working by the day, under the direction of a "driver," a Negro man, who walked about among them, taking care that they left nothing unburned. Mr. X. inspected the ground they had gone over, to see whether the driver had done his duty. It had been sufficiently well burned, but not more than a quarter as much ground had been gone over, he said, as was usually burned in task work— and he thought they had been very lazy, and reprimanded them. The driver made some little apology, but the women offered no reply, keeping steadily and, it seemed, sullenly, on at their work.

In the next field, twenty men, or boys, for none of them looked as if they were full-grown, were plowing, each with a single mule, and a light, New York-made plow. The soil was friable, the plowing easy, and the mules proceeded at a smart pace; the furrows were straight, regular, and well turned. Their task was nominally an acre and a quarter a day; somewhat less actually, as the measure includes the space occupied by the ditches, which are two to three feet wide, running around each quarter of an acre. The plowing gang was superintended by a driver, who was provided with a watch; and while we were looking at them he called out that it was twelve o'clock. The mules were immediately taken from the plows, and the plow-boys mounting them, leapt the ditches, and cantered off to the stables, to feed them. One or two were ordered to take their plows to the blacksmith, for repairs.

The plowmen got their dinner at this time: those not using horses do not usually dine till they have finished their tasks; but this, I believe, is optional with them. They commence work, I was told, at sunrise, and at about eight o'clock have breakfast brought to them in the field, each hand having left a bucket with the cook for that purpose. All who are working in connection, leave their work together, and gather about a fire, where they generally spend about half an hour. The provisions furnished, consist mainly of meal, rice, and vegetables, with salt and molasses, and occasionally bacon, fish, and coffee. The allowance is a peck of meal, or an equivalent quantity of rice per week, to each working hand, old or young, besides small stores. Mr. X. says that he has lately given a less amount of meat than is now usual on plantations, having observed that the general health of the Negroes is not as good as formerly, when no meat at all was customarily given them. (The general impression among planters is, that the Negroes work much better for being supplied with three or four pounds of bacon a week.)

Leaving the rice land, we went next to some of the upland fields, where we found several other gangs of Negroes at work; one entirely of men engaged in ditching; another of women, and another of boys and girls, "listing" an old corn field with hoes. All of them were working by tasks, and were overlooked by Negro drivers. They all labored with greater rapidity and cheerfulness than any slaves I have before seen; and the women struck their hoes as if they were strong, and well able to engage in muscular labor. The expression of their faces was generally repulsive, and their *ensemble* anything but agreeable. The dress of most was uncouth and cumbrous, dirty and ragged; reefed up, as I have once before described, at the hips, so as to show their heavy legs, wrapped round with a piece of old blanket, in lieu of leggings or stockings. Most of them worked with

bare arms, but wore strong shoes on their feet, and handkerchiefs on their heads; some of them were smoking, and each
gang had a fire burning on the ground, near where they were
at work, by which to light their pipes and warm their breakfast.
Mr. X. said this was always their custom, even in summer. To
each gang a boy or girl was also attached, whose business it
was to bring water for them to drink, and to go for anything
required by the driver. The drivers would frequently call back
a hand to go over again some piece of his or her task that had
not been worked to his satisfaction, and were constantly calling to one or another, with a harsh and peremptory voice,
to strike harder, or hoe deeper, and otherwise taking care that
the work was well done. Mr. X. asked if Little Sam ("Tom's
Sue's Sam") worked yet with the "three-quarter" hands, and
learning that he did, ordered him to be put with the full hands,
observing that though rather short, he was strong and stout,
and, being twenty years old, well able to do a man's work.

The field hands are all divided into four classes, according
to their physical capacities. The children beginning as "quarter hands," advancing to "half hands," and then to "three-
quarter hands"; and, finally, when mature, and able-bodied,
healthy, and strong, to "full hands." As they decline in strength,
from age, sickness, or other cause, they retrograde in the scale,
and proportionately less labor is required of them. Many, of
naturally weak frame, never are put among the full hands.
Finally, the aged are left out at the annual classification, and no
more regular field work is required of them, although they are
generally provided with some light, sedentary occupation. I
saw one old woman picking "tailings" of rice out of a heap of
chaff, an occupation at which she was probably not earning
her salt. Mr. X. told me she was a native African, having been
brought when a girl from the Guinea coast. She spoke almost
unintelligibly; but after some other conversation, in which I
had not been able to understand a word she said, he jokingly
proposed to send her back to Africa. She expressed her preference to remain where she was, very emphatically. "Why?" She
did not answer readily, but being pressed, threw up her palsied
hands, and said furiously, "I lubs 'ou, mas'r, oh, I lubs 'ou. I
don't want go 'way from 'ou."

The field hands are nearly always worked in gangs, the strength of a gang varying according to the work that engages it; usually it numbers twenty or more, and is directed by a driver. As on most large plantations, whether of rice or cotton, in eastern Georgia and South Carolina, nearly all ordinary and regular work is performed *by tasks:* that is to say, each hand has his labor for the day marked out before him, and can take his own time to do it in. For instance, in making drains in light, clean meadow land, each man or woman of the full hands is required to dig one thousand cubic feet; in swamp land that is being prepared for rice culture, where there are not many stumps, the task for a ditcher is five hundred feet: while in a very strong cypress swamp, only two hundred feet is required; in hoeing rice, a certain number of rows, equal to one-half or two-thirds of an acre, according to the condition of the land; in sowing rice (strewing in drills), two acres; in reaping rice (if it stands well), three-quarters of an acre; or, sometimes a gang will be required to reap, tie in sheaves, and carry to the stack yard the produce of a certain area, commonly equal to one fourth the number of acres that there are hands working together. Hoeing cotton, corn, or potatoes; one half to one acre. Threshing; five to six hundred sheaves. In plowing rice land (light, clean, mellow soil) with a yoke of oxen, one acre a day, including the ground lost in and near the drains—the oxen being changed at noon. A cooper, also, for instance, is required to make barrels at the rate of eighteen a week. Drawing staves, 500 a day. Hoop poles, 120. Squaring timber, 100 ft. Laying worm fence, 50 panels per hand. Post and rail do., posts set 2½ to 3 ft. deep, 9 ft. apart, nine or ten panels per hand. In getting fuel from the woods, (pine, to be cut and split), one cord is the task for a day. In "mauling rails," the taskman selecting the trees (pine) that he judges will split easiest, one hundred a day, ends not sharpened.

These are the tasks for first-class able-bodied men; they are lessened by one quarter for three-quarter hands, and proportionately for the lighter classes. In allotting the tasks, the drivers are expected to put the weaker hands where (if there is any choice in the appearance of the ground, as where certain rows in hoeing corn would be less weedy than others,) they will be favored.

These tasks certainly would not be considered excessively

hard, by a Northern laborer; and, in point of fact, the more industrious and active hands finish them often by two o'clock. I saw one or two leaving the field soon after one o'clock, several about two; and between three and four, I met a dozen women and several men coming home to their cabins, having finished their day's work.

Under this "Organization of Labor," most of the slaves work rapidly and well. In nearly all ordinary work, custom has settled the extent of the task, and it is difficult to increase it. The driver who marks it out, has to remain on the ground until it is finished, and has no interest in overmeasuring it; and if it should be systematically increased very much, there is danger of a general stampede to the "swamp"—a danger the slave can always hold before his master's cupidity. In fact, it is looked upon *in this region* as a proscriptive right of the Negroes to have this incitement to diligence offered them; and the man who denied it, or who attempted to lessen it, would, it is said, suffer in his reputation, as well as experience much annoyance from the obstinate "rascality" of his Negroes. Notwithstanding this, I have heard a man assert, boastingly, that he made his Negroes habitually perform double the customary tasks. Thus we get a glimpse again of the black side. If he is allowed the power to do this, what may not a man do?

It is the driver's duty to make the tasked hands do their work well. If, in their haste to finish it, they neglect to do it properly, he "sets them back," so that carelessness will hinder more than it will hasten the completion of their tasks.

In the selection of drivers, regard seems to be had to size and strength—at least, nearly all the drivers I have seen are tall and strong men—but a great deal of judgment, requiring greater capacity of mind than the ordinary slave is often supposed to be possessed of, is certainly needed in them. A good driver is very valuable and usually holds office for life. His authority is not limited to the direction of labor in the field, but extends to the general deportment of the Negroes. He is made to do the duties of policeman, and even of police magistrate. It is his duty, for instance, on Mr. X.'s estate, to keep order in the settlement; and, if two persons, men or women, are fighting, it is his duty to immediately separate them, and then to "whip them both."

Before any field of work is entered upon by a gang, the driver who is to superintend them has to measure and stake off the tasks. To do this at all accurately, in irregular-shaped fields, must require considerable powers of calculation. A driver, with a boy to set the stakes, I was told, would accurately lay out forty acres a day, in half-acre tasks. The only instrument used is a five-foot measuring rod. When the gang comes to the field, he points out to each person his or her duty for the day, and then walks about among them, looking out that each proceeds properly. If, after a hard day's labor, he sees that the gang has been overtasked, owing to a miscalculation of the difficulty of the work, he may excuse the completion of the tasks; but he is not allowed to extend them. In the case of uncompleted tasks, the body of the gang begin new tasks the next day, and only a sufficient number are detailed from it to complete, during the day, the unfinished tasks of the day before. The relation of the driver to the working hands seems to be similar to that of the boatswain to the seamen in the navy, or of the sergeant to the privates in the army.

Having generally had long experience on the plantation, the advice of the drivers is commonly taken in nearly all the administration, and frequently they are, *de facto*, the managers. Orders on important points of the plantation economy, I have heard given by the proprietor directly to them, without the overseer's being consulted or informed of them; and it is often left with them to decide when and how long to flow the rice grounds — the proprietor and overseer deferring to their more experienced judgment. Where the drivers are discreet, experienced, and trusty, the overseer is frequently employed merely as a matter of form, to comply with the laws requiring the superintendence or presence of a white man among every body of slaves; and his duty is rather to inspect and report than to govern. Mr. X. considers his overseer an uncommonly efficient and faithful one, but he would not employ him, even during the summer, when he is absent for several months, if the law did not require it. He has sometimes left his plantation in care of one of the drivers for a considerable length of time, after having discharged an overseer; and he thinks it has then been quite as well conducted as ever. His overseer consults the drivers on all important points, and is governed by their advice.

Mr. X. said, that though overseers sometimes punished the Negroes severely, and otherwise ill-treated them, it is their more common fault to indulge them foolishly in their disposition to idleness, or in other ways to curry favor with them, so they may not inform the proprietor of their own misconduct or neglect. He has his overseer bound to certain rules, by written contract; and it is stipulated that he can discharge him at any moment, without remuneration for his loss of time and inconvenience, if he should at any time be dissatisfied with him. One of the rules is, that he shall never punish a Negro with his own hands, and that corporeal punishment, when necessary, shall be inflicted by the drivers. The advantage of this is, that it secures time for deliberation, and prevents punishment being made in sudden passion. His drivers are not allowed to carry their whips with them in the field; so that if the overseer wishes a hand punished, it is necessary to call a driver; and the driver has then to go to his cabin, which is, perhaps, a mile or two distant, to get his whip, before it can be applied.

I asked how often the necessity of punishment occurred.

"Sometimes, perhaps, not once for two or three weeks; then it will seem as if the devil had got into them all, and there is a good deal of it."

As the Negroes finish the labor required of them by Mr. X., at three or four o'clock in the afternoon, they can employ the remainder of the day in laboring for themselves, if they choose. Each family has a half-acre of land allotted to it, for a garden; besides which, there is a large vegetable garden, cultivated by a gardener for the plantation, from which they are supplied, to a greater or less extent. They are at liberty to sell whatever they choose from the products of their own garden, and to make what they can by keeping swine and fowls. Mr. X.'s family have no other supply of poultry and eggs than what is obtained by purchase from his own Negroes; they frequently, also, purchase game from them. The only restriction upon their traffic is a "liquor law." They are not allowed to buy or sell ardent spirits. This prohibition, like liquor laws elsewhere, unfortunately, cannot be enforced; and, of late years, grog shops, at which stolen goods are bought from the slaves, and poisonous liquors

—chiefly the worst whisky, much watered and made stupefying by an infusion of tobacco—are clandestinely sold to them, have become an established evil, and the planters find themselves almost powerless to cope with it. They have, here, lately organized an association for this purpose, and have brought several offenders to trial; but, as it is a penitentiary offense, the culprit spares no pains or expense to avoid conviction—and it is almost impossible, in a community of which so large a proportion is poor and degraded, to have a jury sufficiently honest and intelligent to permit the law to be executed.

This difficulty in the management of slaves is a great and very rapidly increasing one. Everywhere that I have been, I have found the planters provoked and angry about it. A swarm of Jews, within the last ten years, has settled in nearly every Southern town, many of them men of no character, opening cheap clothing and trinket shops; ruining, or driving out of business, many of the old retailers, and engaging in an unlawful trade with the simple Negroes, which is found very profitable.

The law which prevents the reception of the evidence of a Negro in courts, here strikes back, with a most annoying force, upon the dominant power itself. In the mischief thus arising, we see a striking illustration of the danger which stands before the South, whenever its prosperity shall invite extensive immigration, and lead what would otherwise be a healthy competition to flow through its channels of industry.

Mr. X. remarks that his arrangements allow his servants no excuse for dealing with these fellows. He has a rule to purchase everything they desire to sell, and to give them a high price for it himself. Eggs constitute a circulating medium on the plantation. Their par value is considered to be twelve for a dime, at which they may always be exchanged for cash, or left on deposit, without interest, at his kitchen.

Whatever he takes of them that he cannot use in his own family, or has not occasion to give to others of his servants, is sent to town to be resold. The Negroes do not commonly take money for the articles he has of them, but the value of them is put to their credit, and a regular account kept with them. He has a store, usually well supplied with articles that they most want, which are purchased in large quantities, and sold to them at wholesale prices; thus giving them a great advantage in dealing with him rather than with the grog shops. His slaves are sometimes his creditors to large amounts; at the present time he says he owes them about five hundred dollars. A woman has charge of the store, and when there is anything called for that she cannot supply, it is usually ordered, by the next conveyance, of his factors in town.

So far as I have observed, slaves show themselves worthy of trust most where their masters are most considerate and liberal towards them. Far more so, for instance, on the small farms of North Carolina than on the plantations of Virginia and South Carolina. Mr. X.'s slaves are permitted to purchase firearms and ammunition, and to keep them in their cabins; and his wife and daughters reside with him, among them, the doors of the house never locked, or windows closed, perfectly defenseless, and miles distant from any other white family.

On most of the large rice plantations which I have seen in this vicinity, there is a small chapel, which the Negroes call their prayer house. The owner of one of these told me that, having furnished the prayer house with seats having a backrail, his Negroes petitioned him to remove it, because it did not leave them *room enough to pray*. It was explained to me that it is their custom, in social worship, to work themselves up to a great pitch of excitement, in which they yell and cry aloud, and finally, shriek and leap up, clapping their hands and dancing, as it is done at heathen festivals. The backrail they found to seriously impede this exercise.

Mr. X. told me that he had endeavored, with but little success, to prevent this shouting and jumping of the Negroes at their meetings on his plantation, from a conviction that there was not the slightest element of religious sentiment in it. He considered it to be engaged in more as an exciting amusement than from any really religious impulse. In the town churches, except, perhaps, those managed and conducted almost exclusively by Negroes, the slaves are said to commonly engage in religious exercises in a sober and decorous manner; yet, a member of a Presbyterian church in a Southern city told me, that he had seen the Negroes in his own house of worship, during "a season of revival," leap from their seats, throw their arms wildly in the air, shout vehemently and unintelligibly, cry, groan, rend their clothes, and fall into cataleptic trances.

On almost every large plantation, and in every neighborhood of small ones, there is one man who has come to be considered the head or pastor of the local church. The office among the Negroes, as among all other people, confers a certain importance and power. A part of the reverence attaching to the duties is given to the person; vanity and self-confidence are cultivated, and a higher ambition aroused than can usually enter the mind of a slave. The self-respect of the preacher is also often increased by the consideration in which he is held by his master, as well as by his fellows; thus, the preachers generally have an air of superiority to other Negroes; they acquire a remarkable memory of words, phrases, and forms; a curious sort of poetic talent is developed, and a habit is obtained of rhapsodizing and exciting furious emotions, to a great degree spurious and temporary, in themselves and others, through the imagination. I was introduced, the other day, to a preacher, who was represented to be quite distinguished among them. I took his hand, respectfully, and said I was happy to meet him. He seemed to take this for a joke, and laughed heartily. He was a "driver," and my friend said —

"He drives the Negroes at the cotton all the week, and Sundays he drives them at the Gospel — don't you, Ned?"

He commenced to reply in some scriptural phrase, soberly; but before he could say three words, began to laugh again, and reeled off like a drunken man — entirely overcome with merriment. He recovered himself in a moment, and returned to us.

"They say he preaches very powerfully, too."

"Yes, massa! 'kordin' to der grace — *yah! yah!*"

And he staggered off again, with the peculiar hearty Negro guffaw. My friend's tone was, I suppose, slightly humorous, but I was grave, and really meant to treat him respectfully, wishing to draw him into conversation; but he had got the impression that it was intended to make fun of him, and generously assuming a merry humor, I found it impossible to get a serious reply.

A majority of the public houses of worship at the South are

small, rude structures of logs, or rough boards, built by the
united labor or contributions of the people of a large neighborhood or district of country, and are used as places of assembly
for all public purposes. Few of them have any regular clergymen,
but preachers of different denominations go from one to another, sometimes in a defined rotation, or "circuit," so that they
may be expected at each of their stations at regular intervals. A
late report of the Southern Aid Society states that hardly one-
fifth of the preachers are regularly educated for their business,
and that "you would starve a host of them if you debarred them
from seeking additional support for their families by worldly
occupation." In one presbytery of the Presbyterian Church,
which is, perhaps, the richest, and includes the most educated
body of people of all the Southern churches, there are twenty-
one ministers whose wages are not over two hundred and fifty
dollars each. The proportion of ministers, of all sorts, to people,
is estimated at one to thirteen hundred. (In the Free States it is
estimated at one to nine hundred.) The report of this Society
also states, that "within the limits of the United States religious
destitution lies comparatively at the South and Southwest; and
that from the first settlement of the country the North has preserved a decided religious superiority over the South, especially
in three important particulars: in ample supply of Christian
institutions; extensive supply of Christian truth; and thorough
Christian regimen, both in the Church and in the community."
It is added that, "while the Southwestern States have always
needed a stronger arm of the Christian ministry to raise them
up toward a Christian equality with their Northern brethren,
their supply in this respect has always been decidedly inferior."
The reason of this is the same with that which explains the
general ignorance of the people of the South: The effect of
slavery in preventing social association of the whites, and in
encouraging vagabond and improvident habits of life among
the poor.

The two largest denominations of Christians at the South are
the Methodists and Baptists—the last having a numerical
superiority. There are some subdivisions of each, and of the
Baptists especially, the nature of which I do not understand.
Two grand divisions of the Baptists are known as the Hard

Shells and the Soft Shells. There is an intense rivalry and jealousy among these various sects and sub-sects, and the controversy between them is carried on with a bitterness and persistence exceeding anything which I have known at the North, and in a manner which curiously indicates how the terms Christianity, piety, etc., are misapplied to partisanship and conditions of the imagination.

A general want of essential reverence of character seems to be evidenced in the frequent familiar and public use of expressions of rare reverence, and in high-colored descriptions of personal feelings and sentiments, which, if actual, can only be among a man's dearest, most interior and secret, stillest, and most uncommunicable experiences. Men talk in public places, in the churches, and in barrooms, in the stagecoach, and at the fireside, of their personal communions with the Deity, and of the mutations of their harmony with His Spirit, just as they do about their family and business matters. The familiar use of Scripture expressions by the Negroes, I have already indicated. This is not confined to them. A dram seller advertises thus: —

"FAITH WITHOUT WORKS IS DEAD."
In order to engage in a more "honorable" business, I offer for sale, cheap for cash, my stock of
LIQUORS, BAR FIXTURES, BILLIARD TABLE, *&c., &c.*
If not sold privately, by the 20th day of May, I will sell the same at public auction. "Shew me thy faith without thy works, and I will shew thee my faith by my works."

E. KEYSER

At a Sunday dinner table, at a village inn in Virginia, two or three men had taken seats with me, who had, as they said, "been to the preachin'." A child had been baptized, and the discourse had been a defense of infant baptism.

"I'm damned," said one, "ef he teched on the primary significance of baptism, at all — buryin' with Jesus."

"They wus the weakest arguments for sprinklin' that ever I heerd," said another — a hot, red-faced, corpulent man — "and his sermon was two hours long, for when he stopped I looked at my watch. I thought it should be a lesson to me, for I couldn't help going to sleep. Says I to Uncle John, says I—he sot next to me, and I whispered to him—says I, 'When he gits to Bunker Hill, you wake me up,' for I see he was bound to go clean back to the beginnin' of things."

"Uncle John is an Episcopalian, aint he?"

"Yes."

"Well, there aint no religion in that, no how."

"No, there aint."

"Well now, you wouldn't think it, but I've studied into religion a heap in my life."

"Don't seem to have done you much good."

"No it aint, not yet, but I've studied into it, and I know what it is."

"There aint but one way, Benny."

"I know it."

"Repent of your sins, and believe in Christ, and be immersed—that's all."

"I know it."

"Well, I hope the Lord'll bring you to it, 'fore you die."

"Reckon he will—hope so, sure."

"You wouldn't hardly think that fat man was a preacher himself, would you?" said the landlady to me, after they left.

"Certainly not."

"He is, though, but I don't think much of that sort"; and the landlady immediately began to describe to me the religious history of the neighborhood. It was some different here, she said she reckoned, in reply to a remark of mine, from what it was at the North. Most respectable people became pious here before they got to be very old, especially ladies. Young ladies were always gay and went to balls till they were near twenty years old, but from eighteen to twenty-five they generally got religion, and then they stopped right short, and never danced or carried on any after that. Sometimes it wasn't till after they were married, but there weren't many ladies who had children that warn't pious. She herself was an exception, for she had three children and had not got religion yet; sometimes she was frightened to think how old she was—her children growing up about her; but she did so like dancing—she hoped her turn would come — she knew it would — she had a pious and praying mother, and she reckoned her prayers must be heard, and so on.

The religious service which I am about to describe, was held in a less than usually rude meeting house, the boards by which it was enclosed being planed, the windows glazed, and the seats for the white people provided with backs. It stood in a small clearing of the woods, and there was no habitation within two miles of it. When I reached it with my friends, the services had already commenced. Fastened to trees, in a circle about the house, there were many saddled horses and mules, and a few attached to carts or wagons. There were two smoldering camp-fires, around which sat circles of Negroes and white boys, roasting potatoes in the ashes.

In the house were some fifty white people, generally dressed in homespun, and of the class called "crackers," though I was told that some of them owned a good many Negroes, and were by no means so poor as their appearance indicated. About one-third of the house, at the end opposite the desk, was covered by a gallery or cockloft, under and in which, distinctly separated from the whites, was a dense body of Negroes; the men on one side, the women on another. The whites were seated promiscuously in the body of the house. The Negroes present outnumbered the whites, but the exercises at this time seemed to have no reference to them; there were many more waiting about the doors outside, and they were expecting to enjoy a meeting to themselves, after the whites had left the house. They were generally neatly dressed, more so than the majority of the whites present, but in a distinctly plantation or slave style. A few of them wore somewhat expensive articles, evidently of their own selection and purchase; but I observed with some surprise, that not one of the women had a bonnet upon her head, all wearing handkerchiefs, generally of gay patterns, and becomingly arranged. I inquired if this was entirely a matter of taste, and was told that it, no doubt, was generally so, though the masters would not probably allow them to wear bonnets, if they should be disposed to, and should purchase them themselves, as it would be thought presuming. In the towns, the colored women often, but not generally, wear bonnets.

During all the exercises, people of both classes were frequently going out and coming in; the women had brought their babies with them, and these made much disturbance. A Negro girl would sometimes come forward to take a child out; perhaps the child would prefer not to be taken out, and would make loud and angry objections; it would then be fed. Several were allowed to crawl about the floor, carrying handfuls of cornbread and roasted potatoes about with them; one had a fancy to enter the pulpit; which it succeeded in climbing into three times, and was as often taken away, in spite of loud and tearful expostulations, by its father. Dogs were not excluded; and outside, the doors and windows all being open, there was much neighing and braying, unused as were the mules and horses to see so many of their kind assembled.

The preliminary devotional exercises — a Scripture reading, singing, and painfully irreverential and meaningless harangues nominally addressed to the Deity, but really to the audience — being concluded, the sermon was commenced by reading a text, with which, however, it had, so far as I could discover, no further association. Without often being violent in his manner, the speaker nearly all the time cried aloud at the utmost stretch of his voice, as if calling to some one a long distance off; as his discourse was extemporaneous, however, he sometimes returned with curious effect to his natural conversational tone; and as he was gifted with a strong imagination, and possessed of a good deal of dramatic power, he kept the attention of the people very well. There was no argument upon any point that the congregation were likely to have much difference of opinion upon, nor any special connection between one sentence and another; yet there was a constant, sly, sectarian skirmishing, and a frequently recurring cannonade upon French infidelity and socialism, and several crushing charges upon Fourier, the Pope of Rome, Tom Paine, Voltaire, "Roosu," and Joe Smith. The audience were frequently reminded that the preacher did not want their attention for any purpose of his own; but that he demanded a respectful hearing as "the ambassador of Christ." He had the habit of frequently repeating a phrase, or of bringing forward the same idea in a slightly different form, a great many times. The following passage, of which I took notes, presents an example of this, followed by one of the best instances of his dramatic talent that occurred. He was leaning far over the desk, with his arm stretched forward, gesticulating violently, yelling at the highest key, and catching breath with an effort: —

"A—ah! why don't you come to Christ? ah! what's the reason? ah! Is it because he was of *lowly birth?* ah! Is that it? *Is it* because he was born in a manger? ah! Is it because he was of a humble origin? ah! Is it because he was lowly born? a-ha! Is it because, ah!—is it because, ah!—because he was called a Nazarene? Is it because he was born in a stable?—or is it because—because he was of humble origin? Or is it—is it because"—He drew back, and after a moment's silence put his hand to his chin, and began walking up and down the platform of the pulpit, soliloquizing. "It can't be—it can't be—?" Then lifting his eyes and gradually turning towards the audience, while he continued to speak in a low, thoughtful tone: "Perhaps you don't like the messenger—is that the reason? I'm the ambassador of the great and glorious King; it's his invitation, 'taint mine. You musn't mind me. I ain't no account. Suppose a ragged, insignificant little boy should come running in here and tell you, 'Mister, your house's a-fire!' would you mind the ragged, insignificant little boy, and refuse to listen to him, because he didn't look respectable?"

At the end of the sermon he stepped down from the pulpit, and, crossing the house towards the Negroes, said, quietly, as he walked, "I take great interest in the poor blacks; and this evening I am going to hold a meeting specially for you." With this he turned back, and without re-entering the pulpit, but strolling up and down before it, read a hymn, at the conclusion of which, he laid his book down, and speaking for a moment with natural emphasis, said —

"I don't want to create a tumultuous scene, now;—that isn't my intention. I don't want to make an excitement,—that aint what I want,—but I feel that there's some here that I may never see again, ah! and, as I may never have another opportunity, I feel it my duty as an ambassador of Jesus Christ, ah! before I go—" By this time he had returned to the high key and whining yell. Exactly what he felt it his duty to do, I did not understand;

but evidently to employ some more powerful agency of
awakening than arguments and appeals to the understanding;
and, before I could conjecture, in the least, of what sort this was
to be, while he was yet speaking calmly, deprecating excitement, my attention was attracted to several men, who had
previously appeared sleepy and indifferent, but who now
suddenly began to sigh, raise their heads, and *shed tears*—
some standing up, so that they might be observed in doing
this by the whole congregation—the tears running down their
noses without any interruption. The speaker, presently, was
crying aloud, with a mournful, distressed, beseeching shriek,
as if he were himself suffering torture: "Oh, any of you fond
parents, who know that any of your dear, sweet, little ones may
be, oh! at any moment snatched right away from your bosom,
and cast into hell fire, oh! there to suffer torment for ever and
ever, and ever and ever—Oh! come out here and help us pray
for them! Oh, any of you wives that has got an unconverted
husband, that won't go along with you to eternal glory, but is
set upon being separated from you, oh! and taking up his bed
in hell—Oh! I call upon you, if you love him, now to come out
here and jine us in praying for him. Oh, if there's a husband
here, whose wife is still in the bond of iniquity," etc., through
a long category.

It was immediately evident that a large part of the audience
understood his wish to be the reverse of what he had declared,
and considered themselves called upon to assist him; and it was
astonishing to see with what readiness the faces of those who,
up to the moment he gave the signal, had appeared drowsy and
stupid, were made to express distressing excitement, sighing,
groaning, and weeping. Rising in their seats, and walking up to
the pulpit, they grasped each other's hands agonizingly, and
remained, some kneeling, others standing, with their faces
towards the remainder of the assembly. There was great con-
fusion and tumult, and the poor children, evidently impressed
by the terrified tone of the howling preacher, with the expectation of some immediately impending calamity, shrieked,
and ran hither and thither, till Negro girls came forward,
laughing at the imposition, and carried them out.

At length, when some twenty had gathered around the

preacher, and it became evident that no more could be drawn out, he stopped a moment for breath, and then repeated a verse of a hymn, which being sung, he again commenced to cry aloud, calling now upon all the unconverted, who were *willing* to be saved, to kneel. A few did so, and another verse was sung, followed by another more fervent exhortation. So it went on; at each verse his entreaties, warnings, and threats, and the responsive groans, sobs, and ejaculations of his coterie grew louder and stronger. Those who refused to kneel were addressed as standing on the brink of the infernal pit, into which a diabolical divinity was momentarily on the point of satisfying the necessities of his character by hurling them off.

All this time about a dozen of the audience remained standing, many were kneeling, and the larger part had taken their seats — all having risen at the commencement of the singing. Those who continued standing were mainly wild-looking young fellows, who glanced with smiles at one another, as if they needed encouragement to brazen it out. A few young women were evidently fearfully excited, and perceptibly trembled, but for some reason dared not kneel, or compromise, by sitting. One of these, a good-looking and gaily dressed girl, stood near, and directly before the preacher, her lips compressed, and her eyes fixed fiercely and defiantly upon him. He for some time concentrated his force upon her; but she was too strong for him, he could not bring her down. At length, shaking his finger towards her, with a terrible expression, as if he had the power, and did not lack the inclination, to damn her for her resistance to his will, he said: "I tell you this is *the last call!*" She bit her lips, and turned paler, but still stood erect, and defiant of the immense magnetism concentrated upon her; and he gave it up himself, quite exhausted with the effort.

The last verse of the hymn was sung. A comparatively quiet and sober repetition of Scripture phrases, strung together heterogeneously and without meaning, in the form of prayer, followed, a benediction was pronounced, and in five minutes all the people were out of the door, with no trace of the previous excitement left, but most of the men talking eagerly of the price of cotton, and Negroes, and other news.

The Negroes kept their place during all of the tumult; there may have been a sympathetic groan or exclamation uttered by one or two of them, but generally they expressed only the interest of curiosity in the proceedings, such as Europeans might at a performance of the dancing dervishes, an Indian pow-wow, or an exhibition of "psychological" or "spiritual" phenomena, making it very evident that the emotion of the performers was optionally engaged in, as an appropriate part of divine service. There was generally a self-satisfied smile upon their faces; and I have no doubt they felt that they could do it with a good deal more energy and abandon, if they were called upon. I did not wish to detain my companion to witness how they succeeded, when their turn came; and I can only judge from the fact, that those I saw the next morning were so hoarse that they could scarcely speak, that the religious exercises they most enjoy are rather hard upon the lungs, whatever their effect may be upon the soul.

4.

Alabama

Mobile. — I left Savannah for the West, by the Macon road; the train started punctually to a second, at its advertised time; the speed was not great, but regular, and less time was lost unnecessarily, at way-stations, than usually on our Northern roads.

I have travelled more than five hundred miles on the Georgia roads, and I am glad to say that all of them seem to be exceedingly well managed. The speed upon them is not generally more than from fifteen of twenty miles an hour; but it is made, as advertised, with considerable punctuality. The roads are admirably engineered and constructed, and their equipment will compare favorably with that of any other roads on the continent. There are now upwards of twelve hundred miles of railroad in the State, and more building. The Savannah and Macon line — the first built — was commenced in 1834. The increased commerce of the city of Savannah, which followed its completion, stimulated many other railroad enterprises, not only within the State, but elsewhere at the South, particularly in South Carolina. Many of these were rashly pushed forward by men of no experience, and but little commercial judgment; the roads were injudiciously laid out, and have been badly managed, and, of course, have occasioned disastrous losses. The Savannah and Macon road has, however, been very successful. The receipts are now over $1,000,000 annually; the road is well stocked, is out of debt, and its business is constantly increasing; the stock is above par, and the stockholders are receiving eight per cent dividends, with a handsome surplus on hand. It has been always, in a great degree, under the management of Northern men — was engineered, and is still worked chiefly by Northern men, and a large amount of its stock is owned at the North. I am told that most of the mechanics, and of the successful merchants and tradesmen of Savannah came originally from the North, or are the sons of Northern men.

Partly by rail and partly by rapid stagecoaching (the coaches, horses, and drivers again from the North), I crossed the State in about twenty-four hours. The railroad is since entirely completed from Savannah to Montgomery, in Alabama, and is being extended slowly towards the Mississippi; of course with the expectation that it will eventually reach the Pacific, and thus make Savannah "the gate to the commerce of the world." Ship masters will hope that, when either it or its rival in South Carolina has secured that honor, they will succeed, better than they yet have done, in removing the bars, physical and legal, by which commerce is now annoyed in its endeavors to serve them.

At Columbus, I spent several days. It is the largest manufacturing town, south of Richmond, in the Slave States. It is situated at the Falls, and the head of steamboat navigation of the Chattahoochee, the western boundary of Georgia. The water power is sufficient to drive two hundred thousand spindles, with a proportionate number of looms. There are, probat present from fifteen to twenty thousand spindles running. The operatives in the cotton mills are said to be mainly "cracker girls" (poor whites from the country), who earn, in good times, by piecework, from $8 to $12 a month. There are, besides the cotton mills, one woolen mill, one paper mill, a foundry, a cotton gin factory, a machine shop, etc. The laborers in all these are mainly whites, and they are in such a condition that, if temporarily thrown out of employment, great numbers of them are at once reduced to a state of destitution, and are dependent upon credit or charity for their daily food. Public entertainments were being held at the time of my visit, the profits to be applied to the relief of operatives in mills which had been stopped by the effects of a late flood of the river. Yet slavery is constantly boasted to be a perfect safeguard against such distress.

I had seen in no place, since I left Washington, so much gambling, intoxication, and cruel treatment of servants in public, as in Columbus. This, possibly, was accidental; but I must caution persons, travelling for health or pleasure, to avoid stopping in the town. The hotel in which I lodged was disgustingly dirty; the table revolting; the waiters stupid, inattentive, and annoying. It was the stage house; but I was informed that the other public house was no better. There are very good inns at Macon, and at Montgomery, Alabama; and it will be best for an invalid proceeding from Savannah westward, if possible, not to spend a night between these towns.

A day's journey took me from Columbus, through a hilly wilderness, with a few dreary villages, and many isolated cotton farms, with comfortless habitations for black and white upon them, to Montgomery, the capital of Alabama.

Montgomery is a prosperous town, with pleasant suburbs, and a remarkably enterprising population, among which there is a considerable proportion of Northern and foreign-born businessmen and mechanics.

I spent a week here, and then left for Mobile, on the steamboat *Fashion*, a clean and well-ordered boat, with polite and obliging officers. We were two days and a half making the passage, the boat stopping at almost every bluff and landing to take on cotton, until she had a freight of nineteen hundred bales, which was built up on the guards, seven or eight tiers in height, and until it reached the hurricane deck. The boat was thus brought so deep that her guards were in the water, and the ripple of the river constantly washed over them. There are two hundred landings on the Alabama River, and three hundred on the Bigby (Tombeckbee [Tombigbee] of the geographers), at which the boats advertise to call, if required, for passengers or freight. This, of course, makes the passage exceedingly tedious. The so-called landings, however, have not in many cases the slightest artificial accommodations for the purpose of a landing. The boat's hawser, if used, is made fast to a living tree; there is not a sign of a wharf, often no house in sight, and sometimes no distinct road.

The principal town at which we landed was Selma, a pleasant village, in one corner of which I came upon a tall, ill-proportioned, broken-windowed brick barrack; it had no grounds about it, was close upon the highway, was in every way dirty, neglected, and forlorn in expression. I inquired what it was, and was answered, the "Young Ladies' College." There were a number of pretty private gardens in the town, in which I noticed several evergreen oaks, the first I had seen since leaving Savannah.

At Claiborne, another village upon the river, we landed at

nine o'clock on a Sunday night. It is situated upon a bluff, a hundred and fifty feet high, with a nearly perpendicular bank, upon the river. The boat came to the shore at the foot of a plank slideway, down which cotton was sent to it, from a warehouse at the top.

There was something truly Western in the direct, reckless way in which the boat was loaded. A strong gangplank being placed at right angles to the slideway, a bale of cotton was let slide from the top, and, coming down with fearful velocity, on striking the gangplank, it would rebound up and out on to the boat, against a barricade of bales previously arranged to receive it. The moment it struck this barricade, it would be dashed at by two or three men, and jerked out of the way, and others would roll it to its place for the voyage, on the tiers aft. The mate, standing near the bottom of the slide, as soon as the men had removed one bale to what he thought a safe distance, would shout to those aloft, and down would come another. Not unfrequently, a bale would not strike fairly on its end, and would rebound off, diagonally, overboard; or would be thrown up with such force as to go over the barricade, breaking stanchions and railings, and scattering the passengers on the berth deck. Negro hands were sent to the top of the bank, to roll the bales to the side, and Irishmen were kept below to remove them, and stow them. On asking the mate (with some surmisings) the reason of this arrangement, he said—

"The niggers are worth too much to be risked here; if the Paddies are knocked overboard, or get their backs broke, nobody loses anything!"

There were about one hundred passengers on the *Fashion*, besides a number of poor people and Negroes on the lower deck. They were, generally, cotton planters, going to Mobile on business, or emigrants bound to Texas or Arkansas. They were usually well dressed, but were a rough, coarse style of people, drinking a great deal, and most of the time under a little alcoholic excitement. Not sociable, except when the topics of cotton, land, and Negroes, were started; interested, however, in talk about theaters and the turf; very profane; often showing the handles of concealed weapons about their persons, but not quarrelsome, avoiding disputes and altercations, and respectful to one another in forms of words; very ill-informed, except on plantation business; their language ungrammatical, idiomatic, and extravagant. Their grand characteristics — simplicity of motives, vague, shallow, and purely objective habits of thought; and bold, self-reliant movement.

With all their individual independence, I soon could perceive a very great homogeneousness of character, by which they were distinguishable from any other people with whom I had before been thrown in contact; and I began to study it with interest, as the Anglo-Saxon development of the Southwest.

I found that, more than any people I had ever seen, they were unrateable by dress, taste, forms, and expenditures. I was perplexed by finding, apparently united in the same individual, the self-possession, confidence, and the use of expressions of deference, of the well-equipped gentleman, and the coarseness and low tastes of the uncivilized boor — frankness and reserve, recklessness and self-restraint, extravagance, and penuriousness.

There was one man, who "lived, when he was to home," as he told me, "in the Red River Country," in the northeastern part of Texas, having emigrated thither from Alabama, some years before. He was a tall, thin, awkward person, and wore a suit of clothes (probably bought "ready made") which would have better suited a short, fat figure. Under his waistcoat he carried a large knife, with the hilt generally protruding at the breast. He had been with his family to his former home, for a business purpose, and was now returning to his plantation. His wife was a pale and harassed looking woman; and he scarce ever paid her the smallest attention, not even sitting near her at the public table. Of his children, however, he seemed very fond; and they had a Negro servant in attendance upon them, whom he was constantly scolding and threatening. Having been from home for six weeks, his impatience to return was very great, and was constantly aggravated by the frequent and long-continued stoppages of the boat. "Time's money, time's money!" he would be constantly saying, while we were taking on cotton — "time's worth more'n money to me now; a hundred per cent more, 'cause I left my niggers all alone; not a dam white man within four mile on 'em."

I asked how many Negroes he had.

"I've got twenty on 'em to home, and thar they ar! and thar they ar! and thar aint a dam soul of a white fellow within four mile on 'em."

"They are picking cotton, I suppose?"

"No, I got through pickin' 'fore I left."

"What work have they to do, then, now?"

"I set 'em to clairin', but they aint doin' a dam thing—not a dam thing, they aint; that's wat they are doin', that is—not a dam thing. I know that, as well as you do. That's the reason time's an object. I told the capting so, wen I came aboard: says I, 'capting,' says I, 'time is in the objective case with me.' No, sir, they aint doin' a dam solitary thing; that's what they are up to. I know that as well as anybody; I do. But I'll make it up, I'll make it up, when I get thar, now you'd better believe."

The crew of the boat, as I have intimated, was composed partly of Irishmen, and partly of Negroes; the latter were slaves, and were hired of their owners at $40 a month—the same wages paid to the Irishmen. A dollar of their wages was given to the Negroes themselves, for each Sunday they were on the passage. So far as convenient, they were kept at work separately from the white hands; they were also messed separately. On Sunday I observed them dining in a group, on the cotton bales. The food which was given to them in tubs, from the kitchen, was various and abundant, consisting of bean porridge, bacon, cornbread, ship's biscuit, potatoes, duff (pudding), and gravy. There was one knife used only, among ten of them; the bacon was cut and torn into shares; splinters of the bone and of firewood were used for forks; the porridge was passed from one to another, and drank out of the tub; but though excessively dirty and beastlike in their appearance and manners, they were good natured and jocose as usual.

"Heah! you Bill," said one to another, who was on a higher tier of cotton, "pass down de dessart. You! up dar on de hill; de dessart! Augh! don't you know what de dessart be? De duff, you fool."

"Does any of de gemmen want some o' dese potatum?" asked another; and no answer being given, he turned the tub full of potatoes overboard, without any hesitation. It was evident he had never had to think on one day how he should be able to live the next.

Whenever we landed at night or on Sunday, for wood or cotton, there would be many Negroes come on board from the neighboring plantations, to sell eggs to the steward.

Sunday was observed by the discontinuance of public gambling in the cabin, and in no other way. At midnight gambling was resumed, and during the whole passage was never at any other time discontinued, night or day, so far as I saw. There were three men that seemed to be professional sharpers, and who probably played into each other's hands. One young man lost all the money he had with him — several hundred dollars.

5.

The Lower Mississippi

New Orleans. — The steamboat by which I made the passage along the north shore of the Mexican Gulf to New Orleans, was New York built, and owned by a New Yorker; and the Northern usage of selling passage tickets, to be returned on leaving the boat, was retained upon it. I was sitting near a group of Texans and emigrating planters, when a waiter passed along, crying the usual request, that passengers who had not obtained tickets would call at the captain's office for that purpose. "What's that? What's that?" they shouted; "What did he mean? What is it?" "Why, it's a dun," said one. "He is dunnin' on us, sure," continued one and another; and some started from the seats, as if they thought it insulting. "Well, it's the first time I ever was dunned by a nigger, I'll swar," said one. This seemed to place it in a humorous aspect; and, after a hearty laugh, they resumed their discussion of the advantages offered to emigrants in different parts of Texas, and elsewhere.

There were a large number of steerage passengers occupying the main deck, forward of the shaft. Many of them were Irish, late immigrants, but the large majority were slaves, going on to New Orleans to be sold, or moving with their masters to Texas. There was a fiddle or two among them, and they were very merry, dancing and singing. A few, however, refused to join in the amusement, and looked very disconsolate. A large proportion of them were boys and girls, under twenty years of age.

On the forecastle deck there was a party of emigrants, moving with wagons. There were three men, a father and his two sons, or sons-in-law, with their families, including a dozen or more women and children. They had two wagons, covered with calico and bed ticks, supported by hoops, in which they carried their furniture and stores, and in which they also slept at night, the women in one, and the men in the other. They had six horses, two mules, and two pair of cattle with them. I asked the old man why he had taken his cattle along with him, when he was going so far by sea, and found that he had informed himself accurately of what it would cost him to hire or buy cattle at Galveston; and that taking into account the probable delay he would experience in looking for them there, he had calculated that he could afford to pay the freight on them, to have them with him, to go on at once into the country on his arrival, rather than to sell them at Mobile.

"But," said he, "there was one thing I didn't cakulate on, and I don't understand it; the capting cherged me two dollars and a half for 'wherfage.' I don't know what that means, do you? I want to know, because I don't car' to be imposed upon by nobody. I payed it without sayin' a word, 'cause I never travelled on the water before; next time I do, I shall be more sassy." I asked where he was going. Didn't know much about it, he said, but reckoned he could find a place where there was a good range, and plenty of game. If 'twas as good a range (pasture) as 'twas to Alabama when he first came there, he'd be satisfied. After he'd got his family safe through acclimating this time, he reckoned he shouldn't move again. He had moved about a good deal in his life. There was his littlest boy, he said, looking kindly at a poor, thin, blue-faced little child—he reckoned they'd be apt to *leave* him; he had got *tropsical,* and was of mighty weak constitution, nat'rally; 'twouldn't take much to carry him off, and, of course, a family must be exposed a good deal, moving so this time of year. They should try to find some heavy timbered land—good land, and go to clearing; didn't calculate to make any crops the first year—didn't calculate on it, though perhaps they might if they had good luck. They had come from an eastern county of Alabama. Had sold out his farm for two dollars an acre; best land in the district was worth four; land was naturally kind of thin, and now 'twas pretty much all worn out there. He had moved first from North Carolina, with his father. They never made anything to sell but cotton; made corn for their own use. Never had any Negroes; reckoned he'd done about as well as if he had had them; reckoned a little better on the whole. No, he should not work Negroes in Texas. "Niggers is so kerless, and want so much lookin' arter; they is so monstrous lazy; they won't do no work, you know, less you are clus to 'em all the time, and I don't feel like it. I couldn't, at my time of life, begin a-using the lash; and you know they do have to take that, all on 'em — and a heap on't, sometimes."

"I don't know much about it; they don't have slaves where I live."

"Then you come from a Free State; well, they've talked some of makin' Alabamy a Free State."

"I didn't know that."

"O, yes, there was a good deal of talk one time, as if they was goin' to do it right off. O, yes; there was two or three of the States this way, one time, come pretty nigh freein' the niggers — lettin' 'em all go free."

"And what do you think of it?"

"Well, I'll tell you what I think on it; I'd like it if we could get rid on 'em to yonst. I wouldn't like to hev 'em freed, if they was gwine to hang round. They ought to get some country, and put 'em war they could be by themselves. It wouldn't do no good to free 'em, and let 'em hang round, because they is so monstrous lazy; if they hadn't got nobody to take keer on 'em, you see they wouldn't do nothin' but juss nat'rally laze round, and steal, and pilfer, and no man couldn't live, you see, war they was — if they was free, no man couldn't live. And then, I've two objections; that's one on 'em — no man couldn't live — and this ere's the other; Now suppose they was free, you see they'd all think themselves just as good as we; of course they would, if they was free. Now, just suppose you had a family of children: how would you like to hev a nigger feelin' just as good as a white man? how'd you like to hev a nigger steppin' up to your darter? Of course you wouldn't; and that's the reason I wouldn't like to hev 'em free; but I tell you, I don't think it's right to hev 'em slaves so; that's the fac — taant right to keep 'em as they is."

A mechanic, English by birth, who had lived in New Orleans for several years, always going up the river in the summer, to escape the danger of fever in the city, told me that he could lay up money much more rapidly than in New York. The expenses of living were not necessarily greater than in New York. If a man kept house, and provided for himself, he could live much cheaper than at boarding houses. Many unmarried mechanics, therefore, lived with colored mistresses, who were commonly vile and dishonest. He was at a boarding house, where he paid four dollars a week. In New York he had paid three dollars, but the board was not as good as in New Orleans. "The reason," said he, "that people say it costs so much more to live here than in New York is, that what they think treats in New York, they consider necessaries here. Everybody lives freer, and spends their money more willingly here." When he first came to New Orleans, a New England mechanic came with him. He supposed him to have been previously a man of sober habits; but almost immediately after he got to New Orleans, he got into bad ways, and in a few months he was so often drunk, and brought so much scandal on their boarding house, that he was turned out of it. Soon after this, he called on him, and borrowed two dollars. He said he could not live in New Orleans, it was too expensive, and he was going to Texas. This was several years before, and he had not heard from him since. And this he said was a very common course with New England boys, who had been "too carefully brought up at home," when they came to New Orleans. The master mechanics, who bought up slaves, and took contracts for work, he said, made more money than any others. They did so because they did very poor work — poorer than white mechanics could generally be got to do. But nearly all work was done in New Orleans more hastily and carelessly than in New York, though he thought it was bad enough there. The slaveholding bosses could get no white men to work with their slaves, except Irishmen or Germans — no man who had any regard for his position among his fellow-craftsmen would ever let himself be seen working with a Negro. He said I could see any day in Canal Street, "a most revolting sight" — Irishmen waiting on Negro masons. He had seen, one morning as he was going to his work, a Negro carrying some mortar, when another Negro hailed him with a loud laugh: "Hallo! you is turned Irishman, is 'ou?" White working men were rapidly displacing the slaves in all sorts of work, and he hoped and believed it would not be many years before every Negro would be driven out of the town. He thought acclimated white men could do more hard work than Negroes, even in the hottest weather, if they were temperate, and avoided too stimulating food. That, he said, was the general opinion among those of them who stayed over summer. Those who drank much whisky and cordials, and kept up old habits of eating, just as if they were in England, were the ones who complained most of the climate, and who thought white men were not made to work in it. He had stayed as late as July, and returned in September, and he never saw the day in which he could not do as much work as he did in London.

A New Yorker, whom I questioned about this, said: "I have worked through the very hottest weather, steadily, day after day, and done more work than any three niggers in the State, and been no worse for it. A man has only to take some care of himself."

Going to Lafayette, on the top of an omnibus, I heard an Irishman, somewhat over-stimulated, as Irishmen are apt to be, loudly declare himself an Abolitionist: a companion endeavored in vain to stop him, or make him recant, and finally declared he would not ride any further with him if he could not be more discreet.

The *Morehouse* (Louisiana) *Advocate*, in an article abusive of foreigners, thus describes what, if foreign-born working men were not generally so ignorant and easily imposed upon as they are, would undoubtedly be (although they certainly have not yet generally been) their sentiments with regard to slavery:

The great mass of foreigners who came to our shores are laborers, and consequently come in competition with slave labor. It is to their interest to abolish Slavery; and we know full well the disposition of man to promote all things which advance his own interests. These men come from nations where Slavery is not allowed, and they drink in abolition sentiments from their mothers' breasts; they (all the white race) entertain an utter abhorrence of being put on a level with blacks, whether in the field or in the workshop. Could Slavery be abolished, there would be a greater demand for laborers, and the prices of labor must be greatly enhanced. These may be termed the internal evidences of the abolitionism of foreigners.

But we may find near home facts to corroborate these "internal" evidences: It is well known that there exists a great antipathy among the draymen and rivermen of New Orleans (who are almost to a man foreigners) to the participation of slaves in these branches of industry.

It is obvious that free men have very much gained the field of labor in New Orleans to themselves. The majority of the cartmen, hackney coachmen, porters, railroad hands, public waiters, and common laborers, as well as of skilled mechanics, appear to be white men; and of the Negroes employed in those avocations a considerable proportion are free.

This is the case here more than in any other town in the South, although the climate is torrid, and inconvenient or dangerous to strangers; because New Orleans is more extensively engaged in commerce than they are, and because there is, by the passing and sojourning immigration from Europe, constantly in the city a sufficient number of free laborers to sustain, by competition and association with each other, the habits of free-labor communities. It is plainly perceptible that the white working men in New Orleans have more businesslike manners, and more assured self-respect, than those of smaller towns. They are even not without some *esprit du corps.*

As commerce, or any high form of industry requires intelligence in its laborers, slaves can never be brought together in dense communities, but their intelligence will increase to a degree dangerous to those who enjoy the benefit of their labor. The slave must be kept dependent, day by day, upon his master for his daily bread, or he will find, and will declare his independence in all respects, of him. This condition disqualifies the slave for any but the simplest and rudest forms of labor; and every attempt to bring his labor into competition with free labor can only be successful at the hazard of insurrection. Hundreds of slaves in New Orleans must be constantly reflecting and saying to one another, "I am as capable of taking care of myself as this Irish hod carrier, or this German market gardener; why can't I have the enjoyment of my labor as well as they? I am as capable of taking care of my own family as much as they of theirs; why should I be subject to have them taken from me by those other men who call themselves our owners? Our children have as much brains as the children of these white neighbors of ours, who not long ago were cooks and waiters at the hotels; why should they be spurned from the schoolrooms? I helped to build the schoolhouse, and have not been paid for it. One thing I know, if I can't have my rights, I can have my pleasures; and if they won't give me wages I can take them."

I came to Mr. R.'s plantation by a steamboat, late at night. As the boat approached the shore, near his house, her big bell having been rung some ten minutes previously, a Negro came out with a lantern to meet her. The boat's bow was run boldly against the bank; I leaped ashore, the clerk threw out a newspaper and a package, saying to the Negro, "That's for your master, and that's for so-and-so, tell your master, and ask him to give it to him." The boat bounded off at once, by her own elasticity, the starboard wheel was backed for a turn or two, and the next minute the great edifice was driving up the stream again — not a rope having been lifted, nor any other movement having been made on board, except by the pilot and engineer.

"Do you belong to Mr. R.?" I asked the Negro. "Yes, sir: is you going to our house, master?" "Yes." "I'll show you the way, then, sir"; and he conducted me in, leaving the parcels the clerk had thrown out, where they had fallen, on the bank.

A Negro woman prepared a bed for me, waited at the door till I had put out my light, and then returned to tuck in the mosquito bar tightly about the bed. This was merely from custom, as there were no mosquitoes at that season. In the morning the same woman awakened me, opened the curtains, and asked me to take the money which she had found in the pockets of my clothing, while she took it out to be brushed.

Mr. R. is a Southerner by birth, but was educated at the North, where, also, and in foreign countries, he has spent a large part of his life. He is a man of more than usual precision of mind, energetic and humane; and while his Negroes seemed to be better disciplined than any others I had seen, they evidently regarded him with affection, respect, and pride.

He had been ill for some weeks previous to my visit, and when he walked out with me, on the second day, it was the first time since the commencement of his illness that his field hands had seen him.

The first Negroes we met were half a dozen women, who were going up to the nursery to suckle their children — the overseer's bell having been just rung (at eleven o'clock), to call them in from work for that purpose. Mr. R. said that he allowed them two hours to be with their children while nursing at noon, and to leave work an hour earlier at night than the other field-hands. The women all stopped as we met them, and asked, with much animation:

"Oh, master! how is 'ou?"

"Well, I'm getting up. How are you, girls?"

"Oh, we's well, sir."

"The children all well?"

"Yes, master, all but Sukey's, sir."

"Sukey's? What, isn't that well yet?"

"No, master."

"But it's getting well, is it not?"

"Yes, master."

Soon after we met a boy, driving a cart. He pulled up as he came against us, and, taking off his hat, asked, "How is 'ou, master?"

"I'm getting well, you see. If I don't get about, and look after you, I'm afraid we shan't have much of a crop. I don't know what you niggers will do for Christmas money."

"Ha! — look heah, massa! — you jus' go right straight on de ways you's goin'; see suthin' make you laugh, ha! ha!" (meaning the work that had been done while he was ill, and the good promise of a crop).

The plantation contained about nine hundred acres of tillage land, and a large tract of "swamp," or woodland, was attached to it. The tillage land was inclosed all in one field by a strong cypress post and rail fence, and was drained by two canals, five feet deep, running about twenty feet apart, and parallel — the earth from both being thrown together, so as to make a high, dry road between them, straight through the middle of the plantation.

Fronting upon the river, and but six or eight rods from the public road, which everywhere runs close along the shore inside the levee, was the mansion of the proprietor: an old Creole house, the lower story of brick and the second of wood, with a broad gallery, shaded by the extended roof, running all around it; the roof steep, and shedding water on four sides, with ornaments of turned wood where lines met, and broken by several small dormer windows. The gallery was supported by round brick columns, and arches. The parlors, library, and sleeping rooms of the white family were all on the second floor.

Between the house and the street was a yard, planted formally with orange trees and other evergreens. A little on one side of the house stood a large two-story, square dovecote, which is a universal appendage of a sugar planter's house. In the rear of the house was another large yard, in which, irregularly placed, were houses for the family servants, a kitchen, stable, carriage house, smokehouse, etc. Behind this rear yard there was a vegetable garden, of an acre or more, in the charge of a Negro gardener; a line of fig trees were planted along the fence, but all the ground enclosed was intended to be cropped with vegetables for the family, and for the supply of "the people." I was pleased to notice, however, that the Negro gardener had, of his own accord, planted some violets and other flowering plants. From a corner of the court a road ran to the sugar works and the Negro settlement, which were five or six hundred yards from the house.

The Negro houses were exactly like those I have described on the Georgia rice plantation, except that they were provided with broad galleries in front. They were as neat and well-made externally as the cottages usually provided by large manufacturing companies in New England, to be rented to their workmen. The clothing furnished the Negroes, and the rations of bacon and meal, were the same as on other good plantations. During the grinding season extra rations of flour were served, and hot coffee was kept constantly in the sugar house, and the hands on duty were allowed to drink it almost *ad libitum*. They were also allowed to drink freely of the hot *sirop*, of which they were extremely fond. A generous allowance of *sirop*, or molasses, was also given out to them, with their other rations, every week during the winter and early summer. In extremely hot weather it was thought to be unfavorable to health, and was discontinued. Rations of tobacco were also served. At Christmas, a sum of money, equal to one dollar for each hogshead of sugar made on the plantation, was divided among the Negroes. The last year this had amounted to over two dollars a head. It was usually given to the heads of families. If any had been particularly careless or lazy, it was remembered at this Christmas dole. Of course, the effect of this arrangement, small as was the amount received by each person, was to give the laborers a direct interest in the economical direction of their labor: the advantage of it was said to be evident.

Mr. R. had purchased the plantation but three years before, and had afterwards somewhat increased its area by buying out several poor people, who had owned small farms adjoining. He had greatly extended and improved the drainage, and had nearly doubled the force of Negroes employed upon it, adding to the number that he purchased with the land, nearly as many more whom he had inherited, and whom he transferred to it from an old cotton plantation that he had formerly lived upon.

He had considerably more than doubled the stock of mules and oxen; had built entirely new cabins for all the Negroes, and new sugar works and stables. His whole capital, he said, when he first bought the plantation, would not have paid half the price of it and of the cost of stocking it as he had done. Most men when they buy a plantation, he informed me, go very heavily in debt; frequently the purchase is made three quarters on credit.

"Buying a plantation," were his words, "whether a sugar or cotton plantation, in this country, is usually essentially a gambling operation. The capital invested in a sugar plantation of the size of mine ought not to be less than $150,000. The purchaser pays down what he can, and usually gives security for the payment of the balance in six annual installments, with interest (10 per cent per annum) from the date of the purchase. Success in sugar, as well as cotton planting, is dependent on so many circumstances, that it is as much trusting to luck as betting on a throw of dice. If his first crop proves a bad one, he must borrow money of the Jews in New Orleans to pay his first note; they will sell him this on the best terms they can — often at not less than 25 per cent per annum. If three or four bad crops follow one another, he is ruined. But this is seldom the case, and he lives on, one year gaining a little on his debts, but almost as often enlarging them. Three or four years ago there was hardly a planter in Louisiana or Mississippi who was not in very embarrassed circumstances, nearly every one having his crops pledged to his creditors long before they were secured. The good prices and good crops of the last few years have set them all on their legs again; and this year all the jewellers' shops, and stores of rich furniture and dry goods, in New Orleans, were cleared out by the middle of the season, and everybody feels strong and cheerful. I have myself been particularly fortunate; I have made three good crops in succession. Last year I made six hundred and fifty hogsheads of sugar, and twelve hundred barrels of molasses. The molasses alone brought me a sum sufficient to pay all my plantation expenses; and the sugar yields me a clear profit of twenty-five per cent on my whole investment. If I make another crop this year as good as that, I shall be able to discount my outstanding notes, and shall be clear of debt at the end of four years, instead of six, which was all I had hoped for."

On another plantation, which I have since visited, which had a slave population of over two hundred — counted as one hundred field hands — the sugar works cost $40,000, and seven hundred barrels of sugar were made last year. On this plantation there is a steam pump, which drains the rear of the plantation over a levee, when the backwater from the swamp would otherwise prevent perfect drainage.

Mr. R. modestly credited his extraordinary success to "luck"; but I was satisfied, upon examining his improvements, and considering the reasons, which he readily gave for every operation which he showed, or described to me, that intelligence, study, and enterprise had seldom better claims to reward. Adjoining his plantation there was another of nearly twice the size, on which an equal number of Negroes and only half the number of cattle were employed; and the proprietor, I was told, had had rather *bad luck:* he had, in fact, made but little more than half as much sugar as Mr. R. I inquired of the latter if there was any advantage in his soil over that of his neighbor's. "I think not," he replied; "my best cane was made on a piece of land adjoining his, which, before I bought it, was thought unfit for cultivation. The great advantage I had over him last year, mainly arose from my having secured a more complete drainage of all my land."

The soil of the greater part of the plantation was a fine, dark, sandy loam; some of it, at the greatest distance from the river, was lighter in color, and more clayey; and in one part, where there was a very slight depression of the surface over about fifty acres, there was a dark, stiffish soil. It was this to which Mr. R. alluded as having produced his best cane. It had been considered too low, wet, tenacious, and unfertile to be worthy of cultivation by the former owner, and was covered with bushes and weeds when he took it. The improvement had been effected entirely by draining and fall plowing. In fall plowing, as a remedy for tenacity of soil, this gentleman's experience had given him great faith. At various points, on my tour, I found most conflicting opinions upon this point, many (among them the President of a State Agricultural Society) having invariably observed pernicious effects result from it.

The sugarcane is a perennial-rooted plant, and the stalk does not attain its full size, under favorable circumstances, in less growing time than twelve months; and seed does not usually form upon it until the thirteenth or fourteenth month. This function (termed *arrowing*) it only performs in a very hot and steadily hot climate, somewhat rarely even in the West Indies. The plant is, at all stages, extremely susceptible to cold, a moderate frost not only suspending its growth, but disorganizing it so that the chemical qualities of its sap are changed, and it is rendered valueless for sugar making.

As frosts of considerable severity are common in all parts of Louisiana, during three months of the year, of course the sugarcane is there never permitted to attain its full growth. To so much greater perfection does it arrive in the West Indies, that the cane produced on one acre will yield from 3,000 to 6,000 lbs. of sugar, while in Louisiana 1,000 is considered the average obtained. "I could make sugar in the climate of Cuba," said a Louisiana planter to me, "for half the price that, under the most favorable circumstances, it must cost here." In addition to the natural uncongeniality of the climate, the ground on which it grows in Louisiana, being lower than the surface of the river, is much of the time made cold by the infiltration of moisture, it is, therefore, only by reason of the extreme fertility of this alluvial deposit, assisted by a careful method of cultivation, that the cane is forced to a state of maturity which enables it to yield an amount of sugar which, with the assistance of a governmental protection against foreign competition, will be remunerative to the planter.

I must confess that there seems to me room for grave doubt
if the capital, labor, and especially the human life, which have
been and which continue to be spent in converting the swamps
of Louisiana into sugar plantations, and in defending them
against the annual assaults of the river, and the fever and the
cholera, could not have been better employed somewhere else.
It is claimed as a great advantage of slavery, as well as of
protection, that what has been done for this purpose never
would have been done without it. If it would not, the obvious
reason is, that the wages, or prospect of profit would not have
been sufficient to induce free men to undergo the inconveniences and the danger incident to the enterprise. There
is now great wealth in Louisiana; but I question if greater
wealth would not have been obtained by the same expenditure
of human labor, and happiness, and life, in very many other
directions.

Planting commences immediately after the sugar manufacturing season is concluded — usually in January. New or fallow
land is prepared by plowing the whole surface: on this plantation the plow used was made in Kentucky, and was of a very
good model, plowing seven to nine inches deep, with a single
pair of mules. The ground being then harrowed, drills are
opened with a double mould-board plow, seven feet apart.
Cuttings of cane for seed are to be planted in them. These are
reserved from the crop in the autumn, when some of the best
cane on the plantation is selected for this purpose, while still
standing.[1] This is cut off at the roots, and laid up in heaps or
stacks, in such a manner that the leaves and tops protect the
stalks from frost. The heaps are called mattresses; they are two
or three feet high, and as many yards across. At the planting
season they are opened, and the cane comes out moist and
green, and sweet, with the buds or eyes, which protrude at the
joints, swelling. The immature top parts of the stalk are cut off,
and they are loaded into carts, and carried to the ground

---

[1]It is only on the best plantations that the seed cane is selected with this
care. On another plantation that I visited during the planting season I noticed
that the best part of the stalk had been cut off for grinding, and only the less
valuable part saved for seed; and this, I apprehend, is the general practice. The
best cuttings probably produce the most vigorous plants.

prepared for planting. The carts used are large, with high sideboards, and are drawn by three mules — one large one being in the shafts, and two lighter ones abreast, before her. The drivers are boys, who use the whip a great deal, and drive rapidly.

In the field I found the laborers working in three divisions — the first, consisting of light hands, brought the cane by armsful from the cart, and laid it by the side of the furrows; the second planted it, and the third covered it. Planting is done by laying the cuttings at the bottom of the furrow, in such a way that there shall be three always together, with the eyes of each a little removed from those of the others — that is, all "breaking joints." They are thinly covered with earth, drawn over them with hoes. The other tools were so well selected on this plantation, that I expressed surprise at the clumsiness of the hoes, particularly as the soil was light, and entirely free from stones. "Such hoes as you use at the North would not last a Negro a day," said the planter.

Cane will grow for several years from the roots of the old plants, and, when it is allowed to do so, a very considerable part of the expense is avoided; but the vigor of the plant is less when growing from this source than when starting from cuttings, and the crop, when thus obtained, is annually less and less productive, until, after a number of years, depending upon the rigor of the seasons, fresh shoots cease to spring from the stubble. This sprouting of cane from the stools of the last crop is termed "ratooning." In the West India plantations the cane is frequently allowed to ratoon for eight successive crops. In Louisiana it is usual to plant once in three years, trusting to the ratooning for two crops only, and this was the practice on Mr. R.'s plantation. The cost of sugar growing would be very greatly increased if the crop needed planting every year; for all the cane grown upon an acre will not furnish seed for more than four acres — consequently one-twelfth of the whole of each crop has to be reserved for the planting of the following crop, even when two-thirds of this is to be of ratoon cane.

Planting is finished in a favorable season — early in March. Tillage is commenced immediately afterwards, by plowing *from* the rows of young cane, and subsequently continued very much after the usual plans of tillage for potatoes, when planted in drills, with us. By or before the first of July, the crop is all well earthed up, the rows of cane growing from the crest of a rounded bed, seven feet wide, with deep water furrows between each. The cane is at this time five or six feet high; and that growing from each bed forms arches with that of the next, so as to completely shade the ground. The furrows between the beds are carefully cleaned out; so that in the most drenching torrents of rain, the water is rapidly carried off into the drains, and thence to the swamp; and the crop then requires no further labor upon it until frost is apprehended, or the season for grinding arrives.

The nearly three months' interval, commencing at the intensest heat of summer, corresponds in the allotment of labor to the period of winter in Northern agriculture, because the winter itself, on the sugar plantations, is the planting season. The Negroes are employed in cutting and carting wood for boiling the cane juice, in making necessary repairs or additions to the sugar house, and otherwise preparing for the grinding season.

The grinding season is the harvest of the sugar planter; it commences in October, and continues for two or three months, during which time, the greatest possible activity and the utmost labor of which the hands are capable, are required to secure the product of the previous labor of the year. Mr. R. assured me that during the last grinding season nearly every man, woman, and child on his plantation, including the overseer and himself, were on duty fully eighteen hours a day. From the moment grinding first commences, until the end of the season, it is never discontinued: the fires under the boiler never go out, and the Negroes only rest for six hours in the twenty-four, by relays—three-quarters of them being constantly at work.

Notwithstanding the severity of the labor required of them at this time, Mr. R. said that his Negroes were as glad as he was himself to have the time for grinding arrive, and they worked with greater cheerfulness than at any other season. How can those persons who are always so ready to maintain that the slaves work less than free laborers in free countries, and that for that reason they are to be envied by them, account for this? That at Mr. R.'s plantation it was the case that the slaves enjoyed most that season of the year when the hardest labor was required of them, I have, in addition to Mr. R.'s own evidence, good reason to believe, which I shall presently report. And the reason of it evidently is, that they are then better paid; they have better and more varied food and stimulants than usual, but especially they have a degree of freedom, and of social pleasure, and a variety of occupation which brings a recreation of the mind, and to a certain degree gives them strength for, and pleasure in, their labor. Men of sense have discovered that when they desire to get extraordinary exertions from their slaves, it is better to offer them rewards than to whip them; to encourage them, rather than to drive them.

If the season has been favorable, so that the cane is strong, and well matured, it will endure a smart early frost without injury, particularly if the ground is well drained; but as rapidly as possible, after the season has arrived at which frosts are to be expected, the whole crop is cut, and put in mattresses, from which it is taken to the grinding mill as fast as it can be made to use it.

The business of manufacturing sugar is everywhere carried on in connection with the planting of the cane. The shortness of the season during which the cane can be used is the reason assigned for this: the proprietors would not be willing to trust to custom mills to manufacture their produce with the necessary rapidity. If cane should be cultivated in connection with other crops—that is, on small farms, instead of great "sugar only" plantations—neighborhood custom mills would probably be employed. The profit of a sugar plantation is now large, much in proportion to its size (if it be proportionately stocked); because only a very large supply of cane will warrant the pro-prietor in providing the most economical manufacturing apparatus. In 1849 there were 1,474 sugar estates in Louisiana, producing 236,547 hhds. of sugar; but it is thought that half of this quantity was produced on less than 200 estates—that is, that one-eighth of the plantations produced one-half the sugar. The sugar works on some of the large estates cost over $100,000, and many of them manufacture over 1,000,000 lbs. per annum.

The profits of these, under our present tariff, in a favorable season, are immense.

The apparatus used upon the better class of plantations is very admirable, and improvements are yearly being made, which indicate high scientific acquirements, and much mechanical ingenuity on the part of the inventors. The whole process of sugar manufacturing, although chemical analysis proves that a large amount of saccharine is still wasted, has been within a few years greatly improved, principally by reason of the experiments and discoveries of the French chemists, whose labors have been directed by the purpose to lessen the cost of beet sugar. Apparatus for various processes in the manufacture, which they have invented or recommended, has been improved, and brought into practical operation on a large scale on some of the Louisiana plantations, the owners of which are among the most intelligent, enterprising, and wealthy men of business in the United States. Forty-three plantations in the State are now furnished with apparatus constructed in accordance with the best scientific knowledge on the subject; and 914 are driven by steam engines—leaving but 560 to be worked by horse power. Mr. R.'s sugar house, for making brown sugar, was furnished with the best kind of apparatus, at a cost of $20,000. Preparations were making for the addition of works for the manufacture of white loaf sugar, which would cost $20,000 more. I have visited one plantation on which the sugar works are said to have cost over $100,000.

At one corner of Mr. R.'s plantation, there was a hamlet consisting of about a dozen small houses or huts, built of wood or clay, in the old French peasant style. The residents owned small farms, on which they raised a little corn and rice; but Mr. R. described them as lazy vagabonds, doing but little work, and spending much time in shooting, fishing, and play. He wanted much to buy all their land, and get them to move away. He had already bought out some of them, and had made arrangements by which he hoped soon to get hold of the land of some of the rest. He was willing to pay two or three times as much as the property was actually worth, to get them to move off. As fast as he got possession, he destroyed their houses and gardens, removed their fences and trees, and brought all their land into his cane plantation.

Some of them were mechanics. One was a very good mason, and he employed him in building his sugar works and refinery; but he would be glad to get rid of them all, and depend entirely on slave mechanics—of these he had several already, and he could buy more when he needed them.

Why did he so dislike to have these poor people living near him, I asked? Because, he straightway answered, they demoralized his Negroes. Seeing them living in apparent comfort, without much property and without steady labor, the slaves could not help thinking that it was unnecessary for men to work so hard as they themselves were obliged to, and that if they were free they would not work. Besides, the intercourse of these people with the Negroes was not favorable to good discipline. They would get the Negroes to do them little services, and would pay with luxuries which he did not wish his slaves to have. It was better that they never saw anybody off their own plantation; they should, if possible, have no intercourse with any other white men than their owner or overseer; especially, it was desirable that they should not see white men who did not command their respect, and whom they did not always feel to be superior to themselves, and able to command them.

The nuisance of petty traders dealing with the Negroes, and encouraging them to pilfer, which I found everywhere a great annoyance to planters, seems to be greater on the banks of the Mississippi than elsewhere. The traders generally come on boats, which they moor at night on the shore, adjoining the Negro quarters, and float away whenever they have obtained any booty, with very small chance of detection. One day, during my visit at Mr. R.'s, a neighbor called to apprise him that one of these trading boats was in the vicinity, that he might take precautions to prevent his Negroes dealing with it. "The law," he observed, with much feeling, "is entirely inadequate to protect us against these rascals; it rather protects them than us. They easily evade detection in breaking it; and we can never get them punished, except we go beyond or against the law ourselves." To show me how vexatious the evil was, he mentioned that a large brass cock and some pipe had been lately stolen from his sugar works, and that he had ascertained that one of his Negroes had taken it and sold it on board one of these boats for seventy-five cents, and had immediately spent the money, chiefly for whisky on the same boat. It had cost him thirty dollars to replace it. Mr. R. said that he had lately caught one of his own Negroes going towards one of the "chicken thieves" (so the traders' boats are locally called) with a piece of machinery, unscrewed from his sugar works, which had cost him eighty dollars, but which would, very likely, have been sold for a drink. If the Negro had succeeded in reaching the boat, as he would, if a watch had not been kept, he could never have recovered it. There would have been no witnesses to the sale; the stolen goods would have been hid on board until the boat reached New Orleans; or, if, an officer came to search the boat, they would have been dropped into the river, before he got on board.

This neighbor of Mr. R.'s had been educated in France. Conversing on the inconveniences of slavery, he acknowledged that it was not only an uneconomical system, but a morally wrong one; "but," he said, "it was not instituted by us — we are not responsible for it. It is unfortunately fixed upon us; we could not do away with it if we wished; our duty is only to make the best of a bad thing; to lessen its evils as much as we can, so far as we have to do with it individually."

Mr. R. himself also acknowledged slavery to be a very great evil, morally and economically. It was a curse upon the South; he had no doubt at all about it: nothing would be more desirable than its removal, if it were possible to be accomplished. But he did not think it could be abolished without instituting greater evils than those sought to be remedied. Its influence on the character of the whites was what was most deplorable. He was sorry to think that his children would have to be subject to it. He thought that eventually, if he were able to afford it, he should free his slaves and send them to Africa.

When I left Mr. R.'s, I was driven about twenty miles in a buggy, by one of his house servants. He was inclined to be talkative and communicative; and as he expressed great affection and respect for his owner, I felt at liberty to question him on some points upon which I had always previously avoided conversing with slaves. He spoke rapidly, garrulously; and it was only necessary for me to give a direction to his thoughts, by my inquiries. I was careful to avoid leading questions, and not to show such an interest as would lead him to reply guardedly. I charged my memory as much as possible with his very words, when this was of consequence, and made the following record of the conversation within half an hour after I left him.

He first said that he supposed that I would see that he was not a "Creole nigger"; he came from Virginia. He reckoned the Virginia Negroes were better looking than those who were raised here; there were no black people anywhere in the world who were so "well made" as those who were born in Virginia. He asked if I lived in New Orleans; and where? I told him that I lived at the North. He asked:

"Da's a great many brack folks dah, massa?"

"No; very few."

"Da's a great many in Virginny; more'n da is heah?"

"But I came from beyond Virginia — from New York."

He had heard there were a great many black folk in New York. I said there were a good many in the city; but few in the country. Did I live in the country? What people did I have for servants? Thought, if I hired all my labor, it must be very dear. He inquired further about Negroes there. I told him they were all free, and described their general condition; told him what led them to congregate in cities, and what the effect was. He said the Negroes, both slave and free, who lived in New Orleans, were better off than those who lived in the country. Why? Because they make more money, and it is "gayer" there, and there is more "society." He then drew a contrast between Virginia, as he recollected it, and Louisiana. There is but one road in this country. In Virginia, there are roads running in every direction, and often crossing each other. You could see so much more "society," and there was so much more "variety" than here. He would not like now to go back to Virginia to live, because he had got used to this country, and had all his acquaintances here, and knew the ways of the people. He could speak French. He would like to go to New Orleans, though;

would rather live in New Orleans than any other place in the world.

After a silence of some minutes, he said, abruptly—

"If I was free, I would go to Virginia, and see my old mudder." He had left her when he was thirteen years old. He reckoned he was now thirty-three. "I don't well know, dough, exactly, how old I is; but, I rec'lect, de day I was taken away, my ole mudder she tell me I was tirteen year old." He did not like to come away at all; he "felt dreadful bad"; but, now he was used to it, he liked living here. He came across the Blue Ridge, and he recollected that, when he first saw it, he thought it was a dark piece of sky, and he wondered what it would be like when they came close to it. He was brought, with a great many other Negroes, in wagons, to Louisville; and then they were put on board a steamboat, and brought down here. He was sold, and put on this plantation, and had been on it ever since. He had been twice sold, along with it. Folks didn't very often sell their servants away here, as they did in Virginia. They were selling their servants, in Virginia, all the time; but, here, they did not very often sell them, except they run away. When a man would run away, and they could not do anything with him, they always sold him off. The people were almost all French. "Were there any French in New York?" he asked. I told him there were; but not as many as in Louisiana. "I s'pose dah is more of French people in Lusiana, dan dah is anywhar else in all de world—a'nt dah, massa?"

"Except in France."

"Wh's dat, sar?"

"France is the country where all the Frenchmen came from, in the first place."

"Wa's dat France, massa?"

"France is a country across the ocean, the big water, beyond Virginia, where all the Frenchmen first came from; just as the black people all came first from Africa, you know."

"I've heered, massa, dat dey sell one anoder dah, in de fus place. Does you know, sar, was dat so?" This was said very gravely.

I explained the savage custom of making slaves of prisoners of war, and described the constant wars of the native Africans.

I told him that they were better off here than they would be to be the slaves of cruel savages, in Africa. He turned, and looking me anxiously in the face, like a child, asked:

"*Is* de brack folks better off to be here, massa?"

I answered that I thought so; and described the heathenish barbarism of the people of Africa. I made exception of Liberia, knowing that his master thought of some time sending him there, and described it as a place that was settled by Negroes who went back there from this country. He said he had heard of it, and that they had sent a good many free Negroes from New Orleans there.

After a moment's pause, he inquired — very gravely, again:

"*Why is it*, massa, when de brack people is free, dey wants to send 'em away out of dis country?"

The question took me aback. After bungling a little — for I did not like to tell him the white people were afraid to have them stay here — I said that it was thought to be a better place for them there. He replied, he should think, that, when they had got used to this country, it was much better that they should be allowed to stay here. He would not like to go out of this country. He wouldn't like even to go to Virginia now, though Virginia was such a pleasant country; he had been here so long, seemed like this was the best place for him to live. To avoid discussion of the point, I asked what he would do, if he were free?

"If I was free, massa; *if I was free*" (with great animation), "I would — well, sar, de fus thing I would do, if I was free, I would go to work for a year, and get some money for myself, — den — den — den, massa, dis is what I do — I buy me, fus place, a little house, and little lot land, and den — no; den — den — I would go to old Virginny, and see my old mudder. Yes, sar, I would like to do dat fus thing; den, when I com back, de fus thing I'd do, I'd get me a wife; den, I'd take her to my house, and I would live with her dar; and I would raise things in my garden, and take 'em to New Orleans, and sell 'em dar, in de market. Dat's de way I would live, if I was free."

He said, in answer to further inquiries, that there were many free Negroes all about this region. Some were very rich. He pointed out to me three plantations, within twenty miles, owned by colored men. These bought black folks, he said, and had servants of their own. They were very bad masters, very hard and cruel—hadn't any feeling. "You might think, master, dat dey would be good to dar own nation; but dey is not. I will tell you de truth, massa; I know I'se got to answer; and it's a fact, dey is very bad masters, sar. I'd rather be a servant to any man in de world, dan to a brack man. If I was sold to a brack man, I'd drown myself. I would dat—I'd drown myself! dough I shouldn't like to do dat nudder; but I wouldn't be sold to a colored master for anyting."

If he had got to be sold, he would like best to have an American master buy him. The French people did not clothe their servants well; though now they did much better than when he first came to Louisiana. The French masters were very severe, and "dey whip dar niggers most to deff—dey whip de flesh off of 'em."

Nor did they feed them as well as the Americans. "Why, sometimes, massa, dey only gives 'em dry corn—don't give out no meat at all." I told him this could not be so, for the law required that every master would serve out meat to his Negroes. "Oh, but some on 'em don't mind law, if he does say so, massa. Law never here; don't know anything about him. *Very often*, dey only gives 'em dry corn—I knows dat; I sees de niggers. Didn't you see de niggers on our plantation, sar? Well, you nebber see such a good-looking lot of niggers as ours on any of de French plantations, did you, massa? Why, dey all looks fat, and dey's all got good clothes, and dey look as if dey all had plenty to eat, and hadn't got no work to do, ha! ha! ha! Don't dey? But dey does work, dough. Dey does a heap o'work. But dey don't work so hard as dey does on some ob de French plantations. Oh, dey does work *too* hard on dem, sometimes."

"You work hard in the grinding season, don't you?"

"O, yes; den we works hard; we has to work hard den: harder dan any oder time of year. But, I tell 'ou, massa, I likes to hab de grinding season come; yes, I does—rader dan any oder time of year, dough we work so hard den. I wish it was grinding season all de year roun'—only Sundays."

"Why?"

"Because—oh, because it's merry and lively. All de brack people like it when we begin to grind."

"You have to keep grinding Sundays?"

"Yes, can't stop, when we begin to grind, till we get tru."

"You don't often work Sundays, except then?"

"No, massa! nebber works Sundays, except when der crap's weedy, and we want to get tru 'fore rain comes; den, wen we work a Sunday, massa gives us some oder day for holiday— Monday, if we get tru."

He said that, on the French plantations, they oftener work Sundays than on the American. They used to work almost always on Sundays, on the French plantations, when he was first brought to Louisiana; but they did not so much now.

We were passing a hamlet of cottages, occupied by Acadians, or what the planters call *habitans*, poor white French Creoles. The Negroes had always been represented to me to despise the habitans, and to look upon them as their own inferiors; but William spoke of them respectfully; and, when I tempted him to sneer at their indolence and vagabond habits, refused to do so, but insisted very strenuously that they were "very good people," orderly and industrious. He assured me that I was mistaken in supposing that the Creoles, who did not own slaves, did not live comfortably, or that they did not work as hard as they ought for their living. There were no better sort of people than they were, he thought.

He again recurred to the fortunate condition of the Negroes on his master's plantation. He thought it was the best plantation in the State, and he did not believe there was a better lot of Negroes in the State; some few of them, whom his master had brought from his former plantation, were old; but altogether, they were "as right good a lot of niggers" as could be found anywhere. They could do all the work that was necessary to be done on the plantation. On some old plantations they had not nearly as many Negroes as they needed to make the crop, and they "drove 'em awful hard"; but it wasn't so on his master's: they could do all the work, and do it well, and it was the best worked plantation, and made the most sugar to the hand of any plantation he knew of. All the niggers had enough to eat, and were well clothed; their quarters were good, and they got a good many presents. He was going on enthusiastically, when I asked:

"Well, now, wouldn't you rather live on such a plantation than to be free, William?"

"Oh! no, sir, I'd rather be free! Oh, yes, sir, I'd like it better to be free; I would dat, master."

"Why would you?"

"Why, you see, master, if I was free — if I was *free,* I'd have all my time to myself. I'd rather work for myself. Yes. I'd like dat better."

"But then, you know, you'd have to take care of yourself, and you'd get poor."

"No, sir, I would not get poor, I would get rich; for you see, master, then I'd work all the time for myself."

"Suppose all the black people on your plantation, or all the black people in the country were made free at once, what do you think would become of them? — what would they do, do you think? You don't suppose there would be much sugar raised, do you?"

"Why, yes, master, I do. Why not, sir? What would de brack people do? Wouldn't dey hab to work for dar libben? and de wite people own all de land — war dey goin' to work? Dey hire demself right out again, and work all de same as before. And den, wen dey work for demself, dey work harder dan dey do now to get more wages — a heap harder. I tink so, sir. I would do so, sir. I would work for hire. I don't own any land; I hab to work right away again for massa, to get some money."

Perceiving from the readiness of these answers that the subject had been a familiar one with him, I immediately asked: "The black people talk among themselves about this, do they; and they think so generally?"

"Oh! yes, sir; dey talk so; dat's wat dey tink."

"Then they talk about being free a good deal, do they?"

"Yes, sir. Dey — dat is, dey say dey wish it was so; dat's all dey talk, master — dat's all, sir."

His caution was evidently excited, and I inquired no further. We were passing a large old plantation, the cabins of the Negroes upon which were wretched hovels — small, without windows, and dilapidated. A large gang of Negroes were at work by the roadside, planting cane. Two white men were sitting on horseback, looking at them, and a Negro driver was walking among them, with a whip in his hand.

William said that this was an old Creole plantation, and the Negroes on it were worked very hard. There was three times as much land in it as in his master's, and only about the same number of Negroes to work it. I observed, however, that a good deal of land had been left uncultivated the previous year. The slaves appeared to be working hard; they were shabbily clothed, and had a cowed expression, looking on the ground, not even glancing at us, as we passed, and were perfectly silent.

"Dem's all Creole niggers," said William: "ain't no Virginny niggers dah. I reckon you didn't see no such looking niggers as dem on our plantation, did you, master?"

After answering some inquiries about the levee, close inside of which the road continually ran, he asked me about the levee at New York; and when informed that we had not any levee, asked me with a good deal of surprise, how we kept the water out? I explained to him that the land was higher than the water, and was not liable, as it was in Louisiana, to be overflowed. I could not make him understand this. He seemed never to have considered that it was not the natural order of things that land should be lower than water, or that men should be able to live on land, except by excluding water artificially. At length, he said:—

"I s'pose dis heah State is de lowest State dar is in de world. Dar ain't no odder State dat is low so as dis is. I s'pose it is five thousand five hundred feet lower dan any odder State."

"What?"

"I s'pose, master, dat dis heah State is five thousand five hundred feet lower down dan any odder, ain't it, sir?"

"I don't understand you."

"I say dis heah is de lowest ob de States, master. I s'pose it's *five thousand five hundred feet* lower dan any odder; lower *down*, ain't it, master?"

"Yes, it's very low."

This is a good illustration of the childlike quality common in the Negroes, and which in him was particularly noticeable, notwithstanding the shrewdness of some of his observations. Such an apparent mingling of simplicity and cunning, ingenuousness and slyness, detracted much from the weight of his opinions and purposes in regard to freedom. I could not but have a strong doubt if he would keep to his word, if the opportunity were allowed him to try his ability to take care of himself.

6.

Cotton Planters. Red River

The largest part of the cotton crop of the United States is now produced in the Mississippi valley, including the lands contiguous to its great Southern tributary streams, the Red River and others. The proportion of the whole crop which is produced in this region is constantly and very rapidly increasing. This increase is chiefly gained by the forming of new plantations and the transfer of slave labor westward. The common planter of this region lives very differently to those whose plantations I have hitherto described. What a very different person he is, and what a very different thing his plantation is from the class usually visited by travellers in the South, I learned by an extended experience. I presume myself to have been ordinarily well-informed when I started from home, but up to this point in my first journey had no correct idea of the condition and character of the common cotton planters. I use the word common in reference to the whole region: there are some small districts in which the common planter is a rich man—really rich. But over the whole district there are comparatively few of these, and in this and the next chapter, I shall show what the many are—as I found them. I shall draw for this purpose upon a record of experience extending through nearly twelve months, but obtained in different journeys and in two different years.

My first observation of the common cotton planters was had on the steamboat, between Montgomery and Mobile, and has already been described. My second experience among them was on a steamboat bound up Red River.

On a certain Saturday morning, when I had determined upon the trip, I found that two boats, the *Swamp Fox* and the *St. Charles,* were advertised to leave the same evening, for the Red River. I went to the levee, and, finding the *St. Charles* to be the better of the two, I asked her clerk if I could engage a stateroom. There was just one stateroom berth left unengaged; I was requested to place my name against its number on the passenger book; and did so, understanding that it was thus secured for me.

On Wednesday, I found the berth I had engaged occupied by a very strong man, who was not very polite, when I informed him that I believed there was some mistake — that the berth he was using had been engaged to me. I went to the clerk, who said that he was sorry, but that, as I had not stayed on board at night, and had not paid for the berth, he had not been sure that I should go, and he had, therefore, given it to the gentleman who now had it in possession, and whom, he thought, it would not be best to try to reason out of it. He was very busy, he observed, because the boat was going to start at four o'clock; if I would now pay him the price of passage, he would do the best he could for me. When he had time to examine, he could probably put me in some other stateroom, perhaps quite as good a one as that I had lost. Meanwhile he kindly offered me the temporary use of his private stateroom. I inquired if it was quite certain that the boat would get off at four; for I had been asked to dine with a friend, at three o'clock. There was not the smallest doubt of it — at four they would leave. They were all ready, at that moment, and only waited till four, because the agent had advertised that they would — merely a technical point of honor.

But, by some error of calculation, I suppose, she didn't go at four. Nor at five. Nor at six.

At seven o'clock, the *Swamp Fox* and the *St. Charles* were both discharging dense smoke from their chimneys, blowing steam, and ringing bells. It was obvious that each was making every exertion to get off before the other. The captains of both boats stood at the break of the hurricane deck, apparently waiting in great impatience for the mails to come on board.

The *St. Charles* was crowded with passengers, and her decks were piled high with freight. Bumboatmen, about the bows, were offering shells, and oranges, and bananas; and newsboys, and peddlers, and tract distributors, were squeezing about with their wares among the passengers. I had confidence in their instinct; there had been no such numbers of them the previous evenings, and I made up my mind, although past seven o'clock, that the St. Charles would not let her fires go down again.

It was twenty minutes after seven when the captain observed — scanning the levee in every direction, to see if there was another cart or carriage coming towards us — "No use waiting any longer, I reckon: throw off, Mr. Heady." (The *Swamp Fox* did not leave, I afterwards heard, till the following Saturday.)

We backed out, winded round head up, and as we began to breast the current a dozen of the Negro boat hands, standing on the freight, piled up on the low forecastle, began to sing, waving hats and handkerchiefs, and shirts lashed to poles, towards the people who stood on the sterns of the steamboats at the levee. After losing a few lines, I copied literally into my notebook:

Ye see dem boat way dah ahead.
      CHORUS. — *Oahoiohieu.*
De San Charles is arter 'em, dey mus go behine.
      CHO. — *Oahoiohieu.*
So stir up dah, my livelies, stir her up; (pointing to the furnaces).
      CHO. — *Oahoiohieu.*
Dey's burnin' not'n but fat and rosum.
      CHO. — *Oahoiohieu.*
Oh, we is gwine up de Red River, oh!
      CHO. — *Oahoiohieu.*
Oh, we mus part from you dah asho'.
      CHO. — *Oahoiohieu.*
Give my lub to Dinah, oh!
      CHO. — *Oahoiohieu.*
For we is gwine up de Red River.
      CHO. — *Oahoiohieu.*
Yes, we is gwine up de Red River.
      CHO. — *Oahoiohieu.*
Oh, we must part from you dah, oh.
      CHO. — *Oahoiohieu.*

The wit introduced into these songs has, I suspect, been rather overestimated.

As soon as the song was ended, I went into the cabin to remind the clerk to obtain a berth for me. I found two brilliant supper tables reaching the whole length of the long cabin, and a file of men standing on each side of both of them, ready to take seats as soon as the signal was given.

The clerk was in his room, with two other men, and appeared to be more occupied than ever. His manner was, I thought, now rather cool, not to say rude; and he very distinctly informed me that every berth was occupied, and he didn't know where I was to sleep. He judged I was able to take care of myself; and if I was not, he was quite sure that he had too much to do to give all his time to my surveillance. I then went to the commander, and told him that I thought myself entitled to a berth. I had paid for one, and should not have taken passage in the boat, if it had not been promised me. I was not disposed to fight for it, particularly as the gentleman occupying the berth engaged to me was a deal bigger fellow than I, and also carried a bigger knife; but I thought the clerk was accountable to me for a berth, and I begged that he would inform him so. He replied that the clerk probably knew his business; he had nothing to do with it; and walked away from me. I then addressed myself to a second clerk, or sub-officer of some denomination, who more good-naturedly informed me that half the company were in the same condition as myself, and I needn't be alarmed, cots would be provided for us.

As I saw that the supper table was likely to be crowded, I asked if there would be a second table. "Yes, they'll keep on eatin' till they all get through." I walked the deck till I saw those who had been first seated at the table coming out; then going in, I found the table still crowded, while many stood waiting to take seats as fast as any were vacated. I obtained one for myself at length, and had no sooner occupied it than two half-intoxicated and garrulous men took the adjoining stools.

It was near nine o'clock before the tables were cleared away, and immediately afterwards the waiters began to rig a framework for sleeping cots in their place. These cots were simply canvas shelves, five feet and a half long, two wide, and less than two feet apart, perpendicularly. A waiter, whose good will I had purchased at the supper table, gave me a hint to secure one of them for myself, as soon as they were erected, by putting my hat in it. I did so, and saw that others did the same. I chose a cot as near as possible to the midship doors of the cabin, perceiving that there was not likely to be the best possible air, after all the passengers were laid up for the night, in this compact manner.

Nearly as fast as the cots were ready they were occupied. To make sure that mine was not stolen from me, I also, without much undressing, laid myself away. A single blanket was the only bedclothing provided. I had not lain long, before I was driven, by an exceedingly offensive smell, to search for a cleaner neighborhood; but I found all the cots, fore and aft, were either occupied or engaged. I immediately returned, and that I might have a *dernier ressort,* left my shawl in that I had first obtained.

In the forward part of the cabin there was a bar, a stove, a table, and a placard of rules, forbidding smoking, gambling, and swearing in the cabin, and a close company of drinkers, smokers, card players, and constant swearers. I went out, and stepped down to the boiler deck. The boat had been provided with very poor wood, and the firemen were crowding it into the furnaces whenever they could find room for it, driving smaller sticks between the larger ones at the top, by a battering-ram method.

Most of the firemen were Irish born; one with whom I conversed was English. He said they were divided into three watches, each working four hours at a time, and all hands liable to be called, when wooding, or landing, or taking on freight, to assist the deck hands. They were paid now but thirty dollars a month—ordinarily forty, and sometimes sixty—and board. He was a sailor bred. This boatlife was harder than seafaring, but the pay was better, and the trips were short. The regular thing was to make two trips, and then lay up for a spree. It would be too hard upon a man, he thought, to pursue it regularly; two trips "on end" was as much as a man could stand. He must then take a "refreshment." Working this way for three weeks, and then refreshing for about one, he did not think it was unhealthy, no more so than ordinary seafaring. He concluded, by informing me that the most striking peculiarity of the business was, that it kept a man, notwithstanding wholesale periodical refreshment, very dry. He was of opinion that after the information I had obtained, if I gave him at least the price of a single drink, and some tobacco, it would be characteristic of a gentleman.

Going round behind the furnace, I found a large quantity of freight: hogsheads, barrels, cases, bales, boxes, nail rods, rolls of leather, plows, cotton, bale rope, and firewood, all thrown together in the most confused manner, with hot steam pipes, and parts of the engine crossing through it. As I explored further aft, I found Negroes lying asleep, in all postures, upon the freight. A single group only, of five or six, appeared to be awake, and as I drew near they commenced to sing a Methodist hymn, not loudly, as Negroes generally do, but, as it seemed to me, with a good deal of tenderness and feeling; a few white people—men, women, and children—were lying here and there, among the Negroes. Altogether, I learned we had two hundred of these deck passengers, black and white. A stove, by which they could fry bacon, was the only furniture provided for them by the boat. They carried with them their provisions for the voyage, and had their choice of the freight for beds.

As I came to the bows again, and was about to ascend to the cabin, two men came down, one of whom I recognized to have been my cot neighbor. "Where's a bucket?" said he. "By thunder! this fellow was so strong I could not sleep by him, so I stumped him to come down and wash his feet." "I am much obliged to you," said I; and I was, very much; the man had been lying in the cot beneath mine, to which I now returned and soon fell asleep.

I awoke about midnight. There was an unusual jar in the boat, and an evident excitement among people whom I could hear talking on deck. I rolled out of my cot, and stepped out on the gallery. The steamboat *Kimball* was running head-and-head with us, and so close that one might have jumped easily from our paddle box on to her guards. A few other passengers had turned out beside myself, and most of the waiters were leaning on the rail of the gallery. Occasionally a few words of banter passed between them and the waiters of the *Kimball;* below, the firemen were shouting as they crowded the furnaces, and some one could be heard cheering them: "Shove her up, boys! Shove her up! Give her hell!" "She's got to hold a conversation with us before she gets by, anyhow," said one of the

Negroes. "Ye har that ar' whistlin'?" said a white man; "tell
ye thar an't any too much water in her bilers when ye har that."
I laughed silently, but was not without a slight expectant
sensation, which Burke would perhaps have called sublime.
At length the *Kimball* slowly drew ahead, crossed our bow, and
the contest was given up. "De ole lady too heavy," said a waiter;
"if I could pitch a few ton of dat ar freight off her bow, I'd bet
de *Kimball* would be askin' her to show de way mighty quick."

At half-past four o'clock a hand bell was rung in the cabin,
and soon afterwards I was informed that I must get up, that
the servants might remove the cot arrangement, and clear the
cabin for the breakfast table.

Breakfast was not ready till half-past seven. The passengers,
one set after another, and then the pilots, clerks, mates, and
engineers, and then the free colored people, and then the
waiters, chambermaids, and passengers' body servants, having
breakfasted, the tables were cleared, and the cabin swept. The
tables were then again laid for dinner. Thus the greater part
of the cabin was constantly occupied, and the passengers who
had no staterooms were driven to herd in the vicinity of the
card tables and the bar, the lobby (Social Hall, I believe it is
called), in which most of the passengers' baggage was deposited, or to go outside. Every part of the boat, except the
bleak hurricane deck, was crowded; and so large a number of
equally uncomfortable and disagreeable people I think I never
saw elsewhere together. We made very slow progress, landing,
it seems to me, after we entered Red River, at every "bend,"
"bottom," "bayou," "point," and "plantation" that came in
sight; often for no other object than to roll out a barrel of flour,
or a keg of nails; sometimes merely to furnish newspapers to
a wealthy planter, who had much cotton to send to market,
and whom it was therefore desirable to please.

On the third day, just after the dinner bell had rung, and most
of the passengers had gone into the cabin, I was sitting alone
on the gallery, reading a pamphlet, when a well-dressed
middle-aged man accosted me.

"Is that the book they call *Uncle Tom's Cabin,* you are
reading, sir?"

"No, sir."

"I did not know but it was; I see that there are two or three gentlemen on board that have got it. I suppose I might have got it in New Orleans: I wish I had. Have you ever seen it, sir?"

"Yes, sir."

"I'm told it shows up slavery in very high colors."

"Yes, sir, it shows the evils of slavery very strongly."

He took a chair near me, and said that, if it represented extreme cases as if they were general, it was not fair.

Perceiving that he was disposed to discuss the matter, I said that I was a Northern man, and perhaps not well able to judge; but that I thought that a certain degree of cruelty was necessary to make slave labor generally profitable, and that not many were disposed to be more severe than they thought necessary. I believed there was little wanton cruelty. He answered, that Northern men were much mistaken in supposing that slaves were generally ill-treated. He was a merchant, but he owned a plantation, and he just wished I could see his Negroes. "Why, sir," he continued, "my niggers' children all go regularly to a Sunday school, just the same as my own, and learn verses, and catechism, and hymns. Every one of my grown-up niggers are pious, every one of them, and members of the church. I've got an old man that can pray—well, sir, I only wish I had as good a gift at praying! I wish you could just hear him pray. There are cases in which niggers are badly used; but they are not common. There are brutes everywhere. You have men, at the North, who whip their wives—and they kill them sometimes."

"Certainly, we have, sir; there are plenty of brutes at the North; but our law, you must remember, does not compel women to submit themselves to their power. A wife, cruelly treated, can escape from her husband, and can compel him to give her subsistence, and to cease from doing her harm. A woman could defend herself against her husband's cruelty, and the law would sustain her."

"It would not be safe to receive Negroes' testimony against white people; they would be always plotting against their masters, if you did."

"Wives are not always plotting against their husbands."

"Husband and wife is a very different thing from master and slave."

"Your remark, that a bad man might whip his wife, suggested an analogy, sir."

"If the law was to forbid whipping altogether, the authority of the master would be at an end."

"And if you allow bad men to own slaves, and allow them to whip them, and deny the slave the privilege of resisting cruelty, do you not show that you think it is necessary to permit cruelty, in order to sustain the authority of masters, in general, over their slaves? That is, you establish cruelty as a necessity of slavery—do you not?"

"No more than of marriage, because men may whip their wives cruelly."

"Excuse me, sir; the law does all it can, to prevent such cruelty between husband and wife; between master and slave it does not, because it cannot, without weakening the necessary authority of the master—that is, without destroying slavery. It is, therefore, a fair argument against slavery, to show how cruelly this necessity, of sustaining the authority of cruel and passionate men over their slaves, sometimes operates."

He asked what it was Uncle Tom "tried to make out."

I narrated the Red River episode, and asked if such things could not possibly occur.

"Yes," replied he, "but very rarely. I don't know a man, in my parish, that could do such a thing. There are two men, though, in———, bad enough to do it, I believe; but it isn't a likely story, at all. In the first place, no colored woman would be likely to offer any resistance, if a white man should want to seduce her."

After further conversation, he said, that a planter had been tried for injuring one of his Negroes, at the court in his parish, the preceding summer. He had had a favorite, among his girls, and suspecting that she was unduly kind to one of his men, in an anger of jealousy he mutilated him. There was not sufficient testimony to convict him; "but," he said, "everybody believes he was guilty, and ought to have been punished. Nobody thinks there was any good reason for his being jealous of the boy."

I remarked that this story corroborated *Uncle Tom's Cabin;* it showed that it was all possible.

"Ah!" he answered, "but then nobody would have any respect for a man that treated his niggers cruelly."

I wondered, as I went in to dinner, and glanced at the long rows of surly faces, how many men there were there whose passions would be much restrained by the fear of losing the respect of their neighbors.

My original purpose had been to go high up Red River at this time, but the long delay in the boat's leaving New Orleans, and her slow passage, obliged me to change my plans. The following year, I returned, in company with my brother, as narrated in *The Texas Journey*. Some portion of what follows is taken from that volume.

At a place called Alexandria, our progress was arrested by falls in the river which cannot be passed by boats at low stages of the water. The village is every bit a Southern one—all the houses being one story in height, and having an open verandah before them, like the English towns in the West Indies. It contains, usually, about 1,000 inhabitants, but this summer had been entirely depopulated by the yellow fever. Of 300 who remained, 120, we were told, died. Most of the runaway citizens had returned, when we passed, though the last case of fever was still in uncertain progress.

It has apparently not the best reputation for morality. At Natchitoches, the next village above on the river, a couple of men were waiting for their breakfast at the inn, when one, who looked and spoke more like a New Englander than a Southerner, said to the other, whom I presumed to be an Alexandrian —possibly Elder Slocum himself:—

"I had a high old dream, last night."

"What was it?"

"Dreamt I was in hell."

"Rough country?"

"Boggy—sulphur bogs. By and by I cum to a great pair of doors. Something kinder drew me right to 'em, and I had to open 'em, and go in. As soon as I got in, the doors slammed to, behind me, and there I see old boss devil lying asleep, on a red-hot sofy. He woke up, and rubbed his eyes, and when he see me, he says, 'Halloo! that you?' 'Yes, sir,' says I. 'Where'd you

come from?' says he. 'From Alexandria, sir,' says I. 'Thought
so,' says he, and he took down a big book, and wrote something
in to't with a red-hot spike. 'Well, sir, what's going on now in
Alexandria?' says he. 'Having a "protracted meeting" there,
sir,' says I. 'Look here, my friend,' says he, 'you may stop
lyin', now you've got here.' 'I aint lyin', sir,' says I. 'Oh!' says
he, 'I beg your pardon; I thought it was Alexandria on Red
River, you meant.' 'So it was,' says I, 'and they are having a
protracted meeting there, sure as you're alive.' 'Hell they
are!' says he, jumpin' right up; 'boy, bring my boots!' A little
black devil fetched him a pair of hot brass boots, and he began
to draw 'em on. 'Whose doin' is that?' says he. 'Elder Slocum's,
sir,' says I. 'Elder Slocum's! Why in hell couldn't you have said
so, before?' says he. 'Here, boy, take away these boots'; and he
kicked 'em off, and laid down again."

French blood rather predominates in the population in the
vicinity of Natchitoches, but there is also a considerable amount
of the Spanish and Indian mongrel breed. These are often
handsome people, but vagabonds, almost to a man. Scarcely
any of them have any regular occupation, unless it be that of
herding cattle; but they raise a little maize, and fish a little,
and hunt a little, and smoke and lounge a great deal, and are
very regular in their attendance on divine worship, at the
cathedral.

In the public barroom I heard a person, who I suppose would
claim the appellation of a gentleman, narrating how he had
overreached a political opponent, in securing the "Spanish
vote" at an election, and it appeared from the conversation that
it was considered entirely, and as a matter of course, purchas-
able by the highest bidder. A man who would purchase votes
at the North, would, at least, be careful not to mention it so
publicly.

We spent several days in Natchitoches, purchasing horses
and completing the preparations for our vagrant life in Texas.

On the Emigrant Road into Texas. — Five minutes' ride took
us deep into the pines. Natchitoches, and with it all the tumult
and bother of social civilization, had disappeared. Under the
pines and beyond them was a new, calm, free life, upon which

we entered with a glow of enthusiasm, which, however, hardly sufficed to light up a whole day of pine shadows, and many times afterwards glimmered very dull over days on days of cold cornbread and cheerless winter prairies.

For two days, we rode through these pines over a sandy surface, having little rise and fall, watered here and there by small creeks and ponds, within reach of whose overflow, present or past, stand deciduous trees, such as, principally, oaks and cottonwoods, in a firmer and richer soil. Wherever the road crosses or approaches these spots, there is or has been, usually, a plantation.

The road could hardly be called a road. It was only a way where people had passed along before. Each man had taken such a path as suited him, turning aside to avoid, on high ground, the sand; on low ground, the mud. We chose, generally, the un-trodden elastic pavement of pine leaves, at a little distance from the main track.

We overtook, several times in the course of each day, the slow emigrant trains, for which this road, though less frequented than years ago, is still a chief thoroughfare. Inexorable destiny it seems that drags or drives on, always westward, these toilworn people. Several families were frequently moving together, coming from the same district, or chance met and joined, for company, on the long road from Alabama, Georgia, or the Caro-linas. Before you come upon them you hear, ringing through the woods, the fierce cries and blows with which they urge on their jaded cattle. Then the stragglers appear, lean dogs or fainting Negroes, ragged and spiritless. An old granny, hauling on, by the hand, a weak boy—too old to ride and too young to keep up. An old man, heavily loaded, with a rifle. Then the white covers of the wagons, jerking up and down as they mount over a root or plunge into a rut, disappearing, one after another, where the road descends. Then the active and cheery prime Negroes, not yet exhausted, with a joke and a suggestion about tobacco. Then the black pickaninnies, staring, in a confused heap, out at the back of the wagon, more and more of their eyes to be made out among the table legs and bedding, as you get near; behind them, further in, the old people and young moth-

ers, whose turn it is to ride. As you get by, the white mother
and babies, and the tall, frequently ill-humored master, on
horseback, or walking with his gun, urging up the black driver
and his oxen. As a scout ahead, is a brother, or an intelligent
slave, with the best gun, on the lookout for a deer or a turkey.
We passed in the day perhaps one hundred persons attached to
these trains, probably an unusual number; but the immigration
this year had been retarded and condensed by the fear of yellow
fever, the last case of which, at Natchitoches, had indeed begun
only the night before our arrival. Our chances of danger were
considered small, however, as the hard frosts had already come.
One of these trains was made up of three large wagons, loaded
with furniture, babies, and invalids, two or three light wagons,
and a gang of twenty able field hands. They travel ten or fifteen
miles a day, stopping wherever night overtakes them. The
masters are plainly dressed, often in homespun, keeping their
eyes about them, noticing the soil, sometimes making a remark
on the crops by the roadside; but generally dogged, surly, and
silent. The women are silent too, frequently walking, to relieve
the teams; and weary, haggard, mud bedraggled, forlorn, and
disconsolate, yet hopeful and careful. The Negroes, mud-in-
crusted, wrapped in old blankets or gunny bags, suffering from
cold, plod on, aimless, hopeless, thoughtless, more indifferent,
apparently, than the oxen, to all about them.

We met, in course of the day, numerous cotton wagons, two
or three sometimes together, drawn by three or four pairs of
mules or oxen, going slowly on toward Natchitoches or Grand
Ecore, each managed by its Negro driver. The load is commonly
five bales (of 400 lbs. each), and the cotton comes in this tedious
way, over execrable roads, distances of 100 and even 150 miles.
It is usually hauled from the eastern tier of Texan counties to the
Sabine; but this year there had been no rise of water in the
rivers, and from all this region it must be carried to Red River.
The distance from the Sabine is here about fifty miles, and the
cost of this transportation about one cent a pound; the freight
from Grand Ecore to New Orleans from one to one and a quarter
cents. If hauled 150 miles in this way, as we were told, the profit
remaining, after paying the charges of transportation and com-

mission, all amounting to about five cents, must be exceedingly small in ordinary years.

At night we met three or four of these teams half-mired in a swamp, distant some quarter of a mile one from another, and cheering themselves in the dark with prolonged and musical "Yohoi's," sent ringing through the woods. We got through this with considerable perplexity ourselves, and were very glad to see the light of the cabin where we had been recommended to stop.

This was "Mrs. Stokers'," about half way to the Sabine. We were received cordially, every house here expecting to do inn duty, but were allowed to strip and take care of our own horses, the people by no means expecting to do landlord's duty, but taking guests on sufferance. The house was a double log cabin — two log erections, that is, joined by one long roof, leaving an open space between. A gallery, extending across the whole front, serves for a pleasant sitting room in summer, and for a toilet room at all seasons. A bright fire was very welcome. Supper, consisting of pork, fresh and salt, cold cornbread, and boiled sweet potatoes, was served in a little lean-to behind the house. After disposing of this we were shown to our room, the other cabin, where we whiled away our evening, studying, by the light of the great fire, a book of bear stories, and conversing with the young man of the family, and a third guest. The room was open to the rafters, and had been built up only as high as the top of the door upon the gallery side, leaving a huge open triangle to the roof, through which the wind rushed at us with a fierce swoop, both while we were sitting at the fire and after we retreated to bed. Owing to this we slept little, and having had a salt supper, lay very thirsty upon the deep feather bed. About four o'clock an old Negro came in to light the fire. Asking him for water, we heard him breaking the ice for it outside. When we washed in the piazza the water was thick with frost, crusty, and half inclined not to be used as a fluid at all.

After a breakfast, similar in all respects to the supper, we saddled and rode on again. The horses had had a dozen ears of corn, night and morning, with an allowance of fodder (maize leaves). For this the charge was $1.25 each person. This is a fair sample of roadside stopping places in Western Louisiana and

Texas. The meals are absolutely invariable, save that fresh pork and sweet potatoes are frequently wanting. There is always, too, the black decoction of the South called coffee, than which it is often difficult to imagine any beverage more revolting. The bread is made of cornmeal, stirred with water and salt, and baked in a kettle covered with coals. The corn for breakfast is frequently unhusked at sunrise. A Negro, whose business it is, shells and grinds it in a hand mill for the cook. Should there be any of the loaf left after breakfast, it is given to the traveller, if he wish it, with a bit of pork, for a noon "snack," with no further charge. He is conscious, though, in that case, that he is robbing the hounds, always eagerly waiting, and should none remain, none can be had without a new resort to the crib. Wheat bread, if I am not mistaken, we met with but twice, out of Austin, in our whole journey across the State.

The country was very similar to that passed over the day before, with perhaps rather more of the cultivable loam. A good part of the land had, at some time, been cleared, but much was already turned over to the "old field pines," some of them even fifteen years or more. In fact, a larger area had been abandoned, we thought, than remained under cultivation. With the land, many cabins have, of course, also been deserted, giving the road a desolate air. If you ask, where are the people that once occupied these, the universal reply is, "Gone to Texas."

The plantations occur, perhaps, at an average distance of three of four miles. Most of the remaining inhabitants live chiefly, to appearances, by fleecing emigrants. Every shanty sells spirits, and takes in travellers. We passed through but one village, which consisted of six dwellings. The families obtained their livelihood by the following occupations: one by shoeing the horses of emigrants; one by repairing the wheels of their wagons; one by selling them groceries. The smallest cabin contained a physician. It was not larger than a good-sized medicine chest, but had the biggest sign. The others advertised "corn and fodder." The prices charged for any article sold, or service performed, were enormous; full one hundred per cent over those of New Orleans.

We met Spaniards once or twice on the road, and the population of this district is thought to be one half of Spanish origin.

They have no houses on the road, however, but live in little hamlets in the forest, or in cabins contiguous to each other, about a pond. They make no progress in acquiring capital of their own, but engage in hunting and fishing, or in herding cattle for larger proprietors of the land. For this business they seem to have an hereditary adaptation, far excelling Negroes of equal experience.

The number of cattle raised here is now comparatively small, most of the old herd proprietors having moved on to pastures new in Western Texas. The cane, which is a natural growth of most good soils at the South, is killed if closely fed upon. The blue-joint grass (not the blue grass of Kentucky) takes its place, and is also indigenous upon a poorer class of soils in this region. This is also good food for cattle, but is killed in turn if closely pastured. The ground then becomes bare or covered with shrubs, and the "range" is destroyed. The better class of soils here bear tolerable crops of cotton, but are by no means of value equal to the Red River bottoms or the new soils of any part of Texas. The country is, therefore, here in similar condition to that of the Eastern Slave States. The improvements which the inhabitants have succeeded in making in the way of clearing the forest, fencing and tilling the land, building dwellings, barns, and machinery, making roads and bridges, and introducing the institutions of civilization, not compensating in value the deterioration in the productiveness of the soil, the exhausted land reverts to wilderness.

Eastern Texas. — Shortly after noon rain began to fall from the chilly clouds that had been threatening us, and sleet and snow were soon driving in our faces. Our animals were disposed to flinch, but we were disposed to sleep in Texas, and pushed on across the Sabine. We found use for all our wraps, and when we reached the ferry house our mackintoshes were like a coat of mail with the stiff ice, and trees and fields were covered. In the broad river bottom we noticed many aquatic birds, and the browsing line under the dense mass of trees was almost as clean cut as that of Bushy Park. The river, at its low stage, was only three or four rods across. The old Negro who ferried us over, told us he had taken many a man to the other side, before annexation, who had ridden his horse hard to get beyond the jurisdiction of the States.

If we were unfortunate in this stormy entrance into Texas, we were very fortunate in the good quarters we lighted upon. The ferry has long been known as Gaines's Ferry, but is now the property of Mr. Strather, an adjacent planter, originally from Mississippi, but a settler of long standing. His log house had two stories, and being the first we had met having glass windows, and the second, I think, with any windows at all, takes high rank for comfort on the road. At supper we had capital mallard ducks from the river, as well as the usual Texan diet.

We were detained by the severity of the weather during the following day, and were well entertained with huntsman's stories of snakes, game, and crack shots. Mr. S. himself is the best shot in the county. A rival, who had once a match against him for two thousand dollars, called the day before the trial, and paid five hundred dollars to withdraw. He brought out his rifle for us, and placed a bullet, at one hundred and twenty yards, plump in the spot agreed upon. His piece is an old Kentucky rifle, weighing fourteen pounds, barrel forty-four inches in length, and throwing a ball weighing forty-four to the pound.

A guest, who came in, helped us to pass the day by exciting our anticipations of the West, and by his free and good advice. He confirmed stories we had heard of the danger to slavery in the West by the fraternizing of the blacks with the Mexicans. They helped them in all their bad habits, married them, stole a living from them, and ran them off every day to Mexico. This man had driven stages or herded cattle in every state of the Union, and had a notion that he liked the people and the State of Alabama better than any other. A man would get on faster, he thought, in Iowa, than anywhere else. He had been stage driver in Illinois during the cold winter of 1851–2, and had driven a whole day when the mercury was at its furthest below zero, but had never suffered so much from cold as on his present trip, during a norther on a Western prairie. He was now returning from Alexandria, where he had taken a small drove of horses. He cautioned us, in travelling, always to see our horses fed with our own eyes, and to "hang around" them till they had made sure of a tolerable allowance, and never to leave anything portable within sight of a Negro. A stray blanket was a sure loss.

Mr. S. has two plantations, both on upland, but one under the care of an overseer, some miles from the river. The soil he considers excellent. He averaged, last year, seven and a half bales to the hand; this year, four and a half bales. The usual crop of corn here is thirty bushels (shelled) to the acre.

Hearing him curse the neighboring poor people for stealing hogs, we inquired if thieves were as troublesome here as in the older countries. "If there ever were any hog thieves anywhere," said he, "it's here." In fact, no Slave country, new or old, is free from this exasperating pest of poor whites. In his neighborhood were several who ostensibly had a little patch of land to attend to, but who really, he said, derived their whole lazy subsistence from their richer neighbors' hog droves.

The Negro quarters here, scattered irregularly about the house, were of the worst description, though as good as local custom requires. They are but a rough enclosure of logs, ten feet square, without windows, covered by slabs of hewn wood four feet long. The great chinks are stopped with whatever has come to hand — a wad of cotton here, and a cornshuck there. The suffering from cold within them in such weather as we experienced, must be great. The day before, we had seen a young black girl, of twelve or fourteen years, sitting on a pile of logs before a house we passed, in a driving sleet, having for her only garment a short chemise. It is impossible to say whether such *shiftlessness* was the fault of the master or of the girl. Probably of both, and a part of the peculiar Southern and Southwestern system of "get along," till it comes better weather.

The storm continuing a third day, we rode through it twenty-five miles further to San Augustine. For some distance the country remains as in Louisiana. Then the pines gradually disappear, and a heavy clay soil, stained by an oxide of iron to a uniform brick red, begins. It makes most disagreeable roads, sticking close, and giving an indelible stain to every article that touches it. This tract is known as the Red Lands of Eastern Texas.

On a plantation not far from the river, we learned they had made eight bales to the hand. Mentioning it, afterwards, to a man who knew the place, he said they had planted earlier than their neighbors, and worked night and day, and, he believed, had lied, besides. They had sent cotton both by Galveston and by Grand Ecore, and had found the cost the same, about $8 per bale of 500 lbs.

We called at a plantation offered for sale. It was described in the handbills as having a fine house. We found it a cabin without windows. The proprietor said he had made ten bales to the hand, and would sell with all the improvements, a new gin house, press, etc., for $6 per acre.

The roadside, though free from the gloom of pines, did not cheer up, the number of deserted wrecks of plantations not at all diminishing. The occupied cabins were no better than before. We had entered our promised land; but the oil and honey of gladness and peace were nowhere visible. The people we met were the most sturdily inquisitive I ever saw. Nothing staggered them, and we found our account in making a clean breast of it as soon as they approached.

We rode through the shire town, Milam, without noticing it. Its buildings, all told, are six in number.

We passed several immigrant trains in motion, in spite of the weather. Their aspect was truly pitiful. Splashed with a new coating of red mud, dripping, and staggering, beating still the bones of their long worn-out cattle, they floundered helplessly on.

San Augustine made no very charming impression as we entered, nor did we find any striking improvement on longer acquaintance. It is a town of perhaps fifty or sixty houses, and half a dozen shops. Most of the last front upon a central square acre of neglected mud. The dwellings are clapboarded, and of a much higher class than the plantation dwellings. As to the people, a resident told us there was but one man in the town that was not in the constant habit of getting drunk, and that this gentleman relaxed his Puritanic severity during our stay in view of the fact that Christmas came but once that year.

Late on Christmas eve, we were invited to the window by our landlady, to see the pleasant local custom of The Christmas Serenade. A band of pleasant spirits started from the square, blowing tin horns, and beating tin pans, and visited in succession every house in the village, kicking in doors, and pulling down fences, until every male member of the family had appeared, with appropriate instruments, and joined the merry party. They then marched to the square, and ended the ceremony with a centupled tin row. In this touching commemoration, as strangers, we were not urged to participate.

A gentleman of the neighborhood, addicted, as we knew, to a partiality towards a Rip Van Winkle, tavern-lounging style of living, told us he was himself regarded by many of his neighbors with an evil eye, on account of his "stuck-up" deportment, and his habit of minding too strictly his own business. He had been candidate for representative, and had, he thought, probably been defeated on this ground, as he was sure his politics were right.

Not far from the village stands an edifice, which, having three stories and sashed windows, at once attracted our attention. On inquiry, we learned a story, curiously illustrative of Texan and human life. It appeared that two universities were chartered for San Augustine, the one under the protection of the Methodists, the other of the Presbyterians. The country being feebly settled, the supply of students was short, and great was the consequent rivalry between the institutions. The neighboring people took sides upon the subject so earnestly, that, one fine day, the president of the Presbyterian University was shot down in the street. After this, both dwindled, and seeing death by starvation staring them in the face, they made an arrangement by which both were taken under charge of the fraternity of Masons. The buildings are now used under the style of "The Masonic Institute," the one for boys, the other for girls. The boys occupy only the third story, and the two lower stories are falling to ludicrous decay — the boarding dropping off, and the windows on all sides dashed in.

The Mexican habitations of which San Augustine was once composed, have all disappeared. We could not find even a trace of them.

7.

Eastern Texas and Southeastern Louisiana

Austin. — Before leaving Eastern Texas behind us, I must add a random note or two, the dates of which it would have been uncivil to indicate.

We stopped one night at the house of a planter, now twenty years settled in Eastern Texas. He was a man of some education and natural intelligence, and had, he told us, an income, from the labor of his slaves, of some $4,000. His residence was one of the largest houses we had seen in Texas. It had a second story, two wings and a long gallery. Its windows had been once glazed, but now, out of eighty panes that originally filled the lower windows, thirty only remained unbroken. Not a door in the house had been ever furnished with a latch or even a string; when they were closed, it was necessary to *claw* or to ask some one inside to push open. (Yet we happened to hear a neighbor expressing serious admiration of the way these doors fitted.) The furniture was of the rudest description.

One of the family had just had a hemorrhage of the lungs; while we were at supper, this person sat between the big fireplace and an open outside door, having a window, too, at his side, in which only three panes remained. A norther was blowing, and ice forming upon the gallery outside. Next day at breakfast, the invalid was unable to appear on account of a "bad turn."

On our supper table was nothing else than the eternal fry, pone and coffee. Butter, of dreadful odor, was here added by exception. Wheat flour they never used. It was "too much trouble."

We were waited upon by two Negro girls, dressed in short-waisted, twilled cotton gowns, once white, now looking as if they had been worn by chimney sweeps. The water for the family was brought in tubs upon the heads of these two girls, from a creek, a quarter of a mile distant, this occupation filling nearly all their time.

This gentleman had thirty or forty Negroes, and two legitimate sons. One was an idle young man. The other was, at eight years old, a swearing, tobacco-chewing bully and ruffian. We heard him whipping a puppy behind the house, and swearing between the blows, his father and mother being at hand. His language and tone was an evident imitation of his father's mode of dealing with his slaves.

"I've got an account to settle with you; I've let you go about long enough; I'll teach you who's your master; there, go now, God damn you, but I haven't got through with you yet."

"You stop that cursing," said his father, at length, "it isn't right for little boys to curse."

"What do *you* do when you get mad?" replied the boy; "reckon you cuss some; so now you'd better shut up."

Remarking, one day, at the house of a woman who was brought up at the North, that there was much more comfort at her house than any we had previously stopped at, she told us that the only reason the people didn't have any comfort here was, that they wouldn't *take any trouble* to get anything. Anything that their Negroes could make they would eat; but they would take no pains to instruct them, or to get anything that didn't grow on the plantation. A neighbor of hers owned fifty cows, she supposed, but very rarely had any milk and scarcely ever any butter, simply because his people were too lazy to milk or churn, and he wouldn't take the trouble to make them.

This woman entirely sustained the assertion that Northern people, when they come to the South, have less feeling for the Negroes than Southerners themselves usually have. We asked her (she lived in a village) whether she hired or owned her servants. They owned them all, she said. When they first came to Texas they hired servants, but it was very troublesome; they would take no interest in anything; and she couldn't get along with them. Then very often their owners, on some pretext (ill-treatment, perhaps), would take them away. Then they bought Negroes. It was very expensive: a good Negro girl cost seven or eight hundred dollars, and that, we must know, was a great deal of money to be laid out in a thing that might lie right down the next day and die. They were not much better either than the hired servants.

Folks up North talked about how badly the Negroes were treated; she wished they could see how much work her girls did. She had four of them, and she knew they didn't do half so much work as one good Dutch girl such as she used to have at the North. Oh! the Negroes were the laziest things in creation; there was no knowing how much trouble they gave to look after them. Up to the North, if a girl went out into the garden for anything, when she came back she would clean her feet, but these nigger girls will stump right in and track mud all over the house. What do they care? They'd just as lief clean the mud after themselves as anything else — their time isn't any value to themselves. What do they care for the trouble it gives you? Not a bit. And you may scold 'em and whip 'em — you never can break 'em into better habits.

I asked what were servants' wages when they were hired out to do housework? They were paid seven or eight dollars a month; sometimes ten. She didn't use to pay her girl at the North but four dollars, and she knew she would do more work than any six of the niggers, and not give half so much trouble as one. But you couldn't get any other help here but niggers. Northern folks talk about abolishing slavery, but there wouldn't be any use in that; that would be ridiculous, unless you could some way get rid of the niggers. Why, they'd murder us all in our beds — that's what they'd do. Why, over to Fannin, there was a Negro woman that killed her mistress with an axe, and her two little ones. The people just flocked together, and hung her right up on the spot; they ought to have piled some wood round her, and burned her to death; that would have been a good lesson to the rest. We afterwards heard her scolding one of her girls, the girl made some exculpatory reply, and getting the best of the argument, the mistress angrily told her if she said another word she would have two hundred lashes given her. She came in and remarked that if she hadn't felt so nervous she would have given that girl a good whipping herself; these niggers are so saucy, it's very trying to one who has to take care of them.

Servants are, it is true, "a trial," in all lands, ages, and nations. But note the fatal reason this woman frankly gives for the inevitable delinquencies of slave servants, "Their time isn't any value to themselves!"

The women of Eastern Texas seemed to us, in general, far superior to their lords. They have, at least, the tender hearts and some of the gentle delicacy that your "true Texan" lacks, whether mistresses of slaves, or only of their own frying pan. They are overworked, however, as soon as married, and care gives them thin faces, sallow complexions, and expressions either sad or sour.

Lower Guadalupe. — Not finding a suitable camping place, we stumbled, after dark, into a large plantation upon the river bottom.

The irruption of our train within the plantation fences caused a furious commotion among the dogs and little Negroes, and it was with no little difficulty we could explain to the planter, who appeared with a candle, which was instantly blown out upon the porch, our peaceable intentions. Finally, after a general striking out of Fanny's heels and the master's boots, aided by the throwing of our loose lariats into the confused crowd, the growling and chattering circle about us was sufficiently enlarged and subdued for us to obtain a hearing, and we were hospitably received.

"Ho, Sam! You Tom! here! Call your missus. Suke! if you don't stop that infernal noise I'll have you drowned! Here, Bill! Josh! some of you! why don't you help the gentleman? Bring a lantern here! Packed, are you, sir? Hold on, you there; leave the gun alone. Now, clear out with you, you little devils, every one of you! Is there no one in the house? St! after 'em, Tiger! Can't any of you find a lantern? Where's Bill, to take these horses? What are you doing there? I tell you to be off, now, every one of you! Tom! take a rail and keep 'em off there!"

In the midst of the noise we go through the familiar motions, and land our saddles and hampers upon the gallery, then follow what appears to be the headmost Negro to the stable, and give him a hint to look well out for the horses.

This is our first reintroduction to Negro servants after our German experiences, and the contrast is most striking and disagreeable. Here were thirty or forty slaves, but not an order could be executed without more reiteration, and threats, and oaths, and greater trouble to the master and mistress, than would be needed to get a squadron under way. We heard the master threaten his Negroes with flogging, at least six times, before we went to bed. In the night a heavy rain came up, and he rose, on hearing it, to arrange the cistern spout, cursing again his infernal niggers, who had turned it off for some convenience of their own. In the morning, we heard the mistress scolding her girls for having left articles outside which had been spoiled by the wet, after repeated orders to bring them in. On visiting the stables we found the door fastened by a board leaned against it.

All the animals were loose, except the mule, which I had fastened myself. The rope attached to my saddle was stolen, and a shorter one substituted for it, when I mentioned the fact, by which I was deceived, until we were too far off to return. The master, seeing the horses had yet had no fodder, called to a boy to get some for them, then, countermanding his order, told the boy to call some one else, and go himself to drive the cows out of the garden. Then, to another boy, he said, "Go and pull two or three bundles of fodder out of the stack and give these horses." The boy soon came with two small bundles. "You infernal rascal, couldn't you tote more fodder than that? Go back and bring four or five bundles, and be quick about it, or I'll lick you." The boy walked slowly back, and returned with four bundles more.

But on entering at night we were struck with the air of comfort that met us. We were seated in rocking chairs in a well-furnished room, before a blazing fire, offered water to wash, in a little lean-to bedroom, and, though we had two hours to wait for our supper, it was most excellent, and we passed an agreeable evening in intelligent conversation with our host.

After his curiosity about us was satisfied, we learned from him that, though a young man, he was an old settler, and had made a comfortable fortune by his plantation. His wife gave us a picturesque account of their wagon journey here with their people, and described the hardships, dangers, and privations they had at first to endure. Now they were far more comfortable than they could have ever hoped to have been in the State from which they came. They thought their farm the best cotton land in the world. It extended across a mile of timbered bottom land from the river, then over a mile of bottom prairie, and included a large tract of the big prairie "for range." Their field would produce, in a favorable season, three bales to the acre; ordinarily a bale and a half: the "bale" 400 lbs. They had always far more than their hands could pick. It was much more free from weeds than the States, so much so, that three hands would be needed there to cultivate the same area as two here; that is, with the same hands the crop would be one-third greater.

But so anxious is every one in Texas to give all strangers a favorable impression, that all statements as to the extreme profit and healthfulness of lands must be taken with a grain of allowance. We found it very difficult, without impertinent persistence, to obtain any unfavorable facts. Persons not interested informed us, that from one-third to one-half the cotton crop on some of these rich plantations had been cut off by the worm, on several occasions, and that Negroes suffered much with dysentery and pneumonia.

It cost them very little to haul their cotton to the coast or to get supplies. They had not been more sickly than they would have been on the Mississippi. They considered that their steady sea breeze was almost a sure preventive of such diseases as they had higher up the country.

They always employed German mechanics, and spoke well of them. Mexicans were regarded in a somewhat unchristian tone, not as heretics or heathen, to be converted with flannel and tracts, but rather as vermin, to be exterminated. The lady was particularly strong in her prejudices. White folks and Mexicans were never made to live together, anyhow, and the Mexicans had no business here. They were getting so impertinent, and were so well protected by the laws, that the Americans would just have to get together and drive them all out of the country.

On the Chockolate. — "Which way did you come?" asked some-
one of the old man.

"From ———."

"See anything of a runaway nigger over there, anywhar?"

"No, sir. What kind of a nigger was it?"

"A small, black, screwed-up-faced nigger."

"How long has he been out?"

"Nigh two weeks."

"Whose is he?"

"Judge ——— 's, up here. And he cut the judge right bad.
Like to have killed the judge. Cut his young master, too."

"Reckon, if they caught him, 'twould go rather hard with
him."

"Reckon 'twould. We caught him once, but he got away from
us again. We was just tying his feet together, and he give me
a kick in the face, and broke. I had my six-shooter handy, and
I tried to shoot him, but every barrel missed fire. Been loaded
a week. We shot at him three times with rifles, but he'd got too
far off, and we didn't hit, but we must have shaved him close.
We chased him, and my dog got close to him once. If he'd grip'd
him, we should have got him; but he had a dog himself, and just
as my dog got within about a yard of him, his dog turned and
fit my dog, and he hurt him so bad we couldn't get him to run
him again. We run him close, though, I tell you. Run him out of
his coat, and his boots, and a pistol he'd got. But 'twas getting
towards dark, and he got into them bayous, and kept swimming
from one side to another."

"How long ago was that?"

"Ten days."

"If he's got across the river, he'd get to the Mexicans in two
days, and there he'd be safe. The Mexicans'd take care of him."

"What made him run?"

"The judge gave him a week at Christmas, and when the
week was up, I s'pose he didn't want to go to work again. He
got unruly, and they was a goin' to whip him."

"Now, how much happier that fellow'd 'a' been, if he'd just
stayed and done his duty. He might have just worked and done
his duty, and his master'd 'a' taken care of him, and given him

another week when Christmas come again, and he'd 'a' had nothing to do but enjoy himself again. These niggers, none of 'em, knows how much happier off they are than if they was free. Now, very likely, he'll starve to death, or get shot."

"Oh, the judge treats his niggers too kind. If he was stricter with them, they'd have more respect for him, and be more contented, too."

"Never do to be too slack with niggers."

Southeastern Texas. — We were unable to procure at Houston any definite information with regard to our proposed route. The known roads thence are those that branch northward and westward from their levee, and so thoroughly within lines of business does local knowledge lie, that the eastern shore is completely terra incognita. The roads east were said to be bad after heavy rains, but the season had been dry, and we determined to follow the direct and the distinct road, laid down upon our map.

Now that I am in a position to give preliminary information, however, there is no reason why the reader should enter this region as ignorant as we did.

Our route took us by Harrisburg and San Jacinto to Liberty upon the Trinity; thence by Beaumont to the Sabine at Turner's ferry; thence by the Big Woods and Lake Charles to Opelousas, the old capital of St. Landry Parish, at the western head of the intricate navigation from New Orleans.

This large district, extending from the Trinity River to the bayous of the Mississippi, has, throughout, the same general characteristics, the principal of which are, lowness, flatness, and wetness. The soil is variable, but is in greater part a loose, sandy loam, covered with coarse grasses, forming level prairies, which are everywhere broken by belts of pine forests, usually bordering creeks and bayous, but often standing in islands. The surface is but very slightly elevated above the sea; I suppose, upon an average, less than ten feet. It is, consequently, imperfectly drained, and in a wet season a large proportion is literally covered with water, as in crossing it, even in a dry time, we were obliged to wade through many miles of marshy pools. The river bottoms, still lower than the general level, are subject to constant overflow by tidewater, and what with the fallen timber, the dense undergrowth, the mire quags, the abrupt gullies, the patches of rotten or floating corduroy, and three or four feet of dirty salt water, the roads through them are not such as one would choose for a morning ride. The country is sparsely settled, containing less than one inhabitant to the square mile, one in four being a slave.

The many pools, through which the usual track took us, were swarming with venomous water snakes, four or five black moccasins often lifting at once their devilish heads above the dirty surface, and wriggling about our horses' heels. Beyond the Sabine, alligator holes are an additional excitement, the unsuspicious traveller suddenly sinking through the treacherous surface, and sometimes falling a victim, horse and all, to the hideous jaws of the reptile, while overwhelmed by the engulfing mire in which he lurks.

Upon the whole, this is not the spot in which I should prefer to come to light, burn, and expire; in fact, if the nether regions, as was suggested by the dream gentleman of Natchitoches, be "a boggy country," the avernal entrance might, I should think, with good probabilities, be looked for in this region.

We passed, on both sides the Sabine, many abandoned farms, and the country is but thinly settled. We found it impossible to obtain any information about roads, and frequently went astray upon cattle paths, once losing twenty miles in a day's journey. The people were chiefly herdsmen, cultivating a little cotton upon river banks, but ordinarily only corn, with a patch of cane to furnish household sugar. We tried in vain to purchase corn for our horses, and were told that "folks didn't make corn enough to bread them, and if anybody had corn to give his horse, he carried it in his hat and went out behind somewhere." The herds were in poor condition, and must in winter be reduced to the verge of starvation. We saw a few hogs, converted, by hardship, to figures so unnatural, that we at first took them for goats. Most of the people we met were old emigrants, from Southern Louisiana and Mississippi, and more disposed to gaiety and cheer than the Texan planters. The houses showed a tendency to Louisiana forms, and the table to a French style of serving the jerked beef, which is the general dish of the country.

The meat is dried in strips, over smoky fires, and, if untainted and well prepared, is a tolerably savory food. I hardly know whether to chronicle it as a border barbarism, or a Creolism, that we were several times, in this neighborhood, shown to a bed standing next to that occupied by the host and his wife, sometimes with the screen of a shawl, sometimes without.

We met with one specimen of the Virginia habit of "dipping," or snuff chewing, in the person of a woman who was otherwise neat and agreeable, and observed that a young lady, well-dressed, and apparently engaged, while we were present, in reading, went afterward to light her pipe at the kitchen fire, and had a smoke behind the house.

The condition of the young men appeared to incline decidedly to barbarism. We stopped a night at a house in which a drover, bringing mules from Mexico, was staying; and, with the neighbors who had come to look at the drove, we were thirteen men at table. When speaking with us, all were polite and respectful, the women especially so; but among one another, their coarseness was incredible.

Southwestern Louisiana.—Soon after crossing the Sabine, we entered a "hummock," or tract of more fertile, oak-bearing land, known as the Big Woods. The soil is not rich, but produces cotton, in good seasons nearly a bale to the acre, and the limited area is fully occupied. Upon one plantation we found an intelligent emigrant from Mississippi, who had just bought the place, having stopped on his way into Texas, because the time drew near for the confinement of his wife. Many farms are bought by emigrants, he said, from such temporary considerations: a child is sick, or a horse exhausted; they stop for a few weeks; but summer comes, and they conclude to put in a crop, and often never move again.

From the Big Woods to Opelousas, there was no change in the monotonous scenery. Everywhere extended the immense moist plain, being alternate tracts of grass and pine. Nearer Opelousas, oak appears in groups with the pine, and the soil is darker and more fertile. Here the land was mostly taken up, partly by speculators, in view of the Opelousas Railway, then commenced. But, in all the western portion of the district, the land is still government property, and many of the people squatters. Sales are seldom made, but the estimated price of the land is fifty cents an acre.

Some of the timbered land, for a few years after clearing, yields good crops of corn and sweet potatoes. Cotton is seldom attempted, and sugar only for family use. Oats are sometimes grown, but the yield is small, and seldom thrashed from the straw. We noted one field of poor rye. So wet a region and so warm a climate suggested rice, and, were the land sufficiently fertile, it would, doubtless, become a staple production. It is now only cultivated for home use, the bayou bottoms being rudely arranged for flowing the crop. But without manure no profitable return can be obtained from breaking the prairie, and the only system of manuring in use is that of plowing up occasionally the cow pens of the herdsmen.

The people, after passing the frontier, changed in every prominent characteristic. French became the prevailing language, and French the prevailing manners. The gruff Texan bidding, "Sit up, stranger; take some fry!" became a matter of recollection, of which "Monsieur, la soupe est servie," was the smooth substitute. The good nature of the people was an incessant astonishment. If we inquired the way, a contented old gentleman waddled out and showed us also his wife's house pet, an immense white crane, his big crop of peaches, his old fig tree, thirty feet in diameter of shade, and to his wish of "bon voyage" added for each a bouquet of the jessamines we were admiring. The homes were homes, not settlements on speculation; the house, sometimes of logs, it is true, but hereditary logs, and more often of smooth lumber, with deep and spreading galleries on all sides for the coolest comfort. For form, all ran or tended to run to a peaked and many-chimneyed center, with, here and there, a suggestion of a dormer window. Not all were provided with figs and jessamines, but each had some enclosure betraying good intentions.

The monotonous landscape did not invite to loitering, and we passed but three nights in houses by the road. The first was that of an old Italian-French emigrant, known as "Old Man Corse." He had a name of his own, which he recalled for us, but in forty years it had been lost and superseded by this designation, derived from his birthplace, the island of Corsica. This mixture of nationalities in language must be breeding for future antiquaries a good deal of amusing labor. Next day we were recommended to stop at Jack Bacon's, and, although we would have preferred to avoid an American's, did so rather than go further, and found our Jack Bacon a Creole, named Jacques Béguin.

The distance to Opelousas, our Frenchman told us, was fifteen miles by the road, though only ten miles in a direct line. We found it lined with farms, whose division fences the road always followed, frequently changing its course in so doing at a right angle. The country was very wet and unattractive. About five miles from the town, begin plantations on an extensive scale, upon better soil, and here were large gangs of Negroes at work upon cotton, with their hoes.

At the outskirts of the town, we waded the last pool, and entered, with a good deal of satisfaction, the peaceful shaded streets. Reaching the hotel, we were not so instantly struck as perhaps we should have been, with the overwhelming advantages of civilization, which sat in the form of a landlord, slapping with an agate-headed, pliable cane, his patent leather boots, poised, at easy height, upon one of the columns of the gallery. We were suffered to take off our saddlebags, and to wait until waiting was no longer a pleasure, before civilization, wringing his cane against the floor, but not removing his cigar, brought his patent leathers to our vicinity.

After some conversation, intended as animated upon one side and ineffably indifferent on the other, our horses obtained notice from that exquisitely vague eye, but a further introduction was required before our persons became less than transparent, for the boots walked away, and became again a subject of contemplation upon the column, leaving us, with our saddlebags, upon the steps. After inquiring of a bystander if this glossy individual were the actual landlord, we attacked him in a tone likely to produce either a revolver shot or a room, but whose effect was to obtain a removal of the cigar and a gentle survey, ending in a call for a boy to show the gentlemen to number thirteen.

After an hour's delay, we procured water, and were about

to enjoy very necessary ablutions, when we observed that the door of our room was partly of uncurtained glass. A shirt was pinned to this, and ceremonies were about beginning, when a step came down the passage, and a gentleman put his hand through a broken pane, and lifted the obstruction, wishing "to see what was going on so damn'd secret in number thirteen." When I walked toward him hurriedly, *in puris naturalibus,* he drew back hastily and entered the next room.

On the gallery of the hotel, after dinner, a fine-looking man — who was on the best of terms with every one — familiar with the judge — and who had been particularly polite to me, at the dinner table, said to another:

"I hear you were very unlucky with that girl you bought of me, last year?"

"Yes, I was; very unlucky. She died with her first child, and the child died, too."

"Well, that was right hard for you. She was a fine girl. I don't reckon you lost less than five thousand dollars, when she died."

"No, sir, not a dollar less."

"Well, it came right hard upon you — just beginning so."

"Yes, I was foolish, I suppose, to risk so much on the life of a single woman; but I've got a good start again now, for all that. I've got two right likely girls; one of them's got a fine boy, four months old, and the other's with child — and old Pine Knot's as hearty as ever."

"Is he? Hasn't been sick at all, eh?"

"Yes; he was sick very soon after I bought him of you; but he got well soon."

"That's right. I'd rather a nigger would be sick early, after he comes into this country; for he's bound to be acclimated, sooner or later, and the longer it's put off, the harder it goes with him."

The man was a regular Negro trader. He told me that he had a partner in Kentucky, and that they owned a farm there, and another one here. His partner bought Negroes, as opportunity offered to get them advantageously, and kept them on their Kentucky farm; and he went on occasionally, and brought the surplus to their Louisiana plantation — where he held them for sale.

An intelligent man whom I met here, and who had been travelling most of the time during the last two years in Louisiana, having business with the planters, described the condition of the new slaveholders and the poorer planters as being very miserable.

He had sometimes found it difficult to get food, even when he was in urgent need of it, at their houses. The lowest class live much from hand to mouth, and are often in extreme destitution. This was more particularly the case with those who lived on the river; those who resided on the prairies were seldom so much reduced. The former now live only on those parts of the river to which the back swamp approaches nearest; that is, where there is but little valuable land, that can be appropriated for plantation purposes. They almost all reside in communities, very closely housed in poor cabins. If there is any considerable number of them, there is to be always found, among the cluster of their cabins, a church, and a billiard and a gambling room—and the latter is always occupied, and play going on.

They almost all appear excessively apathetic, sleepy, and stupid, if you see them at home; and they are always longing and waiting for some excitement. They live for excitement, and will not labor, unless it is violently, for a short time, to gratify some passion.

This was as much the case with the women as the men. The women were often handsome, stately, and graceful, and, ordinarily, exceedingly kind; but languid, and incredibly indolent, unless there was a ball, or some other excitement, to engage them. Under excitement, they were splendidly animated, impetuous, and eccentric. One moment they seemed possessed by a devil, and the next by an angel.

The Creoles are inveterate gamblers—rich and poor alike. The majority of wealthy Creoles, he said, do nothing to improve their estate; and are very apt to live beyond their income. They borrow and play, and keep borrowing to play, as long as they can; but they will not part with their land, and especially with their home, as long as they can help it, by any sacrifice.

The men are generally dissolute. They have large families, and a great deal of family affection. He did not know that they had more than Anglo-Saxons; but they certainly manifested a great deal more, and, he thought, had more domestic happiness. If a Creole farmer's child marries, he will build a house for the new couple, adjoining his own; and when another marries, he builds another house — so, often his whole front on the river is at length occupied. Then he begins to build others, back of the first — and so, there gradually forms a little village, wherever there is a large Creole family, owning any considerable piece of land. The children are poorly educated, and are not brought up to industry, at all.

The planters living near them, as their needs increase, lend them money, and get mortgages on their land, or, in some way or other, if it is of any value, force them to part with it. Thus they are every year reduced, more and more, to the poorest lands; and the majority now are able to get but a very poor living, and would not be able to live at all in a Northern climate. They are nevertheless — even the poorest of them — habitually gay and careless, as well as kind-hearted, hospitable, and dissolute — working little, and spending much of their time at church, or at balls, or the gaming table.

There are very many wealthy Creole planters, who are as cultivated and intelligent as the better class of American planters, and usually more refined. The Creoles, he said, did not work their slaves as hard as the Americans; but, on the other hand, they did not feed or clothe them nearly as well, and he had noticed universally, on the Creole plantations, a large number of "used-up hands" — slaves, sore and crippled, or invalided for some cause. On all sugar plantations, he said, they work the Negroes excessively, in the grinding season; often cruelly. Under the usual system, to keep the fires burning, and the works constantly supplied, eighteen hours' work was required of every Negro, in twenty-four — leaving but six for rest. The work of most of them, too, was very hard. They were generally, during the grinding season, liberally supplied with food and coffee, and were induced, as much as possible, to make a kind of frolic of it; yet, on the Creole plantations, he thought they did not, even in the grinding season, often get meat.

I remarked that the law, in Louisiana, required that meat should be regularly served to the Negroes.

"O, those laws are very little regarded."

"Indeed?"

"Certainly. Suppose you are my neighbor; if you maltreat your Negroes, and tell me of it, or I see it, am I going to prefer charges against you to the magistrates? I might possibly get you punished according to law; but if I did, or did not, I should have you, and your family and friends, far and near, for my mortal enemies. There is a law of the State that Negroes shall not be worked on Sundays; but I have seen Negroes at work almost every Sunday, when I have been in the country, since I have lived in Louisiana. I spent a Sunday once with a gentleman, who did not work his hands at all on Sunday, even in the grinding season; and he had got some of his neighbors to help him build a school house, which was used as a church on Sunday. He said, there was not a plantation on either side of him, as far as he could see, where the slaves were not generally worked on Sunday; but that, after the church was started, several of them quit the practice, and made their Negroes go to the meeting. This made others discontented; and after a year or two, the planters voted new trustees to the school, and these forbid the house to be used for any other than school purposes. This was done, he had no doubt, for the purpose of breaking up the meetings, and to lessen the discontent of the slaves which were worked on Sunday.

It was said that the custom of working the Negroes on Sunday was much less common than formerly; if so, he thought that it must have formerly been universal.

He had lived, when a boy, for several years on a farm in Western New York, and afterwards, for some time, at Rochester, and was well acquainted with the people generally, in the valley of the Genesee.

I asked him if he thought, among the intelligent class of farmers and planters, people of equal property lived more happily in New York or Louisiana. He replied immediately, as if he had carefully considered the topic, that, with some rare exceptions, farmers worth forty thousand dollars lived in far greater comfort, and enjoyed more refined and elegant leisure, than planters worth three hundred thousand, and that farmers of the ordinary class, who labored with their own hands, and were worth some six thousand dollars, in the Genesee valley, lived in far greater comfort, and in all respects more enviably, than planters worth forty thousand dollars in Louisiana. The contrast was especially favorable to the New York farmer, in respect to books and newspapers. He might travel several days, and call on a hundred planters, and hardly see in their houses more than a single newspaper apiece, in most cases; perhaps none at all: nor any books, except a Bible, and some government publications, that had been franked to them through the post office, and perhaps a few religious tracts or school books.

The most striking difference that he observed between the Anglo-Americans of Louisiana and New York, was the impulsive and unreflective habit of the former, in doing business. He mentioned, as illustrative of this, the almost universal passion among the planters for increasing their Negro stock. It appeared evident to him, that the market price of Negroes was much higher than the prices of cotton and sugar warranted; but it seemed as if no planter ever made any calculation of that kind. The majority of planters, he thought, would always run in debt to the extent of their credit for Negroes, whatever was asked for them, without making any calculation of the reasonable prospects of their being able to pay their debts. When any one made a good crop, he would always expect that his next one would be better, and make purchases in advance upon such expectation. When they were dunned, they would attribute their inability to pay, to accidental short crops, and always were going ahead risking everything, in confidence that another year of luck would favor them, and a big crop make all right.

If they had a full crop, probably there would be good crops everywhere else, and prices would fall, and then they would whine and complain, as if the merchants were to blame for it, and would insinuate that no one could be expected to pay his debts when prices were so low, and that it would be dangerous to press such an unjust claim. And, if the crops met with any misfortune, from floods, or rot, or vermin, they would cry about it like children when rain fell upon a holiday, as if they had never thought of the possibility of such a thing, and were very hard used.

He had talked with many sugar planters who were strong

Cuba war and annexation men, and had rarely found that any of these had given the first thought to the probable effect the annexation of Cuba would have on their home interests. It was mainly a romantic excitement and enthusiasm, inflamed by senseless appeals to their patriotism and their combativeness. They had got the idea, that patriotism was necessarily associated with hatred and contempt of any other country but their own, and the only foreigners to be regarded with favor were those who desired to surrender themselves to us. They did not reflect that the annexation of Cuba would necessarily be attended by the removal of the duty on sugar, and would bring them into competition with the sugar planters of that island, where the advantages for growing cane were so much greater than in Louisiana.

Washington [Louisiana]. — The inn, here, when we arrived, was well filled with guests, and my friend and I were told that we must sleep together. In the room containing our bed there were three other beds; and although the outside of the house was pierced with windows, nowhere more than four feet apart, not one of them opened out of our room. A door opened into the hall, another into the dining room, and at the side of our bed was a window into the dining room, through which, betimes in the morning, we could, with out heads on our pillows, see the girls setting the breakfast tables. Both the doors were provided with glass windows, without curtains. Hither, about eleven o'clock, we "retired." Soon afterwards, hearing something moving under the bed, I asked, "Who's there?" and was answered by a girl, who was burrowing for eggs; part of the stores of the establishment being kept in boxes, in this convenient locality. Later, I was awakened by a stranger attempting to enter my bed. I expostulated, and he replied that it was his bed, and nobody else had a right to his place in it. Who was I, he asked, angrily, and where was his partner? "Here I am," answered a voice from another bed; and without another word, he left us. I slept but little, and woke feverish, and with a headache, caused by the want of ventilation.

While at the dinner table, a man asked, as one might at the North, if the steamer had arrived, if there had been "any fights today?" After dinner, while we were sitting on the gallery, loud cursing, and threatening voices were heard in the direction of the barroom, which, as at Natchitoches, was detached, and at a little distance from the hotel. The company, except myself and the other New Yorker, immediately ran towards it. After ten minutes, one returned, and said—

"I don't believe there'll be any fight; they are both cowards."

"Are they preparing for a fight?"

"O, yes; they are loading pistols in the coffee room, and there's a man outside, in the street, who has a revolver and a knife, and who is challenging another to come out. He swears he'll wait there till he does come out; but in my opinion he'll think better of it, when he finds that the other feller's got pistols, too."

"What's the occasion of the quarrel?"

"Why, the man in the street says the other one insulted him this morning, and that he had his hand on his knife, at the very moment he did so, so he couldn't reply. And now he says he's ready to talk with him, and he wants to have him come out, and as many of his friends as are a mind to, may come with him; he's got enough for all of 'em, he says. He's got two revolvers, I believe."

We did not hear how it ended; but, about an hour afterwards, I saw three men, with pistols in their hands, coming from the barroom.

The next day, I saw, in the streets of the same town, two boys running from another, who was pursuing them with a large, open dirk knife in his hand, and every appearance of ungovernable rage in his face.

The boat, for which I was waiting, not arriving, I asked the landlady—who appeared to be a German Jewess—if I could not have a better sleeping room. She showed me one, which she said I might use for a single night; but, if I remained another, I must not refuse to give it up. It had been occupied by another gentleman, and she thought he might return the next day, and would want it again; and, if I remained in it, he would be very angry that they had not reserved it for him, although they were under no obligation to him. "He is a dangerous man," she observed, "and my husband, he's a quick-tempered man, and, if they get to quarrelling about it, there'll be knives about, sure. It always frightens me to see knives drawn."

A Texas drover, who stayed overnight at the hotel, being asked, as he was about to leave in the morning, if he was not going to have his horse shod, replied:

"No sir! it'll be a damn'd long spell 'fore I pay for having a horse shod. I reckon, if God Almighty had thought it right hosses should have iron on thar feet, he'd a put it thar himself. I don't pretend to be a pious man myself; but I a'nt a-goin' to run agin the will of God Almighty, though thar's some, that calls themselves ministers of Christ, that does it."

8.

The Exceptional Large Planters

The first night after leaving Natchez I found lodging with a German, who, when I inquired if he could accommodate me, at once said, "Yes, sir, I make it *a business* to lodge travellers."

He had a little farm, and owned four strong Negro men and a woman with several children. All his men, however, he hired out as porters or servants in Natchez, employing a white man, a native of the country, to work with him on his farm.

To explain the economy of this arrangement, he said that one of his men earned in Natchez $30 a month clear of all expenses, and the others much more than he could ever make their labor worth to him. A Negro of moderate intelligence would hire, as a house servant, for $200 a year and his board, which was worth $8 a month; whereas he hired this white fellow, who was strong and able, for $10 a month; and he believed he got as much work out of him as he could out of a Negro. If labor were worth so much as he got for that of his Negroes, why did the white man not demand more? Well—he kept him in whisky and tobacco besides his wages, and he was content. Most folks here did not like white laborers. They had only been used to have niggers do their work, and they did not know how to manage with white laborers; but he had no difficulty.

I asked if eight dollars would cover the cost of a man's board? He supposed it might cost him rather more than that to keep the white man; eight dollars was what it was generally reckoned in town to cost to keep a Negro; niggers living in town or near it were expected to have "extras"; out on the plantations, where they did not get anything but bacon and meal, of course it did not cost so much. Did he know what it cost to keep a Negro generally upon the plantations? It was generally reckoned, he said, that a nigger ought to have a peck of meal and three pounds of bacon a week; some didn't give so much meat, but he thought it would be better to give them more.

"You are getting rich," I said. "Are the Germans generally,

hereabouts, doing well? I see there are a good many in Natchez."

"O yes; anybody who is not too proud to work can get rich here."

The next day, having ridden thirty tedious miles through a somber country, with a few large plantations, about six o'clock I called at the first house standing upon or near the road which I had seen for some time, and solicited a lodging. It was refused, by a woman. How far was it to the next house? I asked her. Two miles and a half. So I found it to be, but it was a deserted house, falling to decay, on an abandoned plantation. I rode several miles further, and it was growing dark, and threatening rain, before I came in sight of another. It was a short distance off the road, and approached by a private lane, from which it was separated by a grass plot. A well dressed man stood between the gate and the house. I stopped and bowed to him, but he turned his back upon me and walked to the house. I opened a gate and rode in. Two men were upon the gallery, but as they paid no attention to my presence when I stopped near them, I doubted if either were the master of the house. I asked, "Could I obtain a lodging here tonight, gentlemen?" One of them answered, surlily, "No." I paused a moment that they might observe me — evidently a stranger benighted, with a fatigued horse, and then asked, "Can you tell me, sir, how far it is to a public house?" "I don't know," replied the same man. I again remained silent a moment. "No public houses in this section of the country, I reckon, sir," said the other. "Do you know how far it is to the next house on the road, north of this?" "No," answered one. "You'll find one about two miles, or two miles and a half from here," said the other. "Is it a house in which I shall be likely to get a lodging, do you know?" "I don't know, I'm sure."

"Good night, gentlemen; you'll excuse me for troubling you. I am entirely a stranger in this region."

A grunt, or inarticulate monosyllable, from one of them, was the only reply, and I rode away, glad that I had not been fated to spend an evening in such company.

Soon afterward I came to a house and stables close upon the road. There was a man on the gallery playing the fiddle. I asked, "Could you accommodate me here tonight, sir?" He stopped fiddling, and turned his head toward an open door, asking, "Wants to know if you can accommodate him?" "Accommodate him with what?" demanded a harsh-toned woman's voice. "With a bed of course — what do you s'pose — ho! ho! ho!" and he went on fiddling again. I had, during this conversation, observed ranges of Negro huts behind the stables, and perceived that it must be the overseer's house of the plantation at which I had previously called. "Like master, like man," I thought, and rode on, my inquiry not having been even answered.

I met a Negro boy on the road, who told me it was about two miles to the next house, but he did not reckon that I would get in there. "How far to the next house beyond that?" "About four miles, sir, and I reckon you can get in there, master; I've heerd they did take in travellers to that place."

Soon after this it began to rain and grow dark; so dark that I could not keep the road, for soon finding Belshazzar in difficulty, I got off and discovered that we were following up the dry bed of a small stream. In trying to get back I probably crossed the road, as I did not find it again, and wandered cautiously among trees for nearly an hour, at length coming to open country and a fence. Keeping this in sight, I rode on until I found a gate, entering at which, I followed a nearly straight and tolerable good road full an hour, as it seemed to me, at last coming to a large Negro "settlement."

I passed through it to the end of the rows, where was a cabin larger than the rest, facing on the space between the two lines of huts. A shout brought out the overseer. I begged for a night's lodging; he was silent; I said that I had travelled far, was much fatigued and hungry; my horse was nearly knocked up, and I was a stranger in the country; I had lost my road, and only by good fortune had found my way here. At length, as I continued urging my need, he said —

"Well, I suppose you must stop. Ho, Byron! Here, Byron, take this man's horse, and put him in *my* stable. 'Light, sir, and come in."

Within I found his wife, a young woman, showily dressed — a caricature of the fashions of the day. Apparently, they had both been making a visit to neighbors, and but just come home. I was not received kindly, but at the request of her husband she brought out and set before me some cold cornbread and fat bacon.

Before I had finished eating my supper, however, they both quite changed their manner, and the woman apologized for not having made coffee. The cook had gone to bed and the fire was out, she said. She presently ordered Byron, as he brought my saddle in, to get some "light wood" and make a fire; said she was afraid I had made a poor supper, and set a chair by the fireplace for me as I drew away from the table.

I plied the man with inquiries about his business, got him interested in points of difference between Northern and Southern agriculture, and soon had him in quite a sociable and communicative humor. He gave me much overseer's lore about cotton culture, nigger and cattle maladies, the right way to keep sweet potatoes, etc.; and when I proposed to ride over the plantation with him in the morning, he said he "would be very thankful for my company."

I think they gave up their own bed to me, for it was double, and had been slept in since the sheets were last changed; the room was garnished with pistols and other arms and ammunition, rolls of Negro cloth, shoes and hats, handcuffs, a large medicine chest, and several books on medical and surgical subjects and farriery; while articles of both men's and women's wearing apparel hung against the walls, which were also decorated with some large patent medicine posters. One of them is characteristic of the place and the times.

We had a good breakfast in the morning, and immediately afterward mounted and rode to a very large cotton field, where the whole field force of the plantation was engaged.

It was a first-rate plantation. On the highest ground stood a large and handsome mansion, but it had not been occupied for several years, and it was more than two years since the overseer had seen the owner. He lived several hundred miles away, and the overseer would not believe that I did not know him, for he was a rich man and an honorable, and had several times been where I came from — New York.

The whole plantation, including the swamp land around it,

and owned with it, covered several square miles. It was four miles from the settlement to the nearest neighbor's house. There were between thirteen and fourteen hundred acres under cultivation with cotton, corn, and other hoed crops, and two hundred hogs running at large in the swamp. It was the intention that corn and pork enough should be raised to keep the slaves and cattle. This year, however, it has been found necessary to purchase largely, and such was probably usually the case, though the overseer intimated the owner had been displeased, and he "did not mean to be caught so bad again."

There were 135 slaves, big and little, of which 67 went to field regularly — equal, the overseer thought, to fully 60 prime hands. Besides these, there were 3 mechanics (blacksmith, carpenter, and wheelwright), 2 seamstresses, 1 cook, 1 stable servant, 1 cattle tender, 1 hog tender, 1 teamster, 1 house servant (overseer's cook), and one midwife and nurse. These were all first-class hands; most of them would be worth more, if they were for sale, the overseer said, than the best field hands. There was also a driver of the hoe gang who did not labor personally, and a foreman of the plow gang. These two acted as petty officers in the field, and alternately in the quarters.

There was a nursery for sucklings at the quarters, and twenty women at this time who left their work four times each day, for half an hour, to nurse their young ones. These women, the overseer counted as half hands — that is, expected to do half the day's work of a prime field hand in ordinary condition.

He had just sold a bad runaway to go to Texas, he happened to remark. He was whipping the fellow, when he turned and tried to stab him — then broke from him and ran away. He had him caught almost immediately with the dogs. After catching him, he kept him in irons till he had a chance to sell him. His niggers did not very often run away, he said, because they had found that he was almost sure to catch them. As soon as he saw that one was gone he put the dogs on, and if rain had not just fallen, they would soon find him. Sometimes they did manage to outwit the dogs, but then they almost always kept in the neighborhood, because they did not like to go where they could not sometimes get back and see their families, and he would soon get wind of where they had been; they would come round their quarters to see their families and to get food, and as soon as he knew it, he would find their tracks and put the dogs on again. Two months was the longest time any of them ever kept out. He had dogs trained on purpose to run after niggers, and never let out for anything else.

We found in the field thirty plows, moving together, turning the earth from the cotton plants, and from thirty to forty hoers, the latter mainly women, with a black driver walking about among them with a whip, which he often cracked at them, sometimes allowing the lash to fall lightly upon their shoulders. He was constantly urging them also with his voice. All worked very steadily, and though the presence of a stranger on the plantation must have been a most unusual occurrence, I saw none raise or turn their heads to look at me. Each gang was attended by a "water toter," that of the hoe gang being a straight, sprightly, plump little black girl, whose picture, as she stood balancing the bucket upon her head, shading her bright eyes with one hand, and holding out a calabash with the other to maintain her poise, would have been a worthy study for Murillo.

I asked at what time they began to work in the morning.

"Well," said the overseer, "I do better by my niggers than most. I keep 'em right smart at their work while they do work, but I generally knock 'em off at 8 o'clock in the morning, Saturdays, and give 'em all the rest of the day to themselves, and I always gives 'em Sundays, the whole day. Pickin' time, and when the crap's bad in grass, I sometimes keep 'em to it till about sunset, Saturdays, but I never work 'em Sundays."

"How early do you start them out in the morning, usually?"

"Well, I don't never start my niggers 'fore daylight, 'less 'tis in pickin' time, then maybe I get 'em out a quarter of an hour before. But I keep 'em right smart to work through the day." He showed an evident pride in the vigilance of his driver, and called my attention to the large area of ground already hoed over that morning; well hoed, too, as he said.

"At what time do they eat?" I asked. They ate "their snacks" in their cabins, he said, before they came out in the morning (that is before daylight — the sun rising at this time at a little before five, and the day dawning, probably, an hour earlier);

then at 12 o'clock their dinner was brought to them in a cart—one cart for the plow gang and one for the hoe gang. The hoe gang ate its dinner in the field, and only stopped work long enough to eat it. The plow gang drove its teams to the "weather houses"—open sheds erected for the purpose in different parts of the plantation, under which were cisterns filled with rain water, from which the water toters carried drink to those at work. The mules were fed with as much oats (in straw), corn and fodder as they would eat in two hours; this forage having been brought to the weather houses by another cart. The plowmen had nothing to do but eat their dinner in all this time. All worked as late as they could see to work well, and had no more food nor rest until they returned to their cabins.[1] At half-past nine o'clock the drivers, each on an alternate night, blew a horn, and at ten visited every cabin to see that its occupants were at rest, and not lurking about and spending their strength in fooleries, and that the fires were safe—a very unusual precaution; the Negroes are generally at liberty after their day's work is done till they are called in the morning. When washing and patching were done, wood hauled and cut for the fires, corn ground, etc., I did not learn: probably all chores not of daily necessity were reserved for Saturday. Custom varies in this respect. In general, with regard to fuel for the cabins, the Negroes are left to look out for themselves, and they often have to go to "the swamp" for it, or at least, if it has been hauled, to cut it to a convenient size, after their day's work is done. The allowance of food was a peck of corn and four pounds of pork per week, each. When they could not get "greens" (any vegetables) he generally gave them five pounds of pork. They had gardens, and raised a good deal for themselves; they also had fowls, and usually plenty of eggs.

[1]This would give at this season hardly less than sixteen hours of plodding labor, relieved by but one short interval of rest, during the daylight, for the hoe gang. It is not improbable. I was accustomed to rise early and ride late, resting during the heat of the day, while in the cotton district, but I always found the Negroes in the field when I first looked out, and generally had to wait for the Negroes to come from the field to have my horse fed when I stopped for the night. I am told, however, and I believe, that it is usual in the hottest weather, to give a rest of an hour or two to all hands at noon. I never happened to see it done. The legal limit of a slave's day's work in South Carolina is fifteen hours.

He added, "the man who owns this plantation does more for his niggers than any other man I know. Every Christmas he sends me up a thousand or fifteen hundred dollars' [equal to eight or ten dollars each] worth of molasses and coffee, and tobacco, and calico, and Sunday tricks for 'em. Every family on this plantation gets a barrel of molasses at Christmas."

Besides which, the overseer added, they are able, if they choose, to buy certain comforts for themselves—tobacco for instance—with money earned by Saturday and Sunday work. Some of them went into the swamps on Sunday, and made boards (which means slabs worked out with no other instrument than an axe). One man sold last year as much as fifty dollars' worth.

Finding myself nearer the outer gate than the "quarters," when at length my curiosity was satisfied, I did not return to the house. After getting a clear direction how to find my way back to the road I had been upon the previous day, I said to the overseer, with some hesitation, "You will allow me to pay you for the trouble I have given you?" He looked a little disconcerted by my putting the question in this way, but answered in a matter-of-course tone, "It will be a dollar and a quarter, sir."

This was the only large plantation I had an opportunity of seeing at all closely, over which I was not chiefly conducted by an educated gentleman and slave owner, by whose habitual impressions and sentiments my own were probably somewhat influenced. From what I saw in passing, and from what I heard by chance of others, I suppose it to have been a very favorable specimen of those plantations on which the owners do not reside. A merchant of the vicinity recently in New York tells me that he supposes it to be a fair enough example of plantations of its class. There is nothing remarkable in its management, so far as he had heard. When I asked about the molasses and Christmas presents, he said he reckoned the overseer must have rather stretched that part of his story, but the owner was a very good man. A magistrate of the district, who had often been on the plantation, said in answer to an inquiry from me, that the Negroes were very well treated upon it, though he did not think they were extraordinarily so. His comparison was with plantations in general. He also spoke well of the overseer. He had been a long time on this plantation—I think he said ever since it had begun to be cultivated. This is very rare; it was the only case I met with in which an overseer had kept the same place ten years, and it was a strong evidence of his comparative excellence, that his employer had been so long satisfied with him. Perhaps it was a stronger evidence that the owner of the Negroes was a man of good temper, systematic and thorough in the management of his property.

The condition of the fences, of the mules and tools, and tillage, which would have been considered admirable in the best farming district of New York—the dress of the Negroes and the neatness and spaciousness of their "quarters," which were superior to those of most of the better class of plantations on which the owners reside, all bore testimony to a very unusually prudent and provident policy.

I made no special inquiries about the advantages for education or means of religious instruction provided for the slaves. As there seems to be much public desire for definite information upon that point, I regret that I did not. I did not need to put questions to the overseer to satisfy my own mind, however. It was obvious that all natural incitements to self-advancement had been studiously removed or obstructed, in subordination to the general purpose of making the plantation profitable. Regarding only the balance sheet of the owner's ledger, it was admirable management. I am sorry to have to confess to an impression that it is rare, where this is the uppermost object of the cotton planter, that an equally frugal economy is maintained; and as the general character of the district along the Mississippi, which is especially noticeable for the number of large and very productive plantations which it contains, has now been sufficiently illustrated, I will here present certain observations which I wish to make upon the peculiar aspect of Slavery in that and other districts where its profits to the owners of slaves are most apparent.

9.

The Interior Cotton Districts.
Central Mississippi, Alabama, etc.

June 3rd. — Yesterday I met a well-dressed man upon the road, and inquired of him if he could recommend me to a comfortable place to pass the night.

"Yes, I can," said he; "you stop at John Watson's. He is a real good fellow, and his wife is a nice, tidy woman; he's got a good house, and you'll be as well taken care of there as in any place I know."

"What I am most concerned about is a clean bed," said I.

"Well, you are safe for that, there."

So distinct a recommendation was unusual, and when I reached the house he had described to me, though it was not yet dark, I stopped to solicit entertainment.

In the gallery sat a fine, stalwart man, and a woman, who in size and figure matched him well. Some ruddy, fat children were playing on the steps. The man wore a full beard, which is very uncommon in these parts. I rode to a horse block near the gallery, and asked if I could be accommodated for the night. "Oh, yes, you can stay here if you can get along without anything to eat; we don't have anything to eat but once a week." "You look as if it agreed with you, I reckon I'll try it for one night." "Alight, sir, alight. Why, you came from Texas, didn't you? Your rig looks like it," he said, as I dismounted. "Yes, I've just crossed Texas, all the way from the Rio Grande." "Have you though? Well, I'll be right glad to hear something of that country." He threw my saddle and bags across the rail of the gallery, and we walked together to the stable.

"I hear that there are a great many Germans in the western part of Texas," he said presently.

"There are a great many; west of the Guadalupe, more Germans than Americans born."

"Have they got many slaves?"

"No."

"Well, won't they break off and make a Free State down there, by and by?"

"I should think it not impossible that they might."

"I wish to God they would; I would like right well to go and settle there if it was free from Slavery. You see Kansas and all the Free States are too far north for me; I was raised in Alabama, and I don't want to move into a colder climate; but I would like to go into a country where they had not got this curse of slavery."

He said this not knowing that I was a Northern man. Greatly surprised, I asked, "What are your objections to slavery, sir?"

"Objections! The first's here" (striking his breast); "I never could bring myself to like it. Well, sir, I know slavery is wrong, and God'll put an end to it. It's bound to come to an end, and when the end does come, there'll be woe in the land. And, instead of preparing for it, and trying to make it as light as possible, we are doing nothing but make it worse and worse. That's the way it appears to me, and I'd rather get out of these parts before it comes. Then I've another objection to it. I don't like to have slaves about me. Now, I tell a nigger to go and feed your horse; I never know if he's done it unless I go and see; and if he didn't know I would go and see, and would whip him if I found he hadn't fed him, would he feed him? He'd let him starve. I've got as good niggers as anybody, but I never can depend on them; they will lie, and they will steal, and take advantage of me in every way they dare. Of course they will, if they are slaves. But lying and stealing are not the worst of it. I've got a family of children, and I don't like to have such degraded beings round my house while they are growing up. I know what the consequences are to children, of growing up among slaves."

I here told him that I was a Northern man, and asked if he could safely utter such sentiments among the people of this district, who bore the reputation of being among the most extreme and fanatical devotees of slavery. "I've been told a hundred times I should be killed if I were not more prudent in expressing my opinions, but, when it comes to killing, I'm

as good as the next man, and they know it. I never came the
worst out of a fight yet since I was a boy. I never am afraid to
speak what I think to anybody. I don't think I ever shall be."

"Are there many persons here who have as bad an opinion of
slavery as you have?"

"I reckon you never saw a conscientious man who had been
brought up among slaves who did not think of it pretty much
as I do—did you?"

"Yes, I think I have, a good many."

"Ah, self-interest warps men's minds wonderfully, but I
don't believe there are many who don't think so, sometimes—
it's impossible, I know, that they don't."

Were there any others in this neighborhood, I asked, who
avowedly hated slavery? He replied that there were a good
many mechanics, all the mechanics he knew, who felt slavery
to be a great curse to them, and who wanted to see it brought to
an end in some way. The competition in which they were
constantly made to feel themselves engaged with slave labor
was degrading to them, and they felt it to be so. He knew a
poor, hard-working man who was lately offered the services
of three Negroes for six years each if he would let them learn
his trade, but he refused the proposal with indignation, saying
he would starve before he helped a slave to become a mechanic.
There was a good deal of talk now among them about getting
laws passed to prevent the owners of slaves from having them
taught trades, and to prohibit slave mechanics from being
hired out. He could go out tomorrow, he supposed, and in the
course of a day get two hundred signatures to a paper alleging
that slavery was a curse to the people of Mississippi, and
praying the Legislature to take measures to relieve them of it
as soon as practicable. (The county contains three times as
many slaves as whites.)

He considered a coercive government of the Negroes by the
whites, forcing them to labor systematically, and restraining
them from a reckless destruction of life and property, at present
to be necessary. Of course, he did not think it wrong to hold
slaves, and the profits of their labor were not more than enough
to pay a man for looking after them—not if he did his duty to
them. What was wrong, was making slavery so much worse

than was necessary. Negroes would improve very rapidly, if they were allowed, in any considerable measure, the ordinary incitements to improvement. He knew hosts of Negroes who showed extraordinary talents, considering their opportunities: there were a great many in this part of the country who could read and write, and calculate mentally as well as the general run of white men who had been to schools. There were Colonel ——'s Negroes, some fifty of them; he did not suppose there were any fifty more contented people in the world; they were not driven hard, and work was stopped three times a day for meals; they had plenty to eat, and good clothes; and through the whole year they had from Friday night to Monday morning to do what they liked with themselves. Saturdays, the men generally worked in their patches (private gardens), and the women washed and mended clothes. Sundays, they nearly all went to a Sabbath School which the mistress taught, and to meeting, but they were not obliged to go; they could come and go as they pleased all Saturday and Sunday; they were not looked after at all. Only on Monday morning, if there should any one be missing, or any one should come to the field with ragged or dirty clothes, he would be whipped. He had often noticed how much more intelligent and sprightly these Negroes all were than the common run; a great many of them had books and could read and write; and on Sundays they were smartly dressed, some of them better than he or his wife ever thought of dressing. These things were purchased with the money they made out of their patches, working Saturdays.

There were two other large plantations near him, in both of which the Negroes were turned out to work at half-past three every week-day morning — I might hear the bell ring for them — and frequently they were not stopped till nine o'clock at night, Saturday nights the same as any other. One of them belonged to a very religious lady, and on Sunday mornings at half-past nine she had her bell rung for Sunday School, and after Sunday School they had a meeting, and after dinner another religious service. Every Negro on the plantation was obliged to attend all these exercises, and if they were not dressed clean they were whipped. They were never allowed to go off the plantation, and if they were caught speaking to a Negro from any other place, they were whipped. They could all of them repeat the catechism, he believed, but they were the dullest, and laziest, and most sorrowful looking Negroes he ever saw.

As a general rule, the condition of the slaves, as regards their material comfort, had greatly improved within twenty years. He did not know that it had in other respects. It would not be a bit safer to turn them free to shift for themselves, than it would have been twenty years ago. Of this he was quite confident. Perhaps they were a little more intelligent, knew more, but they were not as capable of self-guidance, not as much accustomed to work and contrive for themselves, as they used to be, when they were not fed and clothed nearly as well as now.

Beyond the excessive labor required of them on some plantations, he did not think slaves were often treated with unnecessary cruelty. It was necessary to use the lash occasionally. Slaves never really felt under any moral obligation to obey their masters. Faithful service was preached to them as a Christian duty, and they pretended to acknowledge it, but the fact was that they were obedient just so far as they saw that they must be to avoid punishment; and punishment was necessary, now and then, to maintain their faith in their master's power. He had seventeen slaves, and he did not suppose that there had been a hundred strokes of the whip on his place for a year past.

He asked if there were many Americans in Texas who were opposed to slavery, and if they were free to express themselves. I said that the wealthy Americans there were all slaveholders themselves; that their influence all went to encourage the use of slave labor, and render labor by whites disreputable. "But are there not a good many Northern men there?" he asked. The Northern men, I replied, were chiefly merchants or speculators, who had but one idea, which was to make money as fast as they could; and nearly all the little money there was in that country was in the hands of the largest slaveholders.

If that was the way of things there, he said, there could not be much chance of its becoming a Free State. I thought the chances were against it, but if the Germans continued to flock into the country, it would rapidly acquire all the characteristic features of a free-labor community, including an abundance and variety of skilled labor, a home market for a variety of crops, denser settlements, and more numerous social, educational, and commercial conveniences. There would soon be a large body of small proprietors, not so wealthy that the stimulus to personal and active industry would have been lost, but yet able to indulge in a good many luxuries, to found churches, schools, and railroads, and to attract thither tradesmen, mechanics, professional men, and artists. Moreover, the laborers who were not landholders would be intimately blended with them in all their interests; the two classes not living dissociated from each other, as was the case generally at the South, but engaged in a constant fulfillment of reciprocal obligations. I told him that if such a character of society could once be firmly and extensively established before the country was partitioned out into these little independent Negro kingdoms, which had existed from the beginning in every other part of the South, I did not think any laws would be necessary to prevent slavery. It might be a Slave State, but it would be a free people.

On coming from my room in the morning, my host met me with a hearty grasp of the hand. "I have slept very little with thinking of what you told me about western Texas. I think I shall have to go there. If we could get rid of slavery in this region, I believe we would soon be the most prosperous people in the world. What a disadvantage it must be to have your ground all frozen up, and to be obliged to fodder your cattle five months in the year, as you do at the North. I don't see how you live. I think I should like to buy a small farm near some town where I could send my children to school—a farm that I could take care of with one or two hired men. One thing I wanted to ask you, are the Germans learning English at all?" "Oh, yes; they teach the children English in their schools." "And have they good schools?" "Wherever they have settled at all closely they have. At New Braunfels they employ American as well as German teachers, and instruction can be had in the classics, natural history, and the higher mathematics." "Upon my word, I think I must go there," he replied. (Since then, as I hear, an educational institution of a high character,

has been established by German influence in San Antonio,
teachers in which are from Harvard.)

When I left he mounted a horse and rode on with me some
miles, saying he did not often find an intelligent man who
liked to converse with him on the question of slavery. It seemed
to him there was an epidemic insanity on the subject. It is
unnecessary to state his views at length. They were precisely
those which used to be common among all respectable men at
the South.

As we rode an old Negro met and greeted us warmly. My
companion hereupon observed that he had never uttered his
sentiments in the presence of a slave, but in some way all
the slaves in the country had, he thought, been informed what
they were, for they all looked to him as their special friend.
When they got into trouble, they would often come to him for
advice or assistance. This morning before I was up, a Negro
came to him from some miles distant, who had been working
for a white man on Sundays till he owed him three dollars,
which, now that the Negro wanted it, he said he could not
pay. He had given the Negro the three dollars, for he thought
he could manage to get it from the white man.

He confirmed an impression I had begun to get of the purely
dramatic character of what passed for religion with most of
the slaves. One of his slaves was a preacher, and a favorite
among them. He sometimes went to plantations twenty miles
away — even further — on a Sunday, to preach a funeral sermon,
making journeys of fifty miles a day on foot. After the sermon,
a hat would be passed round, and he sometimes brought home
as much as ten dollars. He was a notable pedestrian; and once
when he had committed some abominable crime for which he
knew he would have to be punished, and had run away, he
(Mr. Watson) rode after him almost immediately, often got in
sight of him, but did not overtake him until the second day,
when starting early in the morning he overhauled him crossing
a broad, smooth field. When the runaway parson saw that he
could not escape, he jumped up into a tree and called out to
him, with a cheerful voice, "I gin ye a good run dis time,
didn't I, massa?" He was the most rascally Negro, the worst
liar, thief, and adulterer on his place. Indeed, when he was

preaching, he always made a strong point of his own sinfulness, and would weep and bellow about it like a bull of Bashan, till he got a whole camp meeting into convulsions.

The night after leaving Mr. Watson's I was kindly received by a tradesman, who took me, after closing his shop, to his mother's house, a log cabin, but more comfortable than many more pretentious residences at which I passed a night on this journey. For the first time in many months tea was offered me. It was coarse Bohea, sweetened with honey, which was stirred into the tea as it boiled in a kettle over the fire, by the old lady herself, whose especial luxury it seemed to be. She asked me if folks ever drank tea at the North, and when I spoke of green tea said she had never heard of that kind of tea before. They owned a number of slaves, but the young man looked after my horse himself. There was a good assortment of books and newspapers at this house, and the people were quite intelligent and very amiable.

The next day, I passed a number of small Indian farms, very badly cultivated — the corn nearly concealed by weeds. The soil became poorer than before, and the cabins of poor people more frequent. I counted about ten plantations, or Negro-cultivated farms, in twenty miles. A planter, at whose house I called after sunset, said it was not convenient for him to accommodate me, and I was obliged to ride until it was quite dark. The next house at which I arrived was one of the commonest sort of cabins. I had passed twenty like it during the day, and I thought I would take the opportunity to get an interior knowledge of them. The fact that a horse and wagon were kept, and that a considerable area of land in the rear of the cabin was planted with cotton, showed that the family were by no means of the lowest class, yet, as they were not able even to hire a slave, they may be considered to represent very favorably, I believe, the condition of the poor whites of the plantation districts. The whites of the county, I observe, by the census, are three to one of the slaves; in the nearest adjoining county, the proportion is reversed; and within a few miles the soil was richer, and large plantations occurred.

It was raining and nearly nine o'clock. The door of the cabin was open, and I rode up and conversed with the occupant as he stood within. He said that he was not in the habit of taking in travellers, and his wife was about sick, but if I was a mind to put up with common fare, he didn't care. Grateful, I dismounted and took the seat he had vacated by the fire, while he led away my horse to an open shed in the rear—his own horse ranging at large, when not in use, during the summer.

The house was all comprised in a single room, twenty-eight by twenty-five feet in area, and open to the roof above. There was a large fireplace at one end and a door on each side — no windows at all. Two bedsteads, a spinning-wheel, a packing case, which served as a bureau, a cupboard, made of rough hewn slabs, two or three deerskin seated chairs, a Connecticut clock, and a large poster of Jayne's patent medicines, constituted all the visible furniture, either useful or ornamental in purpose. A little girl, immediately, without having had any directions to do so, got a frying pan and a chunk of bacon from the cupboard, and cutting slices from the latter, set it frying for my supper. The woman of the house sat sulkily in a chair tilted back and leaning against the logs, spitting occasionally at the fire, but took no notice of me, barely nodding when I saluted her. A baby lay crying on the floor. I quieted it and amused it with my watch till the little girl, having made "coffee" and put a piece of cornbread on the table with the bacon, took charge of it.

I hoped the woman was not very ill.

"Got the headache right bad," she answered. "Have the headache a heap, I do. Knew I should have it tonight. Been cuttin' brush in the cotton this afternoon. Knew't would bring on my headache. Told him so when I begun."

As soon as I had finished my supper and fed Jude, the little girl put the fragments and the dishes in the cupboard, shoved the table into a corner, and dragged a quantity of quilts from one of the bedsteads, which she spread upon the floor, and presently crawled among them out of sight for the night. The woman picked up the child—which, though still a suckling, she said was twenty-two months old—and nursed it, retaking her old position. The man sat with me by the fire, his back towards her. The baby having fallen asleep was laid away somewhere, and the woman dragged off another lot of quilts from the beds, spreading them upon the floor. Then taking a deep tin pan, she filled it with alternate layers of corncobs and hot embers from the fire. This she placed upon a large block, which was evidently used habitually for the purpose, in the center of the cabin. A furious smoke arose from it, and we soon began to cough. "Most *too* much smoke," observed the man. "Hope 'twill drive out all the gnats, then," replied the woman. (There is a very minute flying insect here, the bite of which is excessively sharp.)

The woman suddenly dropped off her outer garment and stepped from the midst of its folds, in her petticoat; then, taking the baby from the place where she had deposited it, lay down and covered herself with the quilts upon the floor. The man told me that I could take the bed which remained on one of the bedsteads, and kicking off his shoes only, rolled himself into a blanket by the side of his wife. I ventured to take off my cravat and stockings, as well as my boots, but almost immediately put my stockings on again, drawing their tops over my pantaloons. The advantage of this arrangement was that, although my face, eyes, ears, neck, and hands, were immediately attacked, the vermin did not reach my legs for two or three hours. Just after the clock struck two, I distinctly heard the man and the woman, and the girl and the dog scratching, and the horse out in the shed stamping and gnawing himself. Soon afterward the man exclaimed, "Good God Almighty — mighty! mighty! mighty!" and jumping up pulled off one of his stockings, shook it, scratched his foot vehemently, put on the stocking, and lay down again with a groan. The two doors were open, and through the logs and the openings in the roof, I saw the clouds divide and the moon and stars reveal themselves. The woman, after having been nearly smothered by the smoke from the pan which she had originally placed close to her own pillow, rose and placed it on the sill of the windward door, where it burned feebly and smoked lustily, like an altar to the Lares, all night. Fortunately the cabin was so open that it gave us little annoyance, while it seemed to answer the purpose of keeping all flying insects at a distance.

When, on rising in the morning, I said that I would like to

wash my face, water was given me for the purpose in an earthen pie dish. Just as breakfast, which was of exactly the same materials as my supper, was ready, rain began to fall, presently in such a smart shower as to put the fire out and compel us to move the table under the least leaky part of the roof.

At breakfast occurred the following conversation:—

"Are there many niggers in New York?"

"Very few."

"How do you get your work done?"

"There are many Irish and German people constantly coming there who are glad to get work to do."

"Oh, and you have them for slaves?"

"They want money and are willing to work for it. A great many American-born work for wages, too."

"What do you have to pay?"

"Ten or twelve dollars a month."

"There was a heap of Irishmen to work on the railroad; they was paid a dollar a day; there was a good many Americans, too, but mostly they had little carts and mules, and hauled dirt and sich like. They was paid twenty-five or thirty dollars a month and found" [room, board, and other necessities].

"What did they find them?"

"Oh, blanket and shoes, I expect; they put up kind o' tents like for 'em to sleep in altogether."

"What food did they find them?"

"Oh, common food; bacon and meal."

"What do they generally give the niggers on the plantations here?"

"A peck of meal and three pound of bacon is what they call 'lowance, in general, I believe. It takes a heap o' meat on a big plantation. I was on one of William R. King's plantations over in Alabamy, where there was about fifty niggers, one Sunday last summer, and I see 'em weighin' outen the meat. Tell you, it took a powerful heap on it. They had an old nigger to weigh it out, and he warn't no ways partickler about the weight. He just took and chopped it off, middlins, in chunks, and he'd throw them into the scales, and if a piece weighed a pound or two over he wouldn't mind it; he never took none back. Ain't niggers all-fired sassy at the North?"

"No, not particularly."

"Ain't they all free, there? I hearn so."

"Yes."

"Well, how do they get along when they's free?"

"I never have seen a great many, to know their circumstances very well. Right about where I live they seem to me to live quite comfortably; more so than the niggers on these big plantations do, I should think."

"Oh, they have a mighty hard time on the big plantations. I'd ruther be dead than to be a nigger on one of these big plantations."

"Why, I thought they were pretty well taken care of on them."

The man and his wife both looked at me as if surprised, and smiled.

"Why, they are well fed, are they not?"

"Oh, but they work 'em so hard. My God, sir, in pickin' time on these plantations they start 'em to work 'fore light, and they don't give 'em time to eat."

"I supposed they generally gave them an hour or two at noon."

"No, sir; they just carry a piece of bread and meat in their pockets and they eat it when they can, standin' up. They have a hard life on't, that's a fact. I reckon you can get along about as well withouten slaves as with 'em, can't you, in New York?"

"In New York there is not nearly so large a proportion of very rich men as here. There are very few people who farm over three hundred acres, and the greater number—nineteen out of twenty, I suppose—work themselves with the hands they employ. Yes, I think it's better than it is here, for all concerned, a great deal. Folks that can't afford to buy niggers get along a great deal better in the Free States, I think; and I guess that those who could afford to have niggers get along better without them."

"I no doubt that's so. I wish there warn't no niggers here. They are a great cuss to this country, I expect. But 'twouldn't do to free 'em; that wouldn't do nohow!"

"Are there many people here who think slavery a curse to the country?"

"Oh, yes, a great many. I reckon the majority would be right glad if we could get rid of the niggers. But it wouldn't never do to free 'em and leave 'em here. I don't know anybody, hardly, in favor of that. Make 'em free and leave 'em here and they'd steal everything we made. Nobody couldn't live here then."

These views of slavery seem to be universal among people of this class. They were repeated to me at least a dozen times.

"Where I used to live [Alabama], I remember when I was a boy — must ha' been about twenty years ago — folks was dreadful frightened about the niggers. I remember they built pens in the woods where they could hide, and Christmas time they went and got into the pens, 'fraid the niggers was risin'."

"I remember the same time where we was in South Carolina," said his wife; "we had all our things put up in bags, so we could tote 'em, if we heerd they was comin' our way."

They did not suppose the niggers ever thought of rising now, but could give no better reason for not supposing so than that "everybody said there warn't no danger on't now."

Hereabouts the plantations were generally small, ten to twenty Negroes on each; sometimes thirty or forty. Where he used to live they were big ones — forty or fifty, sometimes a hundred on each. He had lived here ten years. I could not make out why he had not accumulated wealth, so small a family and such an inexpensive style of living as he had. He generally planted twenty to thirty acres, he said; this year he had sixteen in cotton and about ten, he thought, in corn. Decently cultivated, this planting should have produced him five hundred dollars' worth of cotton, besides supplying him with bread and bacon — his chief expense, apparently. I suggested that this was a very large planting for his little family; he would need some help in picking time. He ought to have some now, he said; grass and bushes were all overgrowing him; he had to work just like a nigger; this durnation rain would just make the weeds jump, and he didn't expect he should have any cotton at all. There warn't much use in a man's trying to get along by himself; everything seemed to set in agin him. He'd been trying to hire somebody, but he couldn't, and his wife was a sickly kind of a woman.

His wife reckoned he might hire some help if he'd look round sharp.

My horse and dog were as well cared for as possible, and a "snack" of bacon and cornbread was offered me for noon, which has been unusual in Mississippi. When I asked what I should pay, the man hesitated and said he reckoned what I had had, wasn't worth much of anything; he was sorry he could not have accommodated me better. I offered him a dollar, for which he thanked me warmly. It is the first instance of hesitation in charging for a lodging which I have met with from a stranger at the South.

Northern Alabama, June 15th. — I have today reached a more distinctly hilly country — somewhat rocky and rugged, but with inviting dells. The soil is sandy and less frequently fertile; cotton fields are seen only at long intervals, the crops on the small proportion of cultivated land being chiefly corn and oats. I notice also that white men are more commonly at work in the fields than Negroes, and this as well in the cultivation of cotton as of corn.

The larger number of the dwellings are rude log huts, of only one room, and that unwholesomely crowded. I saw in and about one of them, not more than fifteen feet square, five grown persons, and as many children. Occasionally, however, the monotony of these huts is agreeably varied by neat, white, frame houses. At one such, I dined today, and was comfortably entertained. The owner held a number of slaves, but made no cotton. He owned a saw mill, was the postmaster of the neighborhood, and had been in the Legislature.

I passed the night at the second framed house that I saw during the day, stopping early in order to avail myself of its promise of comfort. It was attractively situated on a hilltop, with a peach orchard near it. The proprietor owned a dozen slaves, and "made cotton," he said, "with other crops." He had some of his neighbors at tea and at breakfast; sociable, kindly people, satisfied with themselves and their circumstances, which I judged from their conversation had been recently improving. One coming in, remarked that he had discharged a white laborer whom he had employed for some time past; the others congratulated him on being "shet" of him; all seemed to have noticed him as a bad, lazy man; he had often been seen lounging in the field, rapping the Negroes with his hoe if they didn't work to suit him. "He was about the meanest white man I ever see," said a woman; "he was a heap meaner 'n niggers. I reckon niggers would come somewhere between white folks and such as he." "The first thing I tell a man," said another, "when I hire him, is, 'if there's any whippin' to be done on this place I want to do it myself.' If I saw a man rappin' my niggers with a hoe handle, as I see him, durned if I wouldn't rap him — the lazy whelp."

June 17th. — The country continues hilly, and is well populated by farmers, living in log huts, while every mile or two, on the more level and fertile land, there is a larger farm, with ten or twenty Negroes at work. A few whites are usually working near them, in the same field, generally plowing while the Negroes hoe.

During the afternoon I rode on through a valley, narrow and apparently fertile, but the crops indifferent. The general social characteristics were the same that I met with yesterday.

At night I stopped at a large house having an unusual number of Negro cabins and stables about it. The proprietor, a hearty old farmer, boasted much of his pack of hounds, saying they had pulled down five deer before he had had a shot at them. He was much interested to hear about Texas, the Indians and the game. He reckoned there was "a heap of big varmint out thar."

His crop of cotton did not average two bales to the hand, and corn not twenty bushels to the acre.

He amused me much with a humorous account of an oyster supper to which he had been invited in town, and his attempts to eat the "nasty things" without appearing disconcerted before the ladies.

An old Negro took my horse when I arrived, and half an hour afterward, came to me and asked if I wanted to see him fed. As we walked toward the stables, he told me that he always took care not to forget gentlemen's hosses, and to treat them well; "then," he said, bowing and with emphasis, "they looks out and don't forget to treat me well."

The same Negro was called to serve me as a candlestick at bedtime. He held the candle till I got into bed. As he retired I closed my eyes, but directly afterward, perceiving the light return, I opened them. Uncle Abram was bending over me, holding the candle, grinning with his toothless gums, winking and shaking his head in a most mysterious manner.

"Hush! massa," he whispered. "You hain't got something to drink, in dem saddlebags, has you, sar?"

The farmer told me something about "nigger dogs"; they didn't use foxhounds, but bloodhounds—not pure, he thought, but a cross of the Spanish bloodhound with the common hounds, or curs. There were many men, he said, in the country below here, who made a business of nigger hunting, and they had their horses trained, as well as the dogs, to go over any common fence, or if they couldn't leap it, to break it down. Dogs were trained, when pups, to follow a nigger—not allowed to catch one, however, unless they were quite young, so that they couldn't hurt him much, and they were always taught to hate a Negro, never being permitted to see one except to be put in chase of him. He believed that only two of a pack were kept kenneled all the time—these were old, keen ones, who led the rest when they were out; they were always kept coupled together with a chain, except when trailing. He had seen a pack of thirteen who would follow a trail two days and a half old, if rain had not fallen in the mean time. When it rained immediately after a Negro got off, they had to scour the country where they supposed he might be, till they scented him.

When hard pushed, a Negro always took to a tree; sometimes, however, they would catch him in an open field. When this was the case the hunter called off the dogs as soon as he could, unless the Negro fought—"that generally makes 'em mad (the hunters), and they'll let 'em tear him a spell. The owners don't mind having them kind o' niggers tore a good deal; runaways ain't much account nohow, and it makes the rest more afraid to run away, when they see how they are sarved." If they caught the runaway within two or three days, they got from $10 to $20; if it took a longer time, they were paid more than that; sometimes $200. They asked their own price; if an owner should think it exorbitant, he supposed, he said in reply to an inquiry, they'd turn the nigger loose, order him to make off, and tell his master to catch his own niggers.

Sunday. — I rode on, during the cool of the morning, about eight miles, and stopped for the day, at a house pleasantly situated by a small stream, among wooded hills. During the forenoon, seven men and three women, with their children, gathered at the house. All of them, I concluded, were non-slave-holders, as was our host himself; though, as one told me, "with his five boys he makes a heap more crop than Mrs. ——, who's got forty niggers." "How is that?" "Well, she's a woman, and she can't make the niggers work; she won't have a overseer, and niggers won't work, you know, unless there's somebody to drive 'em."

Our host, when I arrived, had just been pulling weeds out of his potato patch, which he mentioned as an apology for not being a little clean, like the rest.

Besides the company I have mentioned, and the large family of the house, there was another traveller and myself to dinner, and three bountiful tables were spread, one after another.

The traveller was said to be a Methodist preacher, but gave no indication of it, except that he said grace before meat, and used the Hebrew word for Sunday. He was, however, a man of superior intelligence to the others, who were ignorant and stupid, though friendly and communicative. He asked me "what a good nigger man could be bought for in New York"; he didn't seem surprised, or make any further inquiry, when I told him we had no slaves there. Some asked me much about crops, and when I told them that my crops of wheat for six years had averaged twenty-eight bushels, and that I had once reaped forty from a single acre, they were amazed beyond expression, and anxious to know how I "put it in." I described the process minutely, which astonished them still more; and one man said he had often thought they might get more wheat if they put it in differently; he had thought that perhaps more wheat would grow if more seed were sown, but he never tried it. The general practice, they told me, was to sow wheat on ground from which they had taken maize, without removing the maize stumps, or plowing it at all; they sowed three pecks of wheat to the acre, and then plowed it in — that was all. They used the cradle, but had never heard of reaping machines; the crop was from five to ten bushels an acre; ten bushels was extraordinary, six was not thought bad. Of cotton, the ordinary crop was five hundred pounds to the acre, or from one to two bales to a hand. Of maize, usually from ten to twenty bushels to the acre; last year not over ten; this year they thought it would be twenty-five on the best land.

The general admiration of Jude brought up the topic of Negro dogs again, and the clergyman told a story of a man who hunted niggers near where he lived. He was out once with another man, when after a long search, they found the dogs barking up a big cottonwood tree. They examined the tree closely without finding any Negro, and concluded that the dogs must have been foiled, and they were about to go away, when Mr. ———, from some distance off, thought he saw a Negro's leg very high up in the tree, where the leaves and moss were thick enough to hide a man lying on the top of a limb with his feet against the trunk. He called out, as if he really saw a man, telling him to come down, but nothing stirred. He sent for an axe, and called out again, saying he would cut the tree to the ground if he didn't come down. There was no reply. He then cut half through the tree on one side, and was beginning on the other, when the Negro halloed out that if he would stop he would come down. He stopped cutting, and the Negro descended to the lowest limb, which was still far from the ground, and asked the hunter to take away his dogs, and promise they shouldn't tear him. But the hunter swore he'd make no conditions with him after having been made to cut the tree almost down.

The Negro said no more, but retained his position until the tree was nearly cut in two. When it began to totter, he slid down the trunk, the dogs springing upon him as soon as he was within their reach. He fought them hard, and got hold of one by the ear; that made them fiercer, and they tore him till the hunter was afraid they'd kill him, and stopped them.

"Are dogs allowed to tear the Negroes when they catch them?"

"When the hunters come up they always call them off, unless the nigger fights. If the nigger fights 'em that makes 'em mad, and they let 'em tear him good," said the clergyman.

There were two or three young women present, and the young men were sparking with them in the house, sitting on the beds for want of sofas, the chairs being all in use outside; the rest of the company sat on the gallery most of the time, but there was little conversation. It was twice remarked to me, "Sunday's a dull day — nothing to do."

June————. Today, I am passing through a valley of thin, sandy soil, thickly populated by poor farmers. Negroes are rare, but occasionally neat, new houses, with other improvements, show the increasing prosperity of the district. The majority of dwellings are small log cabins of one room, with another separate cabin for a kitchen; each house has a well, and a garden enclosed with palings. Cows, goats, mules and swine, fowls and doves are abundant. The people are more social than those of the lower country, falling readily into friendly conversation with a traveller. They are very ignorant; the agriculture is wretched and the work hard. I have seen three white women hoeing field crops today. A spinning-wheel is heard in every house, and frequently a loom is clanging in the gallery, always worked by women; every one wears homespun. The Negroes have much more individual freedom than in the rich cotton country, and are not unfrequently heard singing or whistling at their work.

Tennessee, June 29th. — At nightfall I entered a broader and more populous valley than I had seen before during the day, but for some time there were only small single room log cabins, at which I was loath to apply for lodging. At length I reached a large and substantial log house with Negro cabins. The master sat in the stoop. I asked if he could accommodate me.

"What do you want?"

"Something to eat for myself and horse, and room to sleep under your roof."

"The wust on't is," he said, getting up and coming toward me, "we haven't got much for your horse."

"You've got corn, I suppose."

"No, hain't got no corn but a little that we want for ourselves, only just enough to bread us till corn comes again."

"Well, you have oats?"

"Hain't got an oat."

"Haven't you hay?"

"No."

"Then I must go further, for my horse can't travel on fodder."

"Hain't got nary fodder nuther."

Fortunately I did not have to go much further before I came to the best house I had seen during the day, a large, neat, white house, with Negro shanties, and an open log cabin in the front yard. A stout, elderly, fine-looking woman, in a cool white muslin dress, sat upon the gallery, fanning herself. Two little Negroes had just brought a pail of fresh water, and she was drinking of it with a gourd, as I came to the gate. I asked if it would be convenient for her to accommodate me for the night, doubtingly, for I had learned to distrust the accommodations of the wealthy slaveholders.

"Oh yes, get down; fasten your horse there, and the niggers will take care of him when they come from their work. Come up here and take a seat."

I brought in my saddlebags.

"Bring them in here, into the parlor," she said, "where they'll be safe."

The interior of the house was furnished with unusual comfort. "The parlor," however, had a bed in it. As we came out, she locked the door.

We had not sat long, talking about the weather (she was suffering much from the heat), when her husband came. He was very hot also, though dressed coolly enough in merely a pair of short-legged, unbleached cotton trousers, and a shirt with the bosom spread open—no shoes nor stockings. He took his seat before speaking to me, and after telling his wife it was the hottest day he ever saw, squared his chair toward me, threw it back so as to recline against a post, and said gruffly, "Good evening, sir; you going to stay here tonight?"

I replied, and he looked at me a few moments without speaking. He was, in fact, so hot that he spoke with difficulty.

At length he got breath and asked abruptly: "You a mechanic, sir, or a dentist, eh — or what?"

Supper was cooked by two young women, daughters of the master of the house, assisted by the two little Negro boys. The cabin in front of the house was the kitchen, and when the bacon was dished up, one of the boys struck an iron triangle at the door. "Come to supper," said the host, and led the way to the kitchen, which was also the supper room. One of the young ladies took the foot of the table, the other seated herself apart by the fire, and actually waited on the table, though the two Negro boys stood at the head and foot, nominally waiters, but always anticipated by the Cinderella, when anything was wanted.

A big lout of a youth who came from the field with the Negroes, looked in, but seeing me, retired. His father called, but his mother said, "'twouldn't do no good — he was so bashful."

Speaking of the climate of the country, I was informed that a majority of the folks went barefoot all winter, though they had snow much of the time four or five inches deep, and the man said he didn't think most of the men about here had more than one coat, and they never wore any in winter except on holidays. "That was the healthiest way," he reckoned, "just to toughen yourself and not wear no coat"; no matter how cold it was, he didn't wear no coat.

The master held a candle for me while I undressed, in a large room above stairs; and gave me my choice of the four beds in it. I found one straw bed (with, as usual, but one sheet), on which I slept comfortably. At midnight I was awakened by some one coming in. I rustled my straw, and a voice said, "Who is there in this room?"

"A stranger passing the night; who are you?"

"All right; I belong here. I've been away and have just come home."

He did not take his clothes off to sleep. He turned out to be an older son who had been fifty miles away, looking after a stray horse. When I went down stairs in the morning, having been wakened early by flies, and the dawn of day through an open window, I saw the master lying on his bed in the "parlor," still asleep in the clothes he wore at supper. His wife was washing her face on the gallery, being already dressed for the day; after using the family towel, she went into the kitchen, but soon returned, smoking a pipe, to her chair in the doorway.

Yet everything betokened an opulent and prosperous man — rich land, extensive field crops, a number of Negroes, and considerable herds of cattle and horses. He also had capital invested in mines and railroads, he told me. His elder son spoke of him as "the squire."

A Negro woman assisted in preparing breakfast (she had probably been employed in the field labor the night before), and both the young ladies were at the table. The squire observed to me that he supposed we could buy hands very cheap in New York. I said we could hire them there at moderate wages. He asked if we couldn't buy as many as we wanted, by sending to Ireland for them and paying their passage. He had supposed we could buy them and hold them as slaves for a term of years, by paying the freight on them. When I had corrected him, he said, a little hesitatingly, "You don't have no black slaves in New York?" "No, sir." "There's niggers there, ain't there, only they're all free?" "Yes, sir." "Well, how do they get along so?" "So far as I know, the most of them live pretty comfortably." (I have changed my standard of comfort lately, and am inclined to believe that the majority of the Negroes at the North live more comfortably than the majority of whites at the South.) "I wouldn't like that," said the old lady. "I wouldn't like to live where niggers was free, they are bad enough when they are slaves: it's hard enough to get along with them here, they're so bad. I reckon that niggers are the meanest critters on earth; they are so mean and nasty" (she expressed disgust and indignation very strongly in her face). "If they was to think themselves equal to we, I don't think white folks could abide it — they're such vile saucy things." A Negro woman and two boys were in the room as she said this.

July 16th. — I stopped last night at the pleasantest house I have yet seen in the highlands; a framed house, painted white, with a log kitchen attached. The owner was a man of superior standing. I judged from the public documents and law books on his table, that he had either been in the Legislature of the State, or that he was a justice of the peace. There were also a good many other books and newspapers, chiefly of a religious character. He used, however, some singularly uncouth phrases common here. He had a store, and carried on farming and stock raising. After a conversation about his agriculture, I remarked that there were but few slaves in this part of the country. He wished that there were fewer. They were not profitable property here, I presumed. They were not, he said, except to raise for sale; but there were a good many people here who would not have them if they were profitable, and yet who were abundantly able to buy them. They were horrid things, he thought; he would not take one to keep it if it should be given to him. 'Twould be a great deal better for the country, he believed, if there was not a slave in it. He supposed it would not be right to take them away from those who had acquired property in them, without any remuneration, but he wished they could all be sent out of the country — sent to Liberia. That was what ought to be done with them. I said it was evident that where there were no slaves, other things being equal, there was greater prosperity than where slavery supplied the labor. He didn't care so much for that, he said; there was a greater objection to slavery than that, in his mind. He was afraid that there was many a man who had gone to the bad world, who wouldn't have gone there if he hadn't had any slaves. He had been down in the nigger counties a good deal, and he had seen how it worked on the white people. It made the rich people, who owned the niggers, passionate and proud, and ugly, and it made the poor people mean. "People that own niggers are always mad with them about something; half their time is spent in swearing and yelling at them."

"I see you have *Uncle Tom's Cabin* here," said I; "have you read it?"

"Oh, yes."

"And what do you think of it?"

"Think of it? I think well of it."

"Do most of the people here in the mountains think as you do about slavery?"

"Well, there's some thinks one way and some another, but there's hardly any one here that don't think slavery's a curse to our country, or who wouldn't be glad to get rid of it."

I asked what the people about here thought of the Nebraska Bill. He couldn't say what the majority thought. Would people moving from here to Nebraska now, be likely to vote for the admission of slavery there? He thought not; "most people would much rather live in a Free State." He told me that he knew personally several persons who had gone to California, and taken slaves with them, who had not been able to bring them back. There were one or two cases where the Negroes had been induced to return, and these instances had been made much of in the papers, as evidence that the slaves were contented.

"That's a great lie," he said; "they are not content, and nine-tenths of 'em would do 'most anything to be free. It's only now and then that slaves, who are treated unusual kind, and made a great deal of, will choose to remain in slavery if freedom is put in their way." He knew one man (giving his name) who tried to bring two slaves back from California, and had got started with them, when some white people suspecting it, went on board the ship and told him it was against the law to hold Negroes as slaves in California, and his Negroes shouldn't go back with him unless they were willing to. Then they went to the slaves and told them they need not return if they preferred to stay, and the slaves said they had wanted very much to go back to North Carolina, yet they would rather remain in California, if they could be free, and so they took them ashore. He had heard the slave owner himself relating this, and cursing the men who interfered. He had told him that they did no more than Christians were obliged to do.

I overtook upon the road, today, three young men of the poorest class. Speaking of the price of land and the profit of farming, one of them said, believing me to be a Southerner—

"We are all poor folks here; don't hardly make enough to keep us in liquor. Anybody can raise as much corn and hogs on the mountains as he'll want to live on, but there ain't no rich people here. Nobody's got any black ones—only three or four; no one's got fifty or a hundred, like as they have down in the East." "It would be better," interrupted another, somewhat fiercely, "there warn't any at all; that's my mind about it; they're no business here; they ought to be in their own country and take care of themselves, that's what I believe, and I don't care who hears it." But let the reader not be deceived by these expressions; they indicate simply the weakness and cowardice of the class represented by these men. It is not slavery they detest; it is simply the Negro competition, and the monopoly of the opportunities to make money by Negro owners, which they feel and but dimly comprehend.

If you meet a man without stopping, the salutation here always is, "How d'ye do, sir?" never "Good morning"; and on parting it is, "I wish you well, sir," more frequently than "Good-bye." You are always commanded to appear at the table, as elsewhere throughout the South, in a rough, peremptory tone, as if your host feared you would try to excuse yourself.

"Come in to supper." "Take a seat." "Some of the fry?" "Help yourself to anything you see that you can eat."

They ask your name, but do not often call you by it, but hail you "Stranger," or "Friend."

Texas is always spoken of in the plural—"the Texies." Bean't the Texies powerful sickly?"

"Ill" is used for "vicious." "Is your horse ill?" "Not that I am aware of. Does he appear so?" "No; but some horses will bite a stranger if he goes to handling on 'em."

"Is your horse ill?" "No, I believe not." "I see he kind o' drapt his ears when I came up, 'zif he was playful."

Everybody I've met in the last three counties—after ascertaining what parts I came from, and which parts I'm going to, where I got my horse, what he cost, and of what breed he is, what breed the dog is, and whether she's followed me all the way from the Texies, if her feet ain't worn out, and if I don't think I'll have to tote her if I go much further, and if I don't want to give her away, how I like the Texies, etc.—has asked me whether I didn't see a man by the name of Baker in the

Texies, who was sheriff of ——— county, and didn't behave
exactly the gentleman, or another fellow by the name of ———,
who ran away from the same county, and cut to the Texies.
I've been asked if they had done fighting yet in the Texies,
referring to the war with Mexico, which was ended ten years
ago. Indeed the ignorance with regard to everything transpiring
in the world outside, and the absurd ideas and reports I hear,
are quite incredible. It cannot be supposed that having been
at home in New York, there should be any one there whom I
do not personally know, or that, having passed through Texas,
I should be unable to speak from personal knowledge of the
welfare of every one in that State.

Northeastern Tennessee, ———. —Night before last I spent
at the residence of a man who had six slaves; last night, at the
home of a farmer without slaves. Both houses were of the best
class common in this region; two-story framed buildings, large,
and with many beds, to accommodate drovers and wagoners,
who, at some seasons, fill the houses which are known to be
prepared with stabling, corn, and beds for them. The slaveholder was much the wealthier of the two, and his house
originally was the finer, but he lived in much less comfort than
the other. His house was in great need of repair, and was much
disordered; it was dirty, and the bed given me to sleep in was
disgusting. He and his wife made the signs of pious people,
but were very morose or sadly silent, when not scolding and
re-ordering their servants. Their son, a boy of twelve, was
alternately crying and bullying his mother all the evening till
bedtime, because his father had refused to give him something
that he wanted. He slept in the same room with me, but did
not come to bed until after I had once been asleep, and then
he brought another boy to sleep with him. He left the candle
burning on the floor, and when, in five minutes after he had got
into bed, a girl came after it, he cursed her with a shocking
volubility of filthy blackguardism, demanding why she had
not come sooner. She replied gently and entreatingly, "I didn't
think you'd have more'n got into bed yet, master John." The
boys were talking and whispering obscenity till I fell asleep
again. The white women of the house were very negligent and

sluttish in their attire; the food at the table badly cooked, and badly served by Negroes.

The house of the farmer without slaves, though not in good repair, was much neater, and everything within was well-ordered and unusually comfortable. The women and girls were clean and neatly dressed; every one was cheerful and kind. There was no servant. The table was abundantly supplied with the most wholesome food—I might almost say the first wholesome food—I have had set before me since I was at the hotel at Natchez; loaf bread for the first time; chickens, stewed instead of fried; potatoes without fat; two sorts of simple preserved fruit, and whortleberry and blackberry tarts. (The first time I have had any of these articles at a private house since I was in Western Texas.) All the work, both within and without the house, was carried on regularly and easily, and it was well done, because done by parties interested in the result, not by servants interested only to escape reproof or punishment.

Doubtless two extreme cases were thus brought together, but similar, if less striking, contrasts are found the general rule, according to my experience. It is a common saying with the drovers and wagoners of this country, that if you wish to be well taken care of, you must not stop at houses where they have slaves.

The man of the last described house was intelligent and an ardent Methodist. The room in which I slept was papered with the "Christian Advocate and Journal," the Methodist paper of New York. At the slaveholder's house, my bedroom was partially papered with "Lottery Schemes."

The free laboring farmer remarked, that, although there were few slaves in this part of the country, he had often said to his wife that he would rather be living where there were none. He thought slavery wrong in itself, and deplorable in its effects upon the white people. Of all the Methodists whom he knew in Northeastern Tennessee and Southwestern Virginia, he believed that fully three-fourths would be glad to join the Methodist Church North, if it were "convenient." They generally thought slavery wrong, and believed it the duty of the church to favor measures to bring it to an end. He was not an Abolitionist, he said; he didn't think slaves could be set free at once, but they ought to be sent back to their own country, and while they were here they ought to be educated. He had perceived that great injustice was done by the people both of the North and South, towards each other. At the South, people were very apt to believe that the Northerners were wanting not only to deprive them of their property, but also to incite the slaves to barbarity and murder. At the North, people thought that the Negroes were all very inhumanely treated. That was not the case, at least hereabouts, it wasn't. If I would go with him to a camp meeting here, or to one of the common Sunday meetings, I would see that the Negroes were generally better dressed than the whites. He believed that they were always well fed, and they were not punished severely. They did not work hard, not nearly as hard as many of the white folks; they were fat and cheerful. I said that I had perceived this, and it was so generally, to a great degree, throughout the country; yet I was sure that on the large plantations it was necessary to treat the slaves with great severity. He "expected" it was so, for he had heard people say, who had been on the great rice and cotton plantations in South Carolina, that the Negroes were treated very hard, and he knew there was a man down here on the railroad, a contractor, who had some sixty hands which he had hired in Old Virginny ("that's what we call Eastern Virginia here"), and everybody who saw them at work, said he drove them till they could hardly stand, and did not give them half what they ought to have to eat. He was opposed to the Nebraska Bill, he said, and to any further extension of slavery, on any pretext; the North would not do its Christian duty if it allowed slavery to be extended; he wished that it could be abolished in Tennessee. He thought that many of the people who went hence to Kansas would vote to exclude slavery, but he wasn't sure that they would do it generally, because they would consider themselves Southerners, and would not like to go against other Southerners. A large part of the emigration from this part of the country went to Indiana, Illinois, and Iowa; those States being preferred to Missouri, because they were Free States. There were fewer slaves hereabouts now, than there were when he was a boy. The people all thought slavery wrong, except, he supposed, some slaveholders who, because they had property in slaves, would try to make out to themselves that it was right. He knew one rich man who had owned a great many slaves. He thought slavery was wrong, and he had a family of boys growing up, and he knew they wouldn't be good for anything as long as he brought them up with slaves; so he had told his slaves that if they wanted to be free, he would free them, send them to Liberia, and give them a hundred dollars to start with, and they had all accepted the offer. He himself never owned a slave, and never would own one for his own benefit, if it were given to him, "first, because it was wrong; and secondly, because he didn't think they ever did a man much good."

I noticed that the neighbors of this man on each side owned slaves; and that their houses and establishments were much poorer than his.